Historical Replica Constructions

VIKINGS: VOLUME 2

Edited by Stephen 'Sven' Wyley

MELBOURNE

Front cover photo: Weaving knife in use for tablet weaving. Photo by Shannon Joyce

Copyright © 2024 by Wyley, Boyle, Delany, Henry, Joyce, Robinson, Sinclair.

All rights reserved. No part of this publication may be reproduced, distributed or transmitted in any form or by any means, including photocopying, recording, or other electronic or mechanical methods, without the prior written permission of the publisher, except in the case of brief quotations embodied in critical reviews and certain other non-commercial uses permitted by copyright law. For permission requests, write to the publisher, addressed *"Attention: Permissions Coordinator"* at the address below.

Wyley, Boyle, Delany, Henry, Joyce, Robinson, Sinclair.
C/- Intertype
Unit 45, 125 Highbury Road
BURWOOD VIC 3125
www.intertype.com.au

Ordering Information:
Quantity sales. Special discounts are available on quantity purchases by corporations, associations, and others. For details, contact the *"Special Sales Department"* at the address above.

Historical replica construction in wood, metal and leather – Viking – Volume 2. Wyley, Boyle, Delany, Henry, Joyce, Robinson, Sinclair.
—1st ed.
ISBN 978-17635027-3-4

Acknowledgements.

Special thanks to the following people for taking their red pen to my manuscript: Rey Croucher, Mikkel Heeschen, Shannon Joyce, Katrina (Kat) Lambert, Robert (Hrothgar) Lock, Josh Orth, Hugh McDonald, Guy Merritt, especially Wayne Robinson and others.

Thanks to the following for assistance with this project:
- Sarah Brown – Ancient Arts Fellowship (Australian Re-enactor);
- Steve Mijatovic – The Wandering Folk (Australian Re-enactor);
- Tomáš Lázeňská – Researcher and member of Marobud (Czech Republic);
- Dianne and John Russell, Chest fitting manufacture;
- Dr. Matthias Simon Toplak (Museum für Archäologie Schloss Gottorf, Leitung Wikinger Museum Haithabu);
- Dr. James Waldron (President and Trustee of Bergen Museum of Art and Science).

The following people have contributed over a long period to the development of the knowledge that has been accumulated in these books;
Jenny and Gary Baker, Dr Peter Beatson, Dr Tim Dawson, Stephen Lowe, Hugh McDonald, Christopher Morgan, Steven Nicol, Wayne Robinson, Robert Schuster, Keith (Chips) Whitehead, Frank Wyley (my dad), and Andrew Young.

And thanks to all the customers and stakeholders associated with '*Sven the Merchant*', without your support and purchases this would never have happened.

We are grateful to all the institutions and individuals listed for permission to reproduce the material in wish they hold copyright. Every effort has been made to determine and contact the copyright holders, we apologise for any omission and we will try to add any necessary acknowledgement in the subsequent editions.

Dedications:

To the Varangians, past, present and future.

Stephen 'Sven' Wyley
Member of the Vlachernai Garrison,
New Varangian Guard Inc. since 1984.

Table of Contents.

Introduction.	9
Blackening iron and steel.	11
Blacksmithing in the Viking Age.	12
Carving in the Viking age.	28
Doing the research.	32
Finger gauge.	34
Lock vs hasp and padlocks.	34
Re-enactor / living history / experimental archaeology.	36
Replicas.	37
Runes and how they were used.	38
Viking chest Lock study.	42
Weaving textiles in the Viking age.	46
Workshop chemical hazards.	51
Workshop set up.	52
The Gamla Lödöse weaving knife.	55
The Oseberg chair.	68
The Hedeby chest.	92
The Winchester lock.	112
The Hørning table.	128
The Gokstad Bed.	143
The Trondheim Hnefatafl board.	171
The Grytøy Whalebone Plaque (Smoothing Board).	191
Coopering – a brief overview.	207
The Oseberg Bucket.	211
The Gokstad Backpack.	256
Part A – The Wooden boards.	263

Part B – Carving on plates.	267
Part C – The Leather work.	270
Hedeby Arrows	292
Appendices.	333
Appendix 1 - Typology of locks.	333
Appendix 2 - Trapezoid chest comparison, updated from Viking – Volume 1 (2021).	334
Appendix 3 – Updated Coppergate Mallet measurements from Viking – Volume 1 (2021).	336
Appendix 4 – Alternative hasp plate for Hedeby chest.	337
Appendix 5 – Hedeby chest – Small version.	338
Appendix 6 – Hedeby chest – Large version.	339
Appendix 7. – Gokstad bed. Wider slat plans – when you need more support.	340
Appendix 8 – Gokstad backpack – Kids version.	341
Appendix 9 – Larger Oseberg chair.	347
Appendix 10 - Gokstad Backpack evaluation.	351
Appendix 11 – Gokstad Backpack – An alternative shoulder strap arrangements for comfort.	353
Appendix 12 – Extant arrow finds.	355
Appendix 13 - Making your own pitch glue.	361
Appendix 14 - Useful conversions.	367
About the authors.	369
Bibliography.	379
Further Reading.	386
Links.	389
Photographs.	404
Drawings.	416
Index	422

Forthcoming works.	423
Previous volumes.	424

Introduction.

The Vikings were known for their fine craftsmanship in metal (the drum shaped broach from Mårten, Gotand, Sweden), wood (the sled and cart of the Oseberg Viking ship burial, Vestfold, Norway), ivory (the Gunhild cross of walrus ivory from Denmark) and stone (Harald Bluetooth's rune stone at Jelling, Denmark) but they also produced many of the mundane items needed for life such as coins, furniture, jewellery, cook and homewares, games, tools, arms and armour, fabric and clothes, musical instruments and various accoutrements.

The Vikings were also traders in all manner of goods and were at one end of the Silk Road, evidenced by the Indian bronze Buddha statue found in Helgö in Sweden, the Caliphate glass cup found in Birka in Sweden and numerous Arabic coins such as those contained in the Hoard of Ralswiek in Germany[1].

The Vikings also mass produced goods for local and international markets in materials like iron, and finished goods like jewellery, combs, soapstone bowls, goods that catered for both the Christian and Pagan market.

We hope you liked Viking Volume 1 (2021) and have come back for more projects. The projects you have completed should have provided you with a chance to hone your skills in preparation for the more difficult projects in this volume.

The first part of this book covers a range of information which will aid you in your future projects including: safety, reasons for replicas, re-enactors and living history; chemical hazards in the

---

[1] The willow basket contained 2211 whole and fragmentary silver coins, mainly from the Abbasid caliphate from the end of the 8th century.

workplace; black smithing; workshop set up; chest lock study; and doing the research.

This volume covers eleven more advanced Viking projects including:

- The Gamla Lödöse weaving knife – Stephen Wyley and Shannon Joyce;
- The Oseberg chair – Darren Delany and Stephen Wyley;
- The Hedeby chest – Stephen Wyley;
- The Winchester chest lock – Stephen Wyley;
- The Hørning table – Stephen Wyley;
- The Gokstad Bed no. 2 – Stephen Wyley and Brodie Henry;
- The Trondheim hnefatafl board – Stephen Wyley;
- The Grytøy smoothing board – Shannon Joyce;
- The Oseberg bucket – Stephen Sinclair;
- The Gokstad backpack – Brodie Henry and Stephen Wyley;
- The Hedeby arrows – Wayne Robinson.

This book assumes a basic level of experience with working with wood, metal, cloth and leather. As you complete the projects your skill will increase, however, safety is paramount. You should not use tools or equipment with which you have no experience, or without the appropriate personal protective equipment. If you are lacking experience or skill it is recommended that you obtain training from your local training institution or a more experienced worker of wood, metal and leather, or when all else fails there is *'YouTube'*. The subject of metal work will be touched upon in more detail in regards to the manufacture, purchase and fitting of metalwork such as chest hinges, hasps and locks. Project dimensions are provided in both metric and imperial measurements, pick one or the other and use it throughout the project.

Blackening iron and steel.

Blackening iron and steel is done to prevent the metal from rusting by providing a protective covering. This can be either of two ways: 1) hot process where the metal is heated and a carbon based compound like oil is applied; and 2) a cold process where a range of chemicals are applied.

For the hot process you will need: tongs, gloves, leather apron, safety glasses, a fire extinguisher, heat source (a forge or gas supply (Liquid Petroleum Gas (LPG) or butane)) and an area that is flame proof, not containing flammable liquids or combustible materials. This involves heating up the metal to a blue heat and applying the oil, this will produce some smoke, so the area should have good air extraction. Beware of the heat, hot objects and fumes given off by the process.

For the cold process you will need to purchase a suitable product which are available on various websites, read the *'safety data sheet'* (SDS) for the chemical hazards before purchasing and use. You will need tongs, gloves, a leather apron, safety glasses and an area which is chemically inert and has good air extraction. You need to ensure that the chemicals are fresh and ready to use in a range of baths, one for the chemical and one for the distilled water to rinse the chemical off the parts. When all else fails, follow the manufacturer's instructions.

Safety tip: Depending on how many chemicals you have you may just want to keep a link bookmarked on your device for accessing copies of SDS' on the internet.

Blacksmithing in the Viking Age.

By Sean "Bjorn" Boyle.

Photo 2. Hammer head making by Bjørn the Blacksmith.

The Riddle of Steel.

In one of the Icelandic sagas[2], the protagonist Kjartan is ambushed and must fight for his life. Several times during the battle his sword bends so he must risk seeking cover to straighten it underfoot. Kjartan left his sword, a gift from a Norwegian King, at home so had to settle for a poor-quality borrowed sword.

Why were some Viking Age blacksmiths able to make superior weapons and others ones that failed in battle? The answer is the mastery of the craft of making and forging iron and steel.

---

[2] Laxdæla saga chapter 49.

Viking Age smithing knowledge and skills were passed down person to person and refined through experience. It was an empirical, not scientific, craft requiring years of practice to master. Temperature was not measured in degrees, nor time in minutes or toughness in pounds per square inch. Instead, they would rely on observable features such as colour, touch, sound, and smell.

Steel is an alloy of iron and 0.3% to 2% carbon. Steel can be hardened through heat treatment, iron cannot, making it superior for hardness and wear-resistance. In general, the higher the carbon content, the harder but less malleable the steel is, too much and it becomes brittle.

All blacksmiths in the Viking Age knew how to make and work iron, but only highly skilled blacksmiths had the knowledge and skills to make and work steel. Forging steel involved more processes and more opportunities for failure.

Skilled smiths combined steel and iron in ways to create tools and weapons superior to ones made solely from iron or steel. High quality swords, for example, were made by forge welding two pieces of steel around an iron core. The steel formed the cutting edges and iron the spine. This produced swords that held their edges longer and flexed rather than broke or bent upon impact.

What follows is an introduction to blacksmithing during the Viking age. Historical references are provided as a starting point for further research.

My hope is that you will be inspired to start your own exploration into historical blacksmithing and maybe even embark on your own journey to unlocking the riddle of steel[3].

---

[3] Although Vikings had a word for steel (*stál*), the written sources almost exclusively use the word for iron (*járn*). For this reason, iron will be used to refer to both iron and steel in historical contexts from now on.

What we know about Viking age smithing - The written evidence.

There are few written references from the Viking age to blacksmithing[4]. Cultural knowledge was preserved orally through storytelling and skaldic poetry, in addition most of the surviving manuscripts were written hundreds of years after the Viking Age.

The Icelandic Sagas, for example, were written down in the 13th and 14th centuries, well after Christianity replaced most pagan beliefs and practices. Many sagas contain stories of heroes, mythical beings, and magic rather than the prosaic details of day-to-day life.

In the Poetic Edda, Wayland is a smith taught his craft by dwarves. Captured and imprisoned by King Nithad, he is forced to make jewellery to fill the king's coffers. As an act of revenge, Wayland kills the king's two sons, turning their skulls into goblets and making jewels from their eyes. He escapes using wings forged in his smithy.

In the Prose Edda, to win a bet with Loki, dwarven brothers Eitri and Brokk forge three magical items: The replicating gold ring *Draupnir* for Odin, the flying boar *Gullinbursti* for Freyr and the hammer *Mjölnir* for Thor. When forging *Mjölnir*, Loki in the form of a gadfly stings Brokk between the eyes causing him to stop pumping his bellows thereby shortening *Mjölnir's* handle.

In the Volsunga saga, Regin is a dwarven smith versed in magic. In his smithy he repairs the broken sword *Gram* for Sigmund who tests its strength by cleaving an anvil in two. Urged by Regin, Sigmund uses *Gram* to slay Regin's brother Fafnir the dragon. Warned that he plans to kill him, Sigmund cuts Regin's head off.

---

[4] A blacksmith is someone who works iron, *"black"* because of the colour of forged iron and "smith" meaning to strike or spread.

Pictorial evidence.

Pictorial carvings in wood, stone and ivory from the Viking Age show us the tools smiths used. One of the most common pictorial representations is a smith with hammer and tongs at his anvil assisted by someone at the bellows.

Photo 3. Dwarven brothers Eitri and Brokk, Hylestad Stave Church Norway, Wikimedia commons.

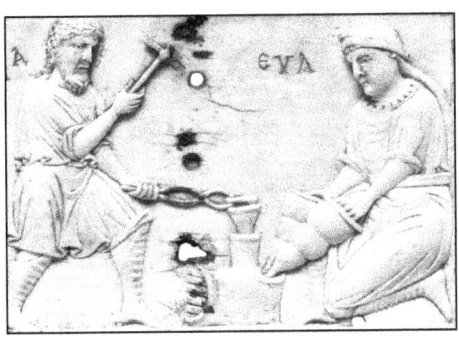

Photo 4. Byzantine ivory casket panel depicting Adam and Eve 10-11C, Met Museum public domain images.

Material evidence.

Fortunately, there are many archaeological finds containing blacksmith's tools to support the written and pictorial evidence. This is partly due to the custom in Viking age Scandinavia for people to be buried with their possessions and because iron tools under the right conditions remain well-preserved for hundreds of years.

Evidence of iron production and forging has also been found at sites that were once farms or settlements, including remnants of furnaces and smelting by-products such as slag and iron bloom fragments.

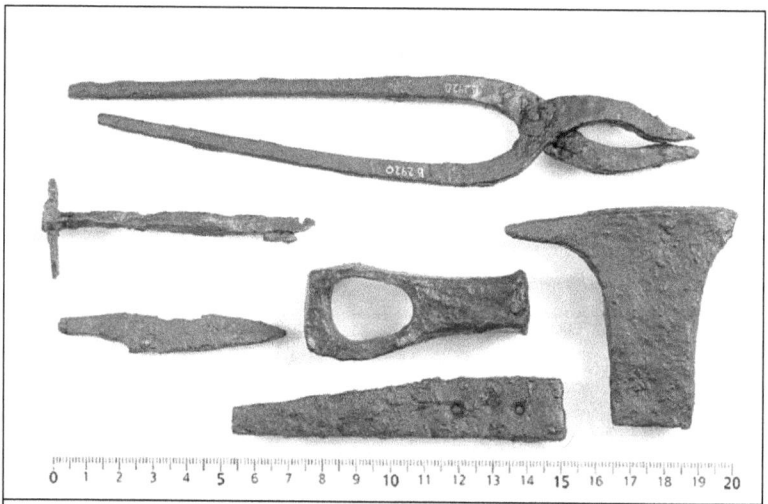

Photo 5. Blacksmith tools from Smoge Norway (900-950 CE). Photo DF.2092 Norway Digital Museum.

Blacksmiths in Viking age society.

Smiths were highly valued members of society. Iron tools were used in most essential activities such as food production, hunting, carpentry, stone masonry, boat building, raiding and warfare.

In the 11th century Latin manuscript Ælfric's Colloquy, a blacksmith proudly states he is the most important craftsman as he makes the tools all the others use:

"How does the ploughman get his plough or his ploughshare, or his goad, but by my craft? How does the fisherman obtain his hook, or the shoemaker his awl, or the tailor his needle, but by my work?"

The other craftsmen agree but don't envy the smith's his job:

"What you say is indeed true; but we all prefer to be guests of the ploughman, rather than yours; for the ploughman gives us bread and drink, and what do you give us in your workshop but sparks of iron, and the noise of hammers striking, and bellows blowing?"

Farmer smiths.
Most people lived on farms. According to Egil's saga, any accomplished farmer was expected to be able to smelt and forge iron. Farmers would have to be able to make and maintain iron farm tools such as axes, ploughs, scythes, and harnesses.

Travelling smiths.
A blacksmith might make a living travelling from farm to farm, setting-up a temporary smithy to make or repair iron tools.

One example might be the famous Mästermyr tool chest which contained more than 80 smithing and carpentry tools. It was discovered by a farmer ploughing his field in 1936 in an area that was once a bog or lake. Was it lost or buried by a travelling smith? We'll never know for sure, but based on its contents, the owner was a multi-skilled smith who worked iron, copper, and bronze.

Settlement smiths.

Trade was the main reason people gathered in large settlements in Viking Age Scandinavia. The major trade centres were Hedeby and Ribe in Denmark, Kaupang in Norway, and Birka in Sweden.

These settlements provided the opportunity for semi-permanent smithies. One such site is the 10th century garrison smithy excavated outside a Birka hill fort which contained evidence of iron production and blacksmithing as well as numerous iron weapons and luxury goods.

Unfortunately, archaeologists have not yet found any sites they can confirm as shipyards. This is unusual as Viking longships required vast amounts of iron to construct. Ships found in burial mounds and recovered from harbours used thousands of iron nails and roves for their clinker construction. This would have required blacksmithing on a large scale.

Essential Smithing Tools.

Any modern-day blacksmith knows you can't have too many pairs of tongs, hammers, or bending/shaping tools. The fact is that most smithing jobs can be done with a small set of essential tools and equipment. All a blacksmith needs to forge iron is a very hot fire, something to hold the iron, something to strike it with and a hard surface to strike it against.

Fuel, Forge and Bellows.

To forge iron, it needs to be heated until red to orange in colour, around 700°C (1300°F). To forge weld two pieces of iron together, a hotter temperature is required, around 1200°C (2192°F), yellow to white in colour.

These temperatures are greater than a normal wood fire can consistently produce, so smiths needed a hotter-burning fuel (charcoal), more oxygen (a bellows) and a contained fire (a forge).

Bellows, *'belgr'* or skin-bags in old Norse, blew air through a hole in a forge stone onto charcoal in a stone or brick forge. The two types used were *bag* and *accordion* bellows.

Photos 6 and 7. Viking Age bellows and hearth stone.
Left: Bag bellows, Byzantine ivory casket. Right: Accordion bellows, Hylestad Stave Church Norway.

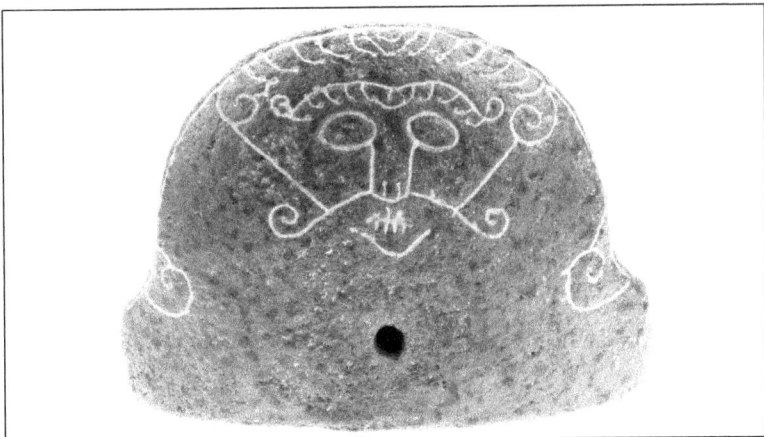

Photo 8. A forge stone depicting the face of Loki. Snaptun Norway (1000 CE), Wikimedia commons.

Anvils.

Iron anvils were small compared to modern anvils. They were typically no more than 20 cm (8 inches) high. Some were even smaller and probably used to make finer items such as jewellery from copper, bronze, silver, or gold.

Anvils were made from a single piece of wrought iron, sometimes with a hardened iron striking surface forge welded to the top. They were usually tapered at the base so they can be fitted into a hole in a block of wood or tree stump.

There is no evidence for cast anvils in this period as the technology to heat iron to its molten state, around 1,500°C (2,732°F), was not yet available.

Iron anvils from this period can be grouped into three types: 1. Rectilinear faced; 2. Rectilinear faced with a bick; 3. Bick only. See Photo 9.

Some anvils had a small circular hole, like the pritchel hole on a modern anvil, used when punching holes or forging nails.

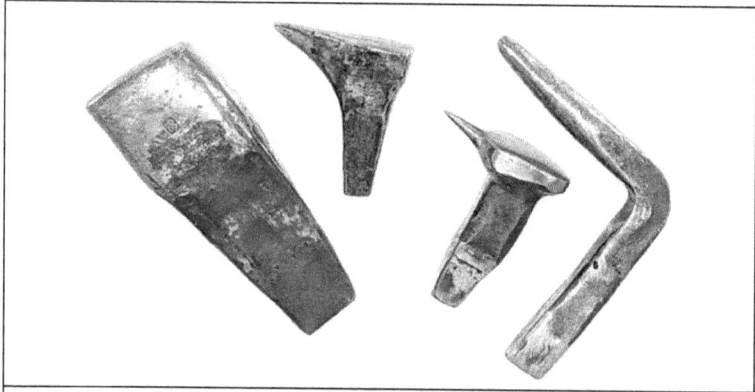

Photo 9. Reproduction Viking Age anvils by Bjørn the Blacksmith. Left to right: Rectilinear, 2 x rectilinear with bick and bick only.

Large stones were also sometimes used as anvils. Examples have been found in Rauðanes Iceland and Rendsburg Northern Germany. In Egil's Saga, Skallagrim rows out to sea and recovers a large stone from the seabed to use as an anvil on his farm.

Where iron was scarce, stone anvils were used by necessity. They might also have been used for the initial crude forging of large pieces of iron and then finished on a smaller iron anvil.

Hammers and Tongs.

Several different types of hammers have been found. The size and shape of a hammer determines its function. The most common type is the single handed cross pein hammer with two faces, one for striking and the pein for spreading hot material.

Sledgehammers were used by strikers and are larger with longer handles. Dog's head hammers, also known as cutler's hammers, have a single face, and were used for more precise hammer work.

Photo 10. Period hammers by Bjørn the Blacksmith. Left to right: Dog's head, small cross pein, large cross pein.

Tongs found to date vary in size but don't vary much in type. The most common type is the mandrel jaw tongs which can handle a wide range of hot materials, which possibly explains the lack of other types.

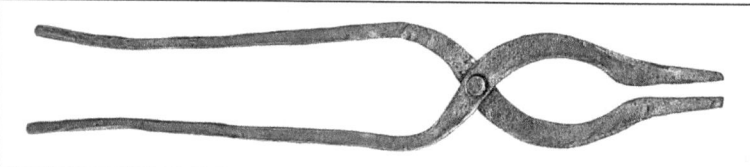

Photo 11. Period mandrel jaw tongs by Bjørn the Blacksmith. The type of tongs occurs most often in archaeological excavations.

Other Smithing Tools.

Other tools are required to either increase the smith's productivity or to forge specific items.

Nail headers.

In the Viking Age the most common way to fasten pieces of wood together was with wood or iron nails.

Iron nails were stronger than wood and although more expensive to make, had the advantage of being able to be peined-over a rove or clinched back into the wood for more secure fastening.

Both nails and rivets were created using nail headers.

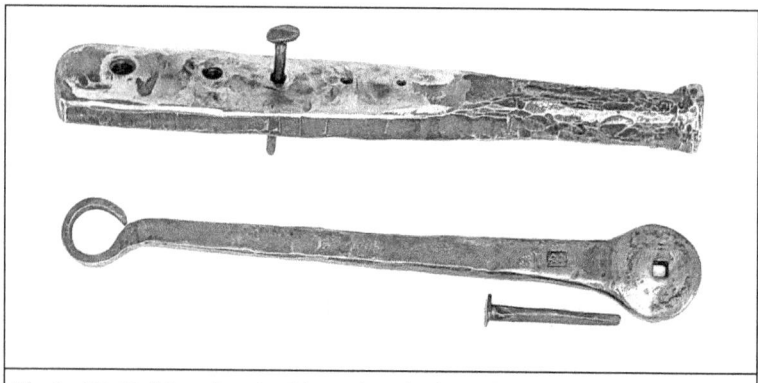

Photo 12. Nail headers by Bjørn the Blacksmith.
Top: For round profiled nails. Bottom: For square profiled nails.

Punches, Drifts, Chisels and Files.

In the Viking Age no tool existed hard enough to drill holes into iron, instead holes were punched into hot iron. These holes could then be widened using a drift for things such as making the eyes of hammers and axes.

Chisels were used with a hammer to cut hot iron. Files were used to cut into, smooth, sharpen and shape both hot and cold iron.

Photo 13. From left to right; a drift, a chisel, two punches, a rove with punched hole and file by Bjørn the Blacksmith.

Essential smithing practices.

Forging.
Forging is the process of heating iron so it becomes malleable, and shaping it using tools such as hammers, anvils, chisels, and punches. Forging requires iron to be heated to at least 700°C (1,300°F) but less than the temperature at which iron burns at around 1,200 °C (2,200 °F) depending on the carbon content.

Smelting.
Smelting is the process of heating iron ore in a furnace to reduce the iron oxides and obtain the iron base metal. Iron is extracted from ore at around 1,250 °C (2,282 °F).

Vikings were traders and raiders so high-quality iron could be sourced from the Far East and South. If you were a farmer or settlement smith though, you would need to know how to make your own iron. The process of smelting iron from iron ore was time-consuming and required large amounts of raw materials.

First, a large amount of charcoal is required for the furnace. If you didn't know someone who made it, you would have to make it yourself from cut tree branches in an earthen charcoal kiln.

Second, collect and prepare iron ore for the smelt. In Scandinavia this was commonly collected from bogs or riverbanks banks[5]. Ore is collected, crushed to a uniform size and roasted in a fire to remove some of the impurities and moisture.

---

[5] Bog iron was the most common form of iron ore available to Viking Age Scandinavians. It is produced in bogs by bacteria that oxidize and concentrate trace amounts of dissolved iron.

Third, you built a bloomery furnace; a chimney-like structure made from clay and a binding fibre such as straw. A wood fire is lit in the furnace before use to set the clay.

Fourth, the smelt begins. The furnace is fired with wood and charcoal and brought to smelting heat by forcing air into the base of the furnace using a bellows. Over many hours a mix of charcoal and iron ore are fed into the top of the furnace and burned. The high heat triggers a chemical reaction that produces an iron bloom which settles to the bottom of the furnace. The bloom is a spongy mixture of iron, steel, and slag (undesirable impurities).

Finally, the iron bloom is removed from the furnace and turned into wrought iron. First the bloom is gently struck with a sledgehammer to remove some slag inclusions and consolidate the remaining material. The bloom is then formed into a wrought iron billet by repeatedly heating, folding, forge welding and hammering. This produces a stronger, more homogeneous iron with a characteristic fibrous appearance. The result is a piece of wrought "*worked*" iron.

All iron produced by smelting iron ore in a charcoal furnace contains at least some carbon introduced from the fuel.

Forge-welding.
This is the process of heating two pieces of iron to a high enough temperature, around 1200°C (2192°F), that when brought together they weld into a single piece or iron.

Iron will weld when it reaches a yellow to white heat, just before it starts to sparkle and burn.

Forge welding is an essential skill required not only to make iron but also to combine smaller pieces of iron to make larger objects.

Heat treatment.

Heat treatment is a set of processes involving heating and cooling steel to achieve desired properties such as hardness, ductility, malleability, or resilience. The three main heat treatment processes are normalising, hardening, and tempering.

> Normalising is a process of heating metal to a specific temperature and slowly letting cool to reduce hardness making it more ductile and easier to work. Normalising is typically required before forging previously heat-treated steel.
>
> Hardening is the process of slowly heating steel to a specific temperature and rapidly cooling it in a quenching liquid to 'lock-in' a hardened state. All sorts of quenching mediums were used in the Viking Age including water, brine, urine, blood, linseed oil or tallow. Different mediums would cool the metal at different rates. Hardening steel increases strength but decreases ductility making it more brittle. The hardening process may also introduce internal stresses that lead to cracks, chips, or brakes.
>
> Tempering is the process of heating steel to just below its hardening temperature, holding it at that temperature and then slowly letting it cool in air. It is done after hardening to relieve internal stresses and to toughen steel so it is more resilient to chips and cracks. Viking Age smiths judge tempering by sight alone. Steel is first heated to a dull red colour, then taken out of fire and air cooled watching for the desired temper colours to appear. Once they appear the steel is quenched to lock-in the temper.

Given the complexity of heat treatment, it is maybe not so surprising to note that many of the Viking Age swords that have undergone metallurgical analysis were found to have not been hardened or tempered.

The temperatures and times involved in heat treatment are highly dependent on the percentage of carbon in the steel, get it wrong and a sword might be too brittle and break or an axe might dull quickly and need to be sharpened after every use.

Knowing how and when to heat treat steel would be an essential part of a master smith's craft. They had no way of knowing the % of carbon present in their iron, so they relied on tried-and-true methods, recipes, and processes to create iron with the best properties for the intended use.

This may include empirical practices we would see as superstitious today but produced the results required. A Medieval source later than the Viking Age, the 14-15th century manuscript *Pol Hausbuch*, has some very specific advice for hardening:

> "Scythes should be hardened in tallow. Files should be quenched in urine, or in linseed oil, or in buck's blood."

The manuscript goes on to explain that the buck (male deer) the blood is extracted from should be in heat or rutting. This is presumably to imbue the file with properties of hardness or toughness from the buck when it is at its most aggressive.

Archaeological finds.

Table 1 – List of examples of blacksmith tool finds.			
Location	Dated:	Collection	Details
Heradsbygd, Hedmark, Norway.	7th century CE	Museum of Cultural History, Norway, C60023	31 items totalling 30 kg (66lp) of iron including axe, hammer, sledgehammer, ore shovel, celts, iron magnifiers, knife blade, drill.
Staraja Ladoga, Russia.	Mid-8th Century CE	Gosudarstvennyj Ermitaž, St.	6 tongs, two hammers, three

		Petersburg, Cat. No. 268, 2551/1-22.	anvils, a pair of shears, various metal work pieces and stock.
Sogndalsdalen, Norway.	800 CE	University Museum of Bergen	Grave with 60 artefacts including blacksmith tools, an axe, a sword, agricultural implements, a razor, scissors, tweezers, a frying pan, and a poker.
Mästermyr, Gotland, Sweden.	1000 CE.	Statens Historiska Museum, Stockholm, 21592.	Wooden chest with over 80 blacksmithing, metal working and carpentry tools.
Bygland, Telemark, Norway.	10th century CE	Universitetets Oldsaksamling, Oslo, C27454.	2 tongs, 5 hammers, 4 anvils, two cold chisels, files, nail iron, casting ladle, etc. and lots of worked pieces, 4 swords, 4 spears, 7 axes, 2 shield bosses, 13 arrow heads.

Carving in the Viking age.

Carving was used in the Viking period to decorate all manner of items from architectural features, furniture, household items and implements, religious objects and memorial stones. Carving was also used for small unique items like figurines of animals such as cats and bears, and toys. Material for carving included wood, ivory, bone, amber and stone. Here are two tables, Table 2 for larger items with an ascribed style to the carving (i.e. Carolingian to Romanesque, and Table 3 for all the other (smaller) carved items.

Table 2. Examples of Carving. (Large pieces).

Dated (CE)	Place	Collection details	Style	Comment
800-850	Oseberg farm, Tonsberg, Vestfold, Norway	Universitetets Oldsaksamling, Olso, K51, 60, 50, 49	a. Baroque b. Flat relief c. Carolingian d. Academician[6]	4* animal headed posts, in a hardwood possible Lime. Maximum height 95cm (37 ½''').
1000	The Cathedral Treasury of Kamien (Pomorski) Poland	Denmark National Museum, Copenhagen	Mammen	Cammin Casket. Material horn, wood and gilt bronze. L. 63cm (24").
Early 10th C.	York Coppergate, England	York City Council, 1977.7.2115	Jelling and English animals	Grave slab fragment in magnesium limestone, L. 23cm (9 1/16").
1050	Lund (Kv Glambeck 4) Sweden	Kulturen, Lund KM 59.126.795	English Winchester and Ringerike	Walking stick with dragon head and interlaced plant decoration, Wood (Maple). L. 98.5cm (38 ¾").
1075	Trondheim, Norway	Vitenskapsmuseeh, Trondheim, N93241/FU433.	Urnes	Decorated spoon, bone, L. 17.5cm (7").

---

[6] The artist was nicknamed the 'Academician' by Shetelig because of the traditional and controlled design of the gently curving animals in the manner of pre- Viking art – James Graham-Campbell, The Viking World, 1980.

Table 3. Examples of Carving (Small).

Date (CE)	Place	Collection details	Comment
800-1090	Svarta Jorden, Birka, Uppland, Sweden.	Swedish History Museum. Inventory No. 8252, subnumber 1. SHM Object Identity - 267204	Amber cat (3 cm (1 $^3/_{16}$") long).
9th C	Øysund, Meløy, Nordland, Norway.	Transø Museum, Ts7587	Figure of a bear, Amber, Height 4.7cm (1 $^7/_8$''').
1000	Snaptun, Jutland, Denmark	Forhistorisk Museum, Moesgård, 72A	Bellows shield with face blow hole for mouth, in soapstone, H 20cm (7 $^7/_8$").
10th C	Staraja Ladoga (Horizon D) obl. St. Petersburg, Russia	Gosudarstvenny Ermitaž, St.Petersburg, LD-117.	Pagan Idol (bearded man) in wood, H 27cm (1 $^1/_{16}$").
10th C	York, Railway Station, England	The Yorkshire Museum, York H110	Snake pendant in Jet, L. 5.2cm (2 1/16").
11th C	Sigtuna, Sweden	Inv. No. 22044, National Historical Museum, Stockholm.	Figure of a male warrior wearing a spangenhelm, sporting a beard and moustache, made from elk horn. L. 22.5cm (8 $^7/_8$").

Doing the research.

As previously mentioned in Viking Volume 1 were the differing levels of research; from examination of extant finds (the best) to relying on Hollywood (the worst). I would like to make the following recommendations for researching:
- Define your search parameters (i.e. location: Gotland, time period: 10th century);
- Utilise both hard and soft copy information;
- Create a library to preserve what you find by,
    - Documenting the web pages you use so you can find them again (i.e. bookmarking),
    - Some information will not be in your first language and translation is a skill in itself, translation services are expensive but there are programs that are available which can be useful, some technical language may not be in your standard bilingual dictionary and will need more research,
    - Avoid buying all the books because it can be expensive, download free copies, try your local library (if you do buy them you could write them off as a business expense…),
    - Don't be offended if a book owner will not lend you a book, it's expensive and people don't always return books (once burned, twice shy),
- Use the Museums;
    - Visit the museums, ask questions, you can ask to see specific pieces,
    - Look at their online catalogues,
    - Email the curators about their collections (some are more helpful than others, always be polite and patient),

- Websites;
    - Use the translate button (not everything will be in your first language),
    - Store digitally or print off and store safely (I recommend plastic sheaths, in a clearly marked folder) with the download date (sites do come and go),
    - Image sharing services like *'Pinterest'* are fine if the material is well and properly labelled so you can find the source,
    - Bookmark links so you can find it again,
    - Google supplies tips for searching:
        1. *"Use the minus (-) sign to exclude multiple words. Use the minus (-) sign to remove multiple words from any search result. ...*
        2. *Use quotes ("") to include results that mention precise terms.*
        3. *Use "site:" to exclude results from specific websites."*
- Use interest groups and forums on the internet, for example;
    - Ancient, Medieval, Renaissance and Colonial Furniture and Woodenware,
    - Viking Gear,
- Don't be put off by the amount of data;
    - Learn to filter out what you don't need and the bad stuff,
    - Don't get distracted by the bling,
- Keep good notes, you can't remember everything
    - Store in a safe & dry place.
    - Use labelled binders/folders with plastic sheaths to store hard copies.

Decades ago the first article I translated was on the Hedeby quiver from German to English using a little red bilingual dictionary, having done leatherwork and archery helped but it was a lot of work.

Good research and document control practices will save you a lot of time, heart ache and should produce great results which can proudly be shared with others in your community and at large.

Finger gauge.

A finger gauge is a basic method of drawing lines on your work by holding a pencil between your pointer finger and your thumb while resting on the middle finger, with the tip of the pencil on the mark previously measured using a ruler and the tip of your pointer finger on the opposite face of the work, then scribe the line with the pencil while keeping pressure on the pencil and the edge of the work.

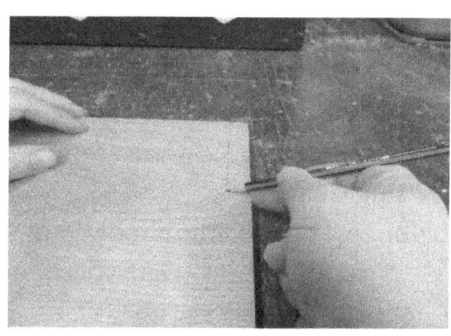

Photo 14. A finger gauge in use to mark out a line in pencil, never use ink.

Lock vs hasp and padlocks.

Most of the extant Viking chests are secured with locks, however, locks were expensive, and so the alternative was a hasp which could secure a chest with a padlock (be it barrel or box padlock).

There are few extant Viking chests that are secured with padlocks, such the second chest from Birka Grave find No. 639, Sweden. There are many part or full remains of padlocks from York, Dublin and the Mastermyr chest had 3 padlocks in it when it was found. There are at least two extant chests from Sweden that date from 1200 CE that were only secured by hasps.
They are:
- the Voxtorp Chest (No. 4094) from the Voxtorp Church, Småland, Sweden, c. 1200, Statens Historiska Museum, Stockholm, Sweden;
- and the Ryadaholm Church chest, Småland, Sweden, c. 1200, Statens Historiska Museum, Stockholm.[7]

Padlocks have been with us from at least the Roman era. From Goodall (2012) we know that:
- Box padlocks were more prevalent pre 1066 CE;
- The barrel padlock was the most common padlock in the Medieval period;
- There are five types of barrel padlock include the following types:
    - A – padlocks with attached tube,
    - B – padlocks with fins and tubes,
    - C – padlocks with 'U' shaped housing,
    - D – padlocks with 'L' shaped arms,
    - E – padlocks with shackles.
- That type B & E were the most popular, with E being the most popular.

From the finds of keys across the Viking world it is clear there are more extant keys than locks that have been found archaeologically.

---
[7] Both chests have similar decorative iron work.

Re-enactor / living history / experimental archaeology.

What is the difference between re-enacting, living history and experimental archaeology? In some cases they overlap and sometimes they are separated by all manner of details.
Living historians (LH) tend to depict certain aspects of a medieval life very well (e.g. a blacksmith with all the tools), and know how to produce replicas of items for use by other LH in their displays. This could include smelting metal, using the metal to make tools (a hammer head or tongs), to make other tools (an axe) which is used to chop down and dress timber to make furniture, which can be used to sit on to make other crafts or cook at the fire.

Whereas a re-enactor is re-enacting a certain event or battle with a determined outcome, so they need to have the gear to portray a type of person that was present and follow a predetermined script normally as part of a public display, such as the Battle of Hasting in 1066 CE.[8]

Experimental archaeology is an approach with academic rigour and reporting used to filling gaps in our knowledge about the past, which cannot be filled through other archaeological research methods. The process involves a process which tests a hypothesis in direct reference to the archaeological record. A good example of experimental archaeology is the comprehensive data set over the lifespan of a reconstructed Viking ship, from the first axe cut into oak logs in 1982 to the last moments on the water in 2016.[9]

---

[8] MrFord4210 (2020)
[9] https://exarc.net/issue-2020-2/ea/roar-ege-lifecycle-reconstructed-viking-ship downloaded 26/08/2021.

Replicas.

Most extant items are not normally found in good condition due to soil conditions, damage from looting, let alone the effects of fire, water and time. The conservator does an amazing job to stop deterioration, clean them up and glue them back together. The items will never look like new, their original use and how they worked may be a mystery. In some cases the original items are too valuable, fragile or damaged to be displayed, let alone taken around the world on display tours. Hence, the uses of replicas which are made using the same materials, tools and techniques as the originals, to the highest levels of craftsmanship and authenticity.

I was commissioned to make a replica of the Lund three-legged stool for the Viking display at the Sydney Maritime Museum. I was provided with all the information, drawings and photographs of the extant remains. For this project I could not just go to my local hardware supplier and purchase a plank of pine and some dowels. No, I sourced a log of a suitable wood, split out a plank, axed it down to the right thickness and shape, augured three holes in the top for three limbs I cut from a suitable tree for the legs, and fitted it together. All skills that came in handy for the fourty stools of the same design the museum wanted for the knowledge interaction area (luckily I could use the planks of prepared timber and dowelling for these.

Some notable replicas are:
- The Antikythera astrolabe (found on a ship wreck dating from 60 BCE of the north east coast of the island of Aigilia, in the Peloponnese Strait;
- The Sutton Hoo helm (from the Anglo-Saxon burial, replica made by the Royal Armoury).

- The various Viking ships that have been reconstructed at the Viking Ship Museum, Roskilde in Denmark.

Runes and how they were used.

The runic alphabet is known as a futh(Þ)ark based on the first six letters. Runes were developed by Germanic tribes and the earliest datable inscription is from 160 Common Era (CE) found in the Vimose bog on the Island of Funen in Denmark (along with five other items from a buckle to a wood plane, now stored in the National Museum of Denmark). There are two types of runes:
- 1) *'Long'* or Danish runes;
- 2) *'Short twig'* or Swedo-Norwegian runes.

Runes were used for short everyday messages, often carved in wood, bone, ivory and stone and used for things like maker's mark, owner identification, love poems, dedications, graffiti showing off, magic or just practicing carving the *'Futhark'*. Here is an example of younger Futhark ᚠᚢᚦᚼᚱᚴ.

Table 5. Examples of Runes and their uses.

Dated (CE)	Place	Find details	Runes	Translation	Reason
160	Vimose bog on the Island of Funen in Denmark	Comb - Asset No 4148, National Museum of Denmark.	Harja	Name of the owner (?)	Ownership
800	Rök, Östergötland, Sweden	Rune stone (Ög 136), 2.4 metres tall, granite.	aft uamuþ stonta runaʀ þar n uarin faþi faþiʀ aft faikion sunu sakum.	After Vämod stand these runes, and Varin carved, the father of a dead son.	Dedication, followed by a long encrypted inscription.
965	Jelling, Jutland, Denmark	• One of two granite rune stones, Height above ground 243cm, raised by King Harald Bluetooth.	Haraldr konungr bað gǫrva kumbl þausi aft Gorm faður sinn auk aft Þórví móður sína. Sá Haraldr es sér vann Danmǫrk alla auk Norveg auk	King Harald had this memorial stone raised to Gorm his father and Thyre his mother. That Harald who won for himself all Denmark and Norway and made the Danes Christians.	Memorial and Showing off.

1000	Gorodišče, near Novgorod, Russia	Bronze amulet, L5.8cm, IIMK, St Petersburg, NOE-83/RG-355.	dani gærði kristna	May you not lack manhood	Magic
Viking era	Istanbul, Turkey	Runic inscription on the balustrade of the Gallery above the floor of the Hagia Sofia.	Halfdan	Halfdan [was here]	Graffiti
Viking era	Gamla Lödöse, Sankt Peder, Västergötland, Sweden	Weaving knife with runic love poem -. SHM 29750 – 542.	mun : þu * mik : man : þik : un : þu : m(e)r : an : þRr	Think of me, I think of you! Love me, I love you!	Love

Security.

My dad had a saying, "*You can't stop a dishonest person being dishonest but you can stop an honest person becoming a thief*" by having good security.

Good security looks like:
- locking your electrical tools in a locked cabinet inside your locked workshop;
- engraving your driver's licence on your tools so that when they turn up the police can identify you as the owner;
- improving your security when you have the opportunity;
- storing your tools in a place where they cannot be seen through the window of your workshop or car;
- ensuring a safe place for your keys, don't store your workshop keys with your house keys.

Storage.

Tool racks, shadow boards, tool boxes keep tools safe from damage and reduce the risk of someone catching a body part on the teeth of a saw, or the corner of a claw hammer. Other storage options include cupboards and draws.

More space to swing a certain animal, which will remain nameless, assists when moving large items or projects about the workshop. More bench space means more convenient space to work.

Only store what material you need on hand in the workshop, use a separate store for timber, metal, or leather not currently in use. Racks are good to store timber flat will mean there is less chance of warping. Store timber in a dry area (avoid mould and direct water damage) by stopping leaks in the roof or rising damp.

Viking chest Lock study.

This is a short Viking chest lock study of 11 extant chest locks from Viking sources that gives a glimpse in the field of lock smithing in the Viking world. There is a need to expand this to other counties for the same period (i.e. the Winchester lock), and produce a typology (aka Peterson). For the current typology of slide locks see Appendix 1.

Table 4. Viking Chest slide locks (where the key is used to slide the slide)

Dated (CE)	Chest and find location	Number of hasps	Hasp position	Key hole	Lock plate shape	Lock type
800 – 850	Oseberg 149 - Norway	3	Left, centre and right	Left of Centre	Rectangle	3A
Late 9th –2nd ½ of 10th century	Fyrkat - Denmark	1	Left	Right of centre with slide snib	Rectangle	1D
1000	Mastermyr - Sweden	2	Left and right	Centre	Rectangle	2A
10th century	Onsild – Denmark, Lock and hasp	1	Left	Right of centre with slide snib	Rectangle	1D
10th century	Hedeby Harbour - Germany	2	Left and right	Centre	Rectangle	2A
10th century	Kaagenden - Denmark	1	Left	Centre - ish	Rectangle	1A
10th century	Lejre – Grave 1160 - Long version - Denmark	2	Left and right	Centre - ish	Rectangle	2A
10th century	Lejre - Grave 321 Casket – Denmark	1	Centre	Unknown	Rectangle	1B

10th century	Hedeby, Germany. Chamber grave 5 – Wooden chest, fittings in iron and bronze.	3	Left, centre and right	Centre	Rectangle	3A
1100	Sweden SHM 21847-4, just the lock plate.	1	Left	Right of centre with slide snib	Rectangle	1D
Viking era	Birka SHM 33140.62 - Sweden	2	Left and right	Centre	Rectangle	2A
Viking era	Birka grave 545 - Sweden	3	Left, centre and right	Centre	Rectangle	3A

Notes: The Hedeby chest is missing the lock but given the shape of the hole in front where the lock was and the remains of two hasps on the lid I believe I can say what type of lock the chest had. Sadly the Oseberg 156 chest was found with no front board, however the Oseberg 178 chest has a spring displacement lock.

Weaving textiles in the Viking age.

By Shannon Joyce.

The process of weaving involves the interlacing of vertical (warp) and horizontal (weft) yarns to form a textile.

Extant examples of textiles from the Viking Age show that tabby (Photo 15) and twill (Photo 16) weave structures were predominantly used with broken twill (Photo 17) and broken diamond twill (Photo 18) being far less common (Ewing, T. 2007, Hayeur Smith, M. 2020, Rabiega, K. 2019).

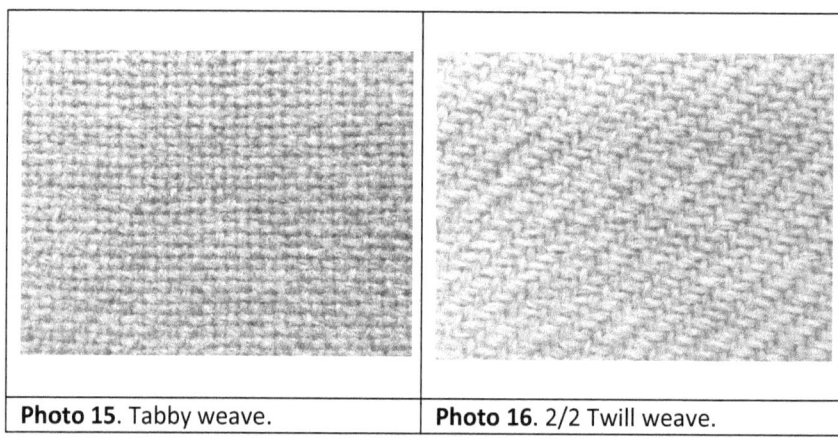

| **Photo 15**. Tabby weave. | **Photo 16**. 2/2 Twill weave. |

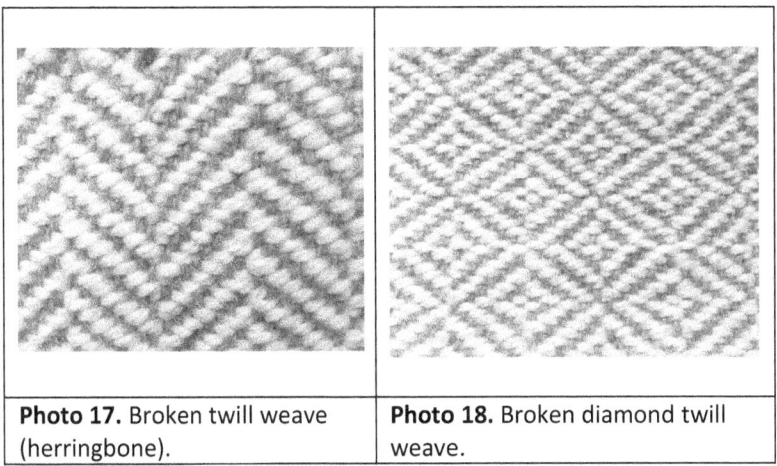

| Photo 17. Broken twill weave (herringbone). | Photo 18. Broken diamond twill weave. |

Evidence suggests[10] that textiles were woven on a warp weighted loom (Drawing 1.). This loom is two vertical posts which hold the cloth beam, shed beam and heddle rods. The warp threads are attached to the cloth beam, usually by way of a tablet woven header, and are attached to weights which provide tension to enable the shifting back and forwards of the heddle rods. Every second warp thread is weighted in front of the shed beam whilst the remainder are weighted straight down behind forming two rows of loom weighted warp threads.

For the weaving of tabby cloth, the warp threads behind the shed beam are attached to a heddle rod using a continuous thread in a process known as knitting the heddles. When the heddle rod is in the neutral position (against the loom upright) these warp threads hang straight down and the natural shed is formed by the shed beam. When the heddle rod is moved forwards and placed in a heddle support it produces an artificial shed enabling the weft yarn to be placed through. The weft is

---

[10] There are no surviving looms from the period however rows of loom weights found in situ are interpreted as evidence of the use of the warp weighted loom (Hayeur Smith, 2020).

then beaten upwards into place with a sword beater and the process is repeated.

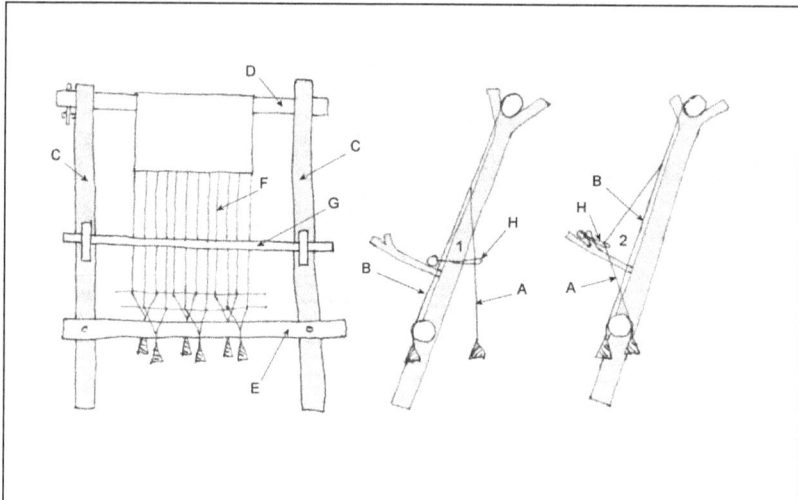

Drawing 1. Diagram of a warp-weighted loom. There are two upright posts (C); they support a horizontal beam (D), which is cylindrical so that the finished cloth can be rolled around it, allowing the loom to be used to weave a piece of cloth taller than the loom, and preserving an ergonomic working height. The warp threads (F, and A and B) hang from the beam and rest against the shed rod (E). The heddle-bar (G) is tied to some of the warp threads (A, but not B), using loops of string called leashes (H). So when the heddle rod is pulled out and placed in the forked sticks protruding from the posts (not lettered, no technical term given in citation), the shed (1) is replaced by the counter-shed (2). By passing the weft through the shed and the counter-shed, alternately, cloth is woven.

There are also extant examples of tablet weaving from the period. This type of weaving can be performed on the warp-weighted loom, on a post loom such as the Oseberg loom or using a backstrap loom. As the name suggests this type of weaving uses square tablets (Photo 19) which create a shed for weaving when turned.

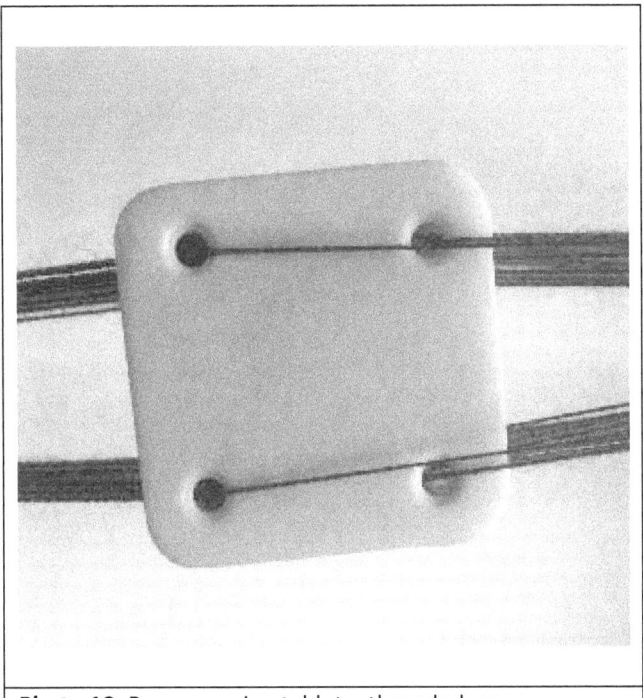
Photo 19. Bone weaving tablet – threaded up.

The combination of tablet threading and the turning sequence forms the braid's pattern. With each turn of the tablets, either backwards or forwards or a combination of both, a different shed is opened and the weft thread is passed through. The tablets are turned again and the previous weft is beaten into place before the weaving of the next weft thread. This process is repeated to produce bands such as those below.

Photo 20. Tablet woven bands based on patterns from Birka (Sweden).

Workshop chemical hazards.

"The dose makes the poison" – Paracelsus (1493 – 1541) a Swiss physician, alchemist and philosopher.

Basically the exposure to toxic substances can make you sick and in the right situation at a certain dose it can kill you, be it acute or chronic. There are a number routes in to the body;
1) Drinking (imagine a mislabelled bottle, a bottle that had sarsaparilla in it but now has dirty turps),
2) Inhalation of dust, vapours or smoke (dust from grinding stone, sanding lead based paint from an object, burning treated timber with arsenic in it, using paint remover with methylene chloride[11] in it),
3) Absorption through the skin (cleaning with acetone on a rag without gloves).

The best control methods involve knowing the hazard, assessing the risks and putting the most appropriate controls in place. For dealing with toxic chemicals always read the safety data sheet (SDS) and follow the hierarchy of control which looks like this;

- Stop using the chemical,
- Replace the chemical with something less toxic,
- Reduce exposure by diluting the chemical,
- Limit exposure time,
- Use engineering by extraction or ventilation,
- Finally the least effective is wearing the most appropriate personal protective equipment (PPE) properly.

---

[11] https://diggersaustralia.com.au/wp-content/uploads/sds/Paint%20Stripper%20v6.pdf downloaded 24 August 2021.

For using respirator you need to do a *'fit test'*[12] and be clean shaven as a beard or stubble will cause a break in the seal and the respirator is useless.

Workshop set up.

The following is some tips, hints and strong suggestions for setting up and running a workshop that is a pleasure to be in and makes the work safe and enjoyable.

Access.
Keep kids, pets and unauthorised adults out of the workshop. Only people with the right to access should be there and there is less chance of someone getting injured if access is denied. There is only some much room and the less people with access the better.
Leave no gaps for vermin, snakes and spiders to enter, always get a professional to deal with snakes, assist spiders out of the workshop, surface spray for cockroaches etc., and bait for mice and rats where appropriate (they love peanut butter).

Electrical.
An *'earth leakage breaker'* on electrical equipment or switchboards, provides a trip switch also known as residual-current device (RCD) or *"Safety switch"* which will save your life. The RCD breaks the **electrical circuit** to protect equipment and to stop serious harm from an electric shock and electrocution (which sadly normally results in a fatality).

---

[12] Fit-testing a respirator measures the effectiveness of the seal between the respirator and the wearer's face.

Plant and equipment.
Equipment set up should make it easy to access and not cause a hazard to other workshop users or equipment, i.e. noise, dust etc. from other machines.

Ergonomics.
Set height of workbench to hip height, lay down rubber fatigue mats on the flow, place tools in racks within easy reach, provide good lighting to reduce eyestrain, and store heavy items between shoulder and knee height.

Good housekeeping.
Good housekeeping means things are not so easily obscured or lost, detritus can make it harder for you to find that nut or nail you have just dropped on the floor.

Lighting (natural, strip, spot) – the finer the work the better light you need.

Free of trip slip and fall hazards (keep floors and walkways clear of slip, trip and fall hazards);
-   Wood chips and sawdust can catch fire from sparks from grinding metal.
-   Dust can be an inhalation hazard, especially those with pre-existing conditions like asthma.

Cleanliness and good housekeeping is paramount to having a safe and productive workshop. Clean up after each type of job (you don't want metal fillings in your wooden table or wooden splinters in your leatherwork).

Waste not, want not for timber:
Keep off cuts to make smaller works and wedges;

- to act as sacrificial timber (backing timber when drilling holes in wood, reduces or eliminates chips and splits;
- cut offs from an Oseberg 178 were used to construct a Fyrkat casket;
- use cheaper timber to practice; techniques, trial pieces and as teaching aids;
- save the expensive timber for the show piece, that special order or gift.

'Clean your work bench at the end of the day and start fresh each new day'.

S.Wyley, 4 January 2015.

The Gamla Lödöse weaving knife.

By Stephen Wyley and Shannon Joyce.

The Gamla Lödöse weaving knife	from Gamla Lödöse, Sankt Peder, Västergötland, Sweden	**When**: Viking – 12th century CE
Stored: Swedish History Museum	**Collection no.**: SHM 29750:542	**Material**: Timber – Juniper
Size: L 220mm (8 $^{21}/_{32}$") x W 34mm (1 $^{11}/_{32}$") down to 15mm ($^{19}/_{32}$"). Thickness from 6mm (¼"") to 14mm (9/16")		

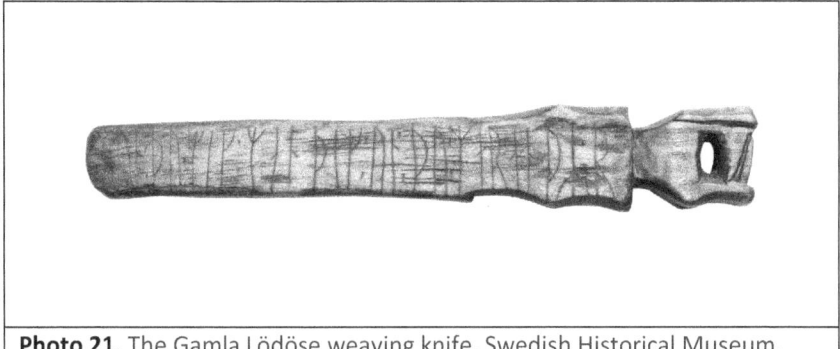

Photo 21. The Gamla Lödöse weaving knife, Swedish Historical Museum.

Introduction.

The weaving knife is made of timber (possibly juniper) from Gamla Lödöse, (Sankt Peder, Västergötland, Sweden. SHM 29750:542) and was found in the centre of Lödöse on the 12th century (CE) level. See Photo 21. Other similar weaving tools were made of timber, whale bone or metal, see comparison Table 6 for details.

Photo 22. The Gamla Lödöse weaving knife, replica in front of the original at the display at the Melbourne Museum (2018).

On one side there is love poem which reads *"mun : þu * mik : man : þik : un : þu : m(e)r : an : þRr"*, in Swedish runes which translates as *"Think of me, I think of you! Love me, I love you!"* On the other side there are two rows of triangular indents running down the centre of the blade, with the points facing the opposite line, with the shape interlocked, which could have been made by using a triangular punch. There is also a set of runes *"brmank"* which are carved in the centre of the blade to one side of the row of triangles, which were carved with less care than the other side and could be interpreted as either as a makers mark or that of the owner.

One end is pierced by a hole which could be used to suspend the knife for storage or as personal ornament, and has a neck leading to the *'blade'* of the knife.

A weaving knife was used to compress the weft threads when weaving by applying pressure via the thin edge to the threads.

This knife is somewhat shorter that other extant finds and could be used for tablet or sprang weaving rather than loom or broad cloth weaving. To be of real use the '*blade*' needs to be much thinner, say about 8mm ($^5/_{16}$")

Photo 23. The Gamla Lödöse weaving knife replica being used for tablet weaving.

Table 6, Weaving equipment comparison.				
Find details	Date (CE)	Overall length	Timber/ material	Stored
England: Kent: Dover: Buckland (Dover) - Anglo-Saxon	Early 6th century	34.5cm (13 $^{37}/_{64}$")	Iron	British Museum, 1963,1108.98
Gamla Lödöse, Sankt Peder, Västergötland, Sweden	Medieval - Viking	22cm (8 $^{21}/_{32}$")	Juniper	Sweden History Museum SHM 29750:542
Grytøy, Trondenes, Troms, Norway	9th century	91.5cm (36 $^{1}/_{32}$")	Whale bone	Historisk Museum, Bergen, B274
Gorodishche, Novrogod, Russia	9th – 10th century	80cm (31 $^{1}/_{2}$")	Timber	Novgorod State Museum
Norway: Møre og Romsdal (county): Romsdalsfjorden: Vestnes: Villa Farm	9th - 10th century	20.30 cm (7$^{63}/_{64}$") (remaining)	Whale bone	British Museum, 1894,1105.45
Beamish and Crawford Brewery site, Cork City, Ireland	1070	30cm (11 $^{13}/_{16}$")	Yew	National Museum of Ireland.

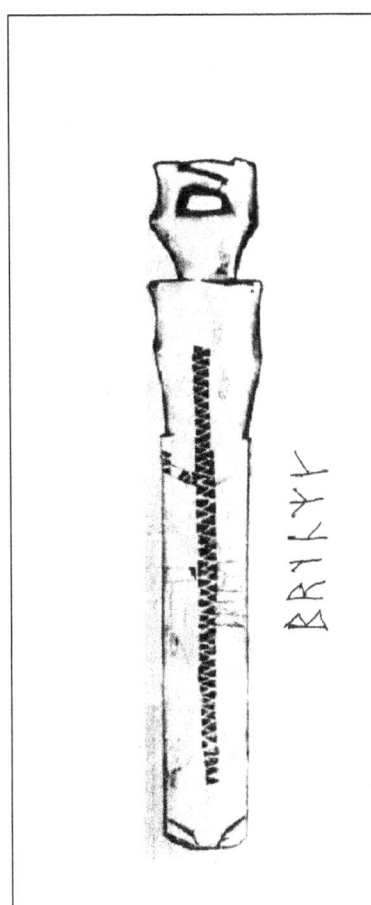

Drawing 2. The Gamla Lödöse weaving knife. The back of the knife in a black and white photograph showing the two rows of interlocked triangles probably made by a triangular punch used on the back. In the centre on the bottom is a set of runes "ᛒ ᚱ ᛅ ᛁ ᛘ ᚴ" (Branmk) in Younger Futhark this could be a maker's or owner's mark.

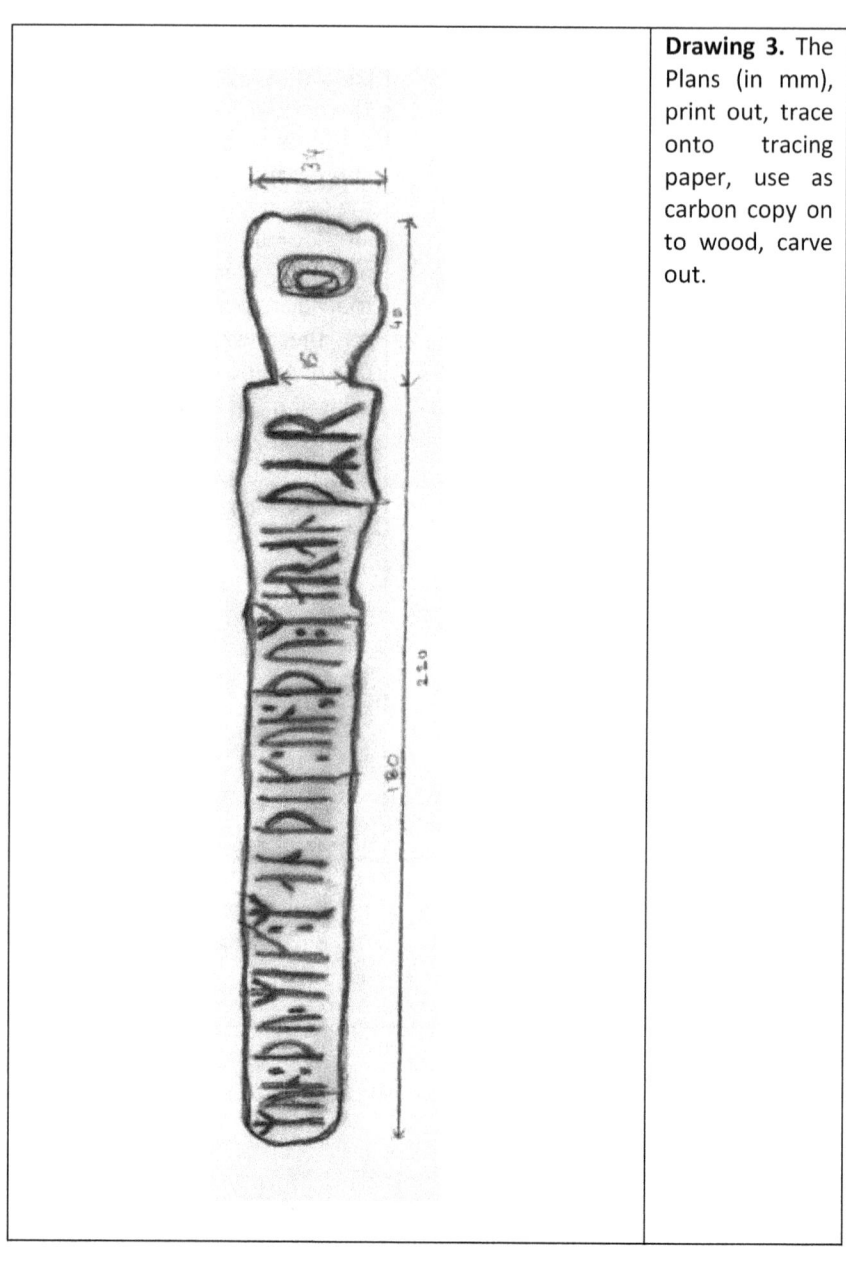

Drawing 3. The Plans (in mm), print out, trace onto tracing paper, use as carbon copy on to wood, carve out.

Materials.

Cutting list is simple: just one piece of timber 220mm (8 5/8") x 34mm (1 3/8"). I used pinus radiata in 19mm ($^3/_4$") thick board. Mineral turpentine and boiled linseed oil (3 parts to 1 part).

Tools.

Ruler, pencil, saw, mallet, draw knife, scrapper, some means of holding the work (i.e. shaving horse, hold down or bench vice), drill and drill bit (I used an 8mm (5/16") drill bit), hammer and modified nail.

Construction Instructions – the body of the weaving knife.

1) Hew a log of wood down to size, or use a plank of wood of the right thickness from your timber supplier.
2) Cut roughly to size.
3) Make a template in tracing paper, transfer shape and decoration to the wood.

Photo 24. Using tracing paper to transfer the outline of the weaving knife onto timber.

4) Refine shape, carve with knife or draw knife, drill hole in handle, clean up surfaces, smooth enough so it will not catch on the threads.
5) Use a template in tracing paper to transfer runes to the wood. See Photos 24 to 26.

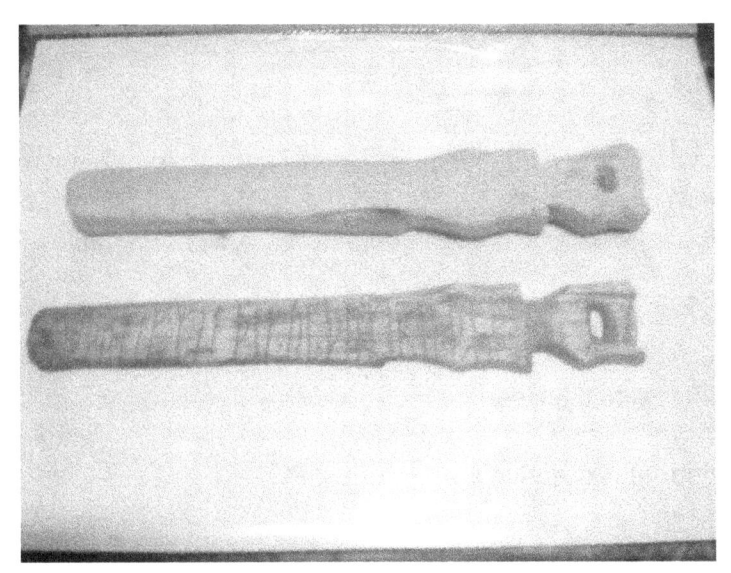

Photo 25. Knife cut out and shape refined to match original.

Photo 26. Runes traced onto blade before cutting.

Construction Instructions – Rune carving.

Tools.

Carving knife (small blade, handle sits in the palm of your hand), or a Stanley knife (spring loaded retractable blade is advisable), or a 'V' gouge and possibly a wooden mallet.

Materials.

Charcoal and linseed oil.

Personal Protective Equipment (PPE).

Leather gloves, leather apron.

Cutting the curved parts may need to be done as two opposing cuts, depending on the grain direction of the timber and the tool used.

I suggest you practice carving the runes on a scrap piece of the same timber used for the weaving knife. When you are confident, carve the runes into the weaving knife.

If the timber is tearing, try chopping down across the grain instead. Remember to have your carving tools mirror-polish sharp.

1) Secure the weaving knife, hold firmly in the opposite hand, resting on a workbench (**not** the kitchen table or your leg) or use a bench stop.

2) Cut slowly with a firm grip on the knife, following the drawn runes, avoid cutting towards any part of your body.
3) Cut a 'V' about 2mm ($^5/_{64}$") deep with two cuts on each part of the rune and remove the sliver of wood.
4) Cut the long part of the rune first, then cut the twig or rounded part of the rune.

If you are using a 'V' gouge, depending on the hardness of the wood you may not need to use a mallet to drive the gouge away from your body through the wood. Using a 'V' gouge is a matter of lining up the bottom of the 'V' on the bottom of the rune and pushing straight or curved as the rune requires at the right angle to remove a sufficient amount of wood.

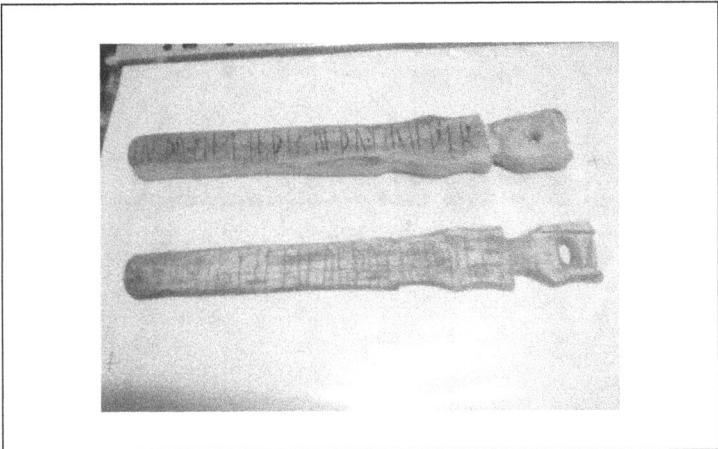

Photo 27. Cut runes highlighted with charcoal.

5)   Rub charcoal into runes to highlight them.
6)   On the reverse side mark out and use a punch and hammer to punch triangular holes in the surface.
7)   Carve the runes "ᛒ ᚱ ᛅ ᚾ ᛘ ᚴ" (Branmk) (Younger Futhark) in the centre on the bottom of the back of the knife, this could be a maker's or owner's mark. See Drawing 2.

8)   Clean up with a scraper, and give a coat of linseed oil, the usual recipe.

Using tracing paper.

For those that have not used tracing paper before, place the tracing paper on top of the drawing, with a pencil copy the design onto the tracing paper, turn the paper over and cover the lines with pencil, place on piece of timber, trace / go over the lines with the pencil, this will transfer the pencil on the other side to the timber.

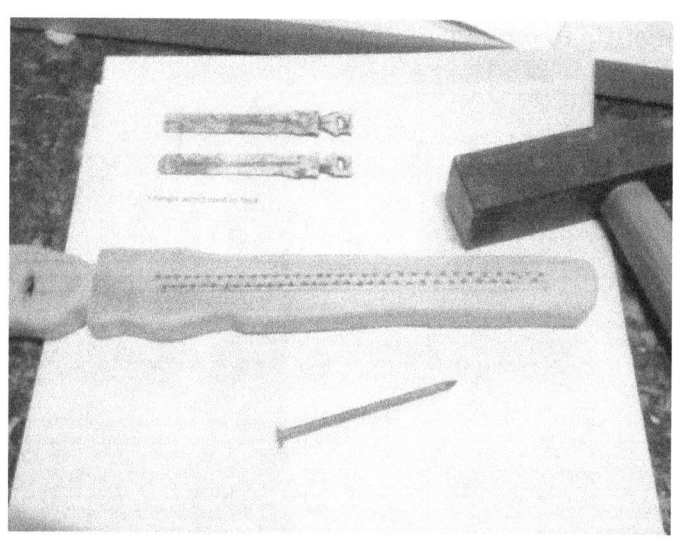

Photo 28. Using a nail with a triangular shaped nail to punch the two rows of triangular shaped nail holes.

Linseed oil.
The usual recipe: 3 parts mineral turpentine (turps) to 1 part boiled linseed oil.

Nail punch.
I made the punch I used from a 40mm (1 1/2") nail by grinding the diamond shaped point to a triangle.

The Oseberg chair.

By Darren Delany and Stephen Wyley.

The Oseberg chair	Oseberg Viking ship burial – Oseberg, Sem, Vestfold, Norway.	**When**: 800 – 850 CE
Stored: Universitetets Oldsaksamling	**Collection no.**: K70	**Material**: Beech
Size: Seat height 41cm (16 $^9/_{64}$"), length 56cm (22 $^3/_{64}$"), width 46cm (18 $^7/_{64}$"). Back height 71cm (27 $^{61}/_{64}$").		

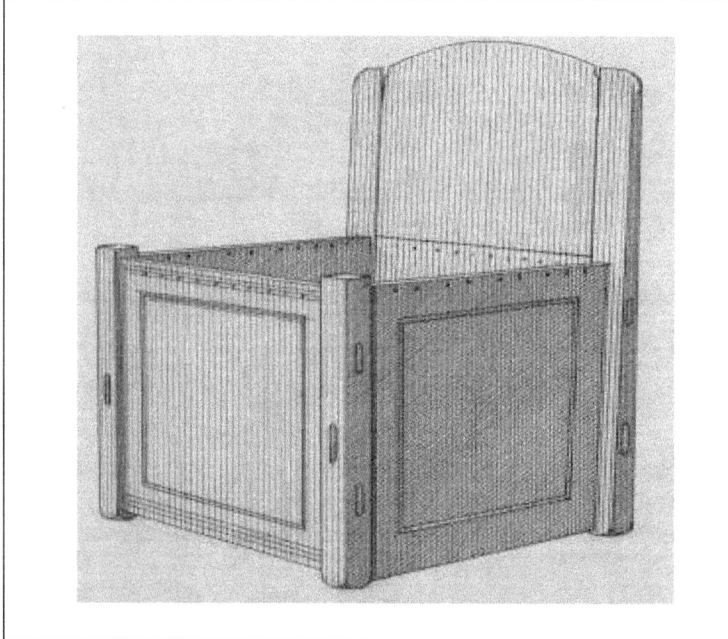

Drawing 4. Drawing of the Oseberg chair.

Photo 29. A replica of the chair in pine.

Introduction.

The Oseberg Viking ship burial (800 – 850 CE) was an extensive find including the ship, a sled, a cart and multiple chests, and the box chair.

The chair consists of four boards, supported by four legs or corner posts. The back and the rear posts slant backwards and continue above the seat. The parts of the chair are joined by mortise and tenon joints.

The boards have recessed areas, surrounded by narrow groves. The recessed areas were painted with multi-coloured animal ornamentation surrounded by geometric borders. The tops of the boards of the front and sides are provided with holes along the top, and across the back at the same height for a woven seat, the material of which was not preserved. There are no similar Viking finds of this design but there are a number of medieval examples. See Table 7.

Table 7. Chair – Comparison of Chair.

Description	Dated CE	Find and collection	Material	Dimensions
Backed chair (only back remains) held together with mortise and tenon joints.	1000 – 1050	Lund (Kv Färgaren 22) Sweden. Kulturen, Lund, KM 53.436:1065	Maple and with a cross piece in beech.	Height 75cm (29 $^{17}/_{32}$"), width 42.5cm (16 $^{47}/_{64}$")
Box chair with carved panels, front legs with horse carving on apex, curved sides run up to back. Seat forms a lid to the box which appears to have had a lock where there is a hole in the front panel. Mortise and tenon joints are clearly shown.	Early 13th century	from Blakar farm in Gudbrandsdalen, Norway.	The staves are made from birch while the panels are from pine.	Unknown.
A pine choir stall with Mickey Mouse ears on the side panel. Side and front panels are relief carved.	13th century	Hol Church, Hallingdal, Kulturhistorisk museum, Oslo. KHM. C17802. There is a Choir stall with ears from Skrautvål, Nord-Aurdal. 13th or 14th century is very similar.	Pine	Height 161 cm (63 $^{25}/_{64}$"), width 71 cm (27 $^{61}/_{64}$"), depth 38 cm (14 $^{61}/_{64}$).

Box chair, gothic carved panels, bottom edge and back carved.	15th century	Halberstadt Cathedral, Halberstadt, Germany	Unknown
Box chair with high back, carved panels and arms decorated with chimeras.	1401 – 1500	Museum of religious art and Mosan art, Liège, Belgium. Inventory number: 512	Unknown	Height 143 cm (56 $^{19}/_{64}$"), Width 77 cm (30 $^{5}/_{16}$"), Depth 53 cm (20 $^{55}/_{64}$")

Materials.

- The original chair is made from beech but I found pine quite good for the job.
- The seat weave, 8mm (3/8") rope in hemp, nettle etc.
- And wood glue, linseed oil, and dowels.

Table 8. Cutting list (L x W x Thickness)	
Front and back (lower)	56 x 41 x 2cm (22 1/16""x 16 ⅛""x ¾"")
Side x 2	48 x 41 x 2cm (18 ⅞"x 16 ⅛"x ¾")
Back (upper)	48 x 30 x 2cm (18 ⅞"x 11 ¾"x ¾")
Front legs x 2	43 x 4 x 4cm (16 ⅞""x 1 ½"x 1 ½""")
Back legs x 2	64 x 6 x 4cm (25 3/16"""x 2 ⅜"" x 1 ½")

Safety tip: Rags used to wipe on linseed oil should be soaked in water afterwards because they can spontaneously combust and start fires.

Tools.

Pencil and ruler, jigsaw (electrical) or coping saw, drill/drill bit (9mm (13/32") for rope holes), hand saw, rasp or knife, and brush for the linseed oil. Mallet (wooden) for persuading the wood to move.

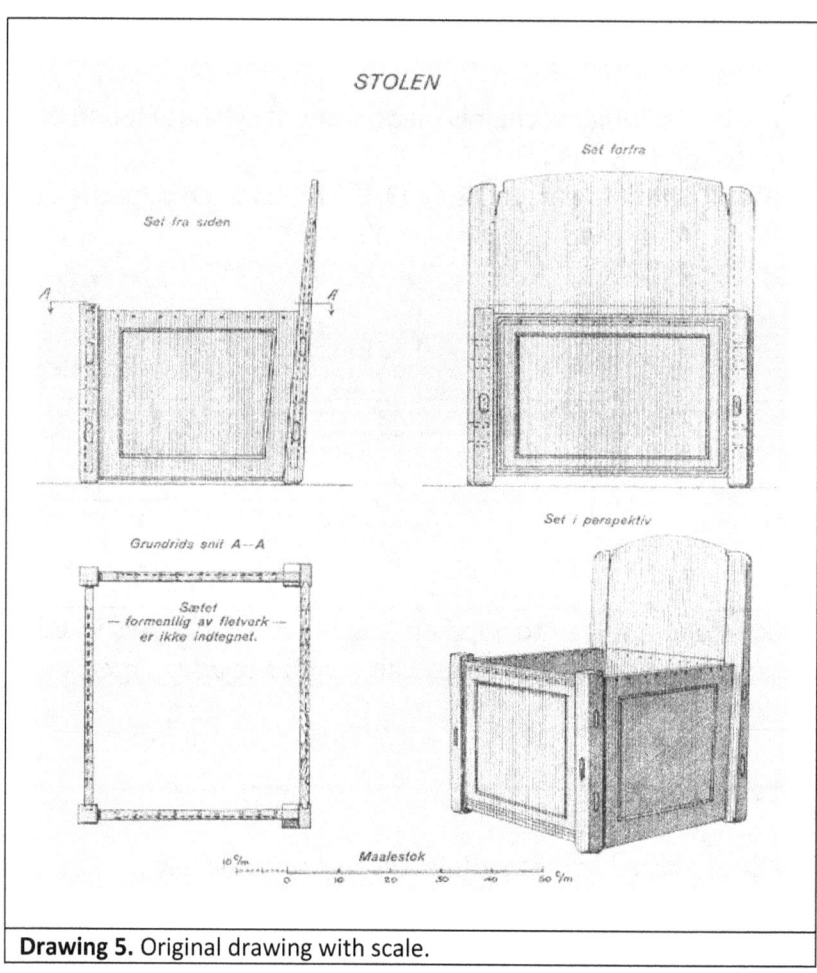

Drawing 5. Original drawing with scale.

Plans are based on the original drawings, see Drawing 5. Obtaining planks in these sizes may prove difficult, so some gluing of planks together will be required. See section in 14th Century Volume 1 for making wider planks.

A larger version of the Oseberg chair is located in Appendix 9 – Larger Oseberg chair.

Construction Instructions.

1. Selecting a suitable piece of timber for the chair free of knots.
2. Mark out timber as per plan using a pencil and ruler. Make sure to avoid cutting through knots.

Front. See Drawing 6 & 7.
1. Mark out, cut out with a saw, and clean up the edges.
2. The central section between the two tenons can be cut out with a jig saw.
3. Chisel out recess with broad chisel, chisel around edge of recess first. Chisel the main part of the recess with the grain down to 2 to 3mm (1/16" - 1/8").
4. Mark out and drill holes for the seat cord along the upper edge, round the edges of holes with a file or counter sink bit (saves on wear and tear on cord).

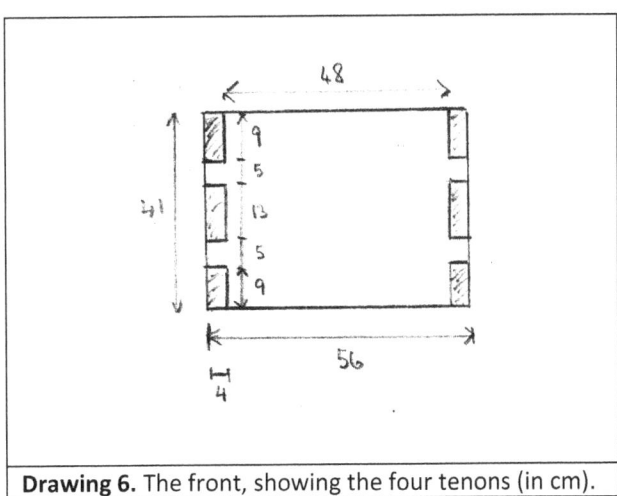

Drawing 6. The front, showing the four tenons (in cm).

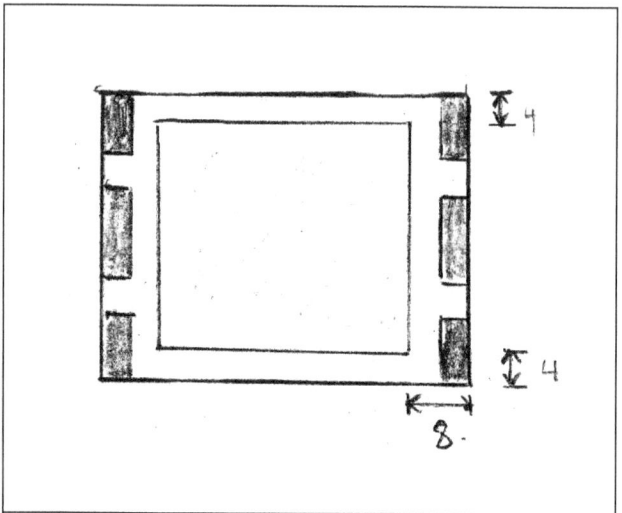

Drawing 7. The front, showing the recessed area (in cm).

Photo 30. Side, showing recess cut 2-3mm ($^5/_{64}$" - $^1/_8$") into outer face of front.

Sides. (reduction in number of mortices and the sloped side). See Drawings 8 & 9.

1. Mark out include sloped right edge, cut out, and clean up.
2. Chisel out recess with broad chisel, chisel around edge of recess first. Chisel the main part of the recess with the grain down to 2 to 3mm (1/16" - 1/8").
3. Mark out and drill holes for the seat cord along the upper edge, round the edges of holes with a file or counter sink bit (saves on wear and tear on cord).

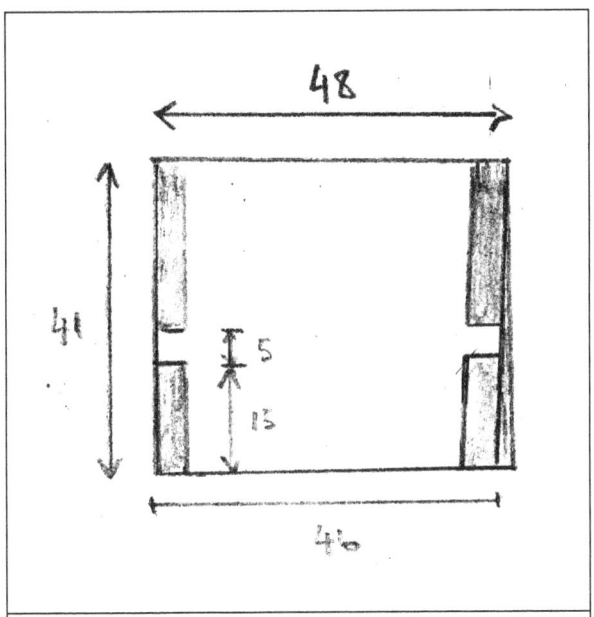

Drawing 8. The side, showing the sloped back and two tenons (in cm).

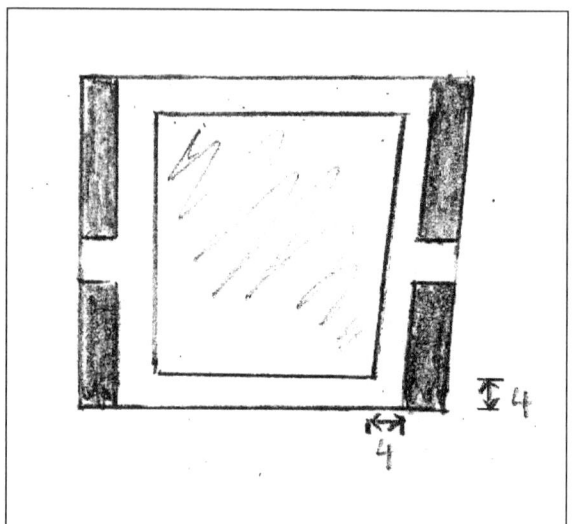

Drawing 9. The side, showing the recessed area (in cm).

Photo 31. Side, showing recess cut 2-3mm (1/16" - 1/8") into outer face of side.

Back (Upper). See Drawings 10 – 12.

1. Mark out and cut to length with a hand saw.
2. Make a template in cardboard to match the curve of the top of the chair. Trace around the template and cut curved top and corner notches.

Back (Lower). See Drawings 10 – 12.

1. Mark out, cut out with a saw, and clean up the edges.
2. The central section between the two tenons can be cut out with a jig saw.
3. Chisel out recess with broad chisel, chisel around edge of recess first. Chisel the main part of the recess with the grain down to 2 to 3mm (1/16" - 1/8").
4. Mark out and drill holes for the seat cord along the upper edge, round the edges of holes with a file or counter sink bit (saves on wear and tear on cord).

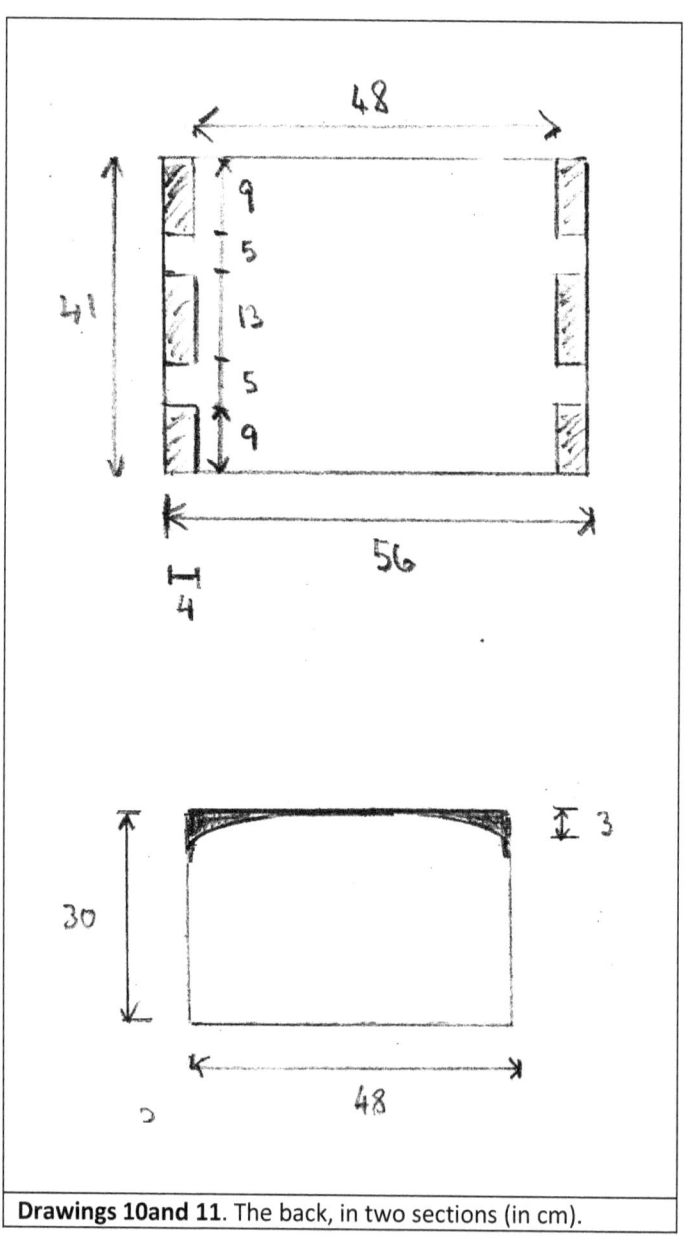

Drawings 10 and 11. The back, in two sections (in cm).

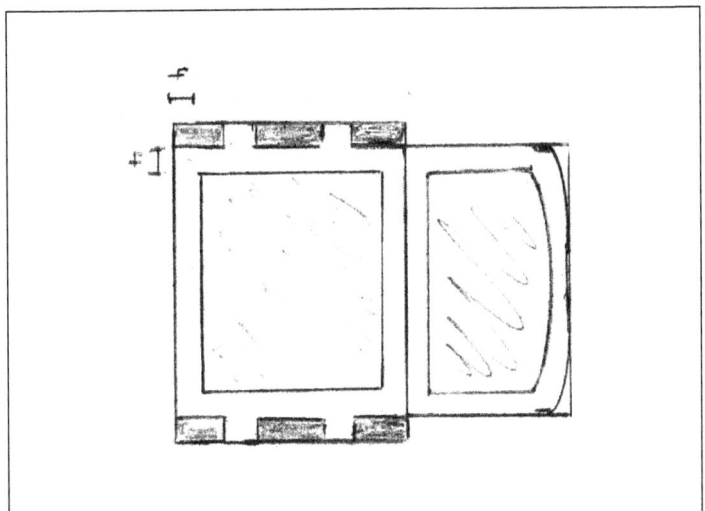

Drawing 12. The back, in two sections connected and the recesses in both sections (in cm).

Photo 32. The back, in two sections connected and the recesses in both sections.

Front legs. See Drawing 13.
1. Mark out, cut to length with a saw, and clean up.
2. Round of edges of leg tops with spoke shave.
3. Mark out and chisel out mortises.
4. Define the edges of the mortice with a chisel.
5. Chisel out mortise while ensuring the sides are straight.
6. When you get to half way through, turn the leg over and repeat the process from the other side of the leg.
7. Mark out and chisel out the slot for the ends of the back, sides and front, 5mm (¼") deep.

Note: this reduces the amount of the damage to the edges of the mortise. Note: A drill with a spade bit (a few mm less than the hole) may be used to remove most of the mortise, followed up by a clean-up with a sharp chisel.

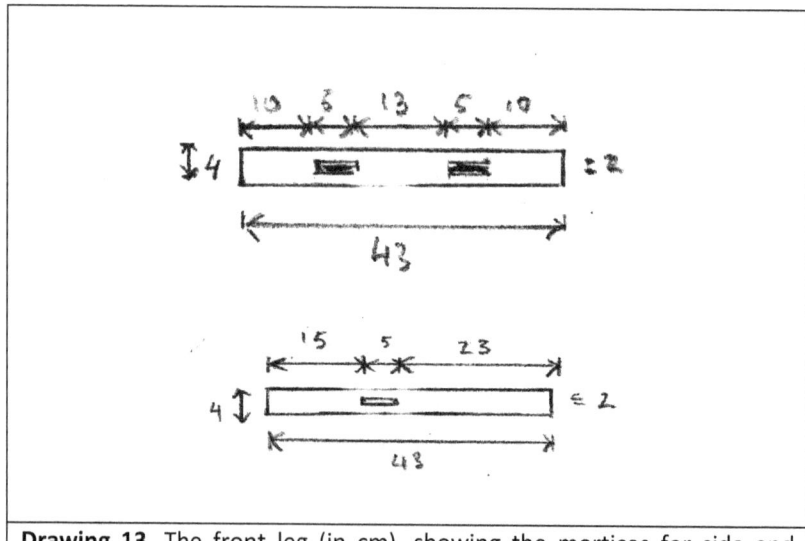

Drawing 13. The front leg (in cm), showing the mortices for side and front tenons.

Photo 33. The front legs with mortises.

Photo 34. The front legs getting the rebate chiselled out.

Back legs. See Drawings 14 and 15.
1. Mark out with a slope on the bottom end of the legs.
2. Use a cross saw to cut to length.
3. Use a rip saw to cut down to the right width.
4. Clean up surfaces with a plane and scraper.
5. Mark out and chisel out mortise.
    a. Define the edges of the mortice with a chisel.
    b. Chisel out mortise while ensuring the sides are straight.
    c. Half way down, turn the leg over and repeat the process from the other side of the leg. Note; this reduces the amount of the damage to the edges of the mortise. Note: A drill with a spade bit (a few mm less that the mortise) may be used to remove most of the mortise.
    d. Check mortise and tenon joints on a regular basis. The joint should be snug but not overly tight.
    e. Dry fit together back and back legs with gentle taps with a wooden mallet.

Note: Remember the backwards slope towards the legs. Be wary when working close to the edges.

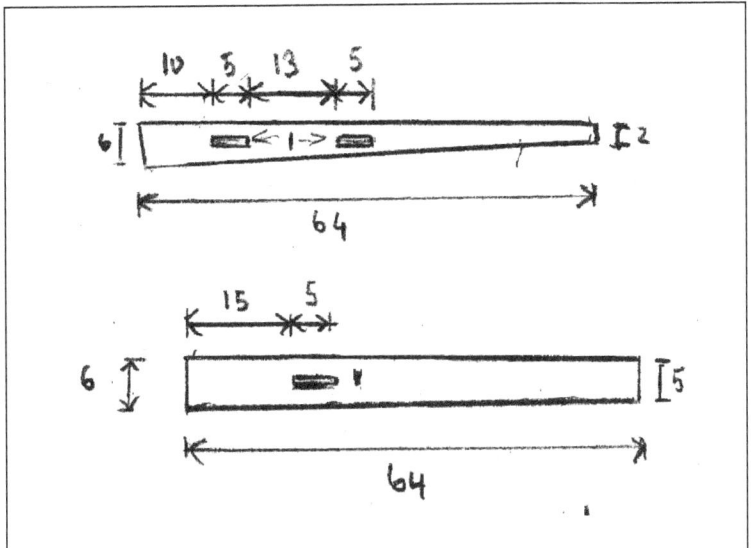

Drawing 14. The back leg, showing the mortices for side and back tenons (in cm).

Photo 35. The back tenons are marked out only to 1cm (3/8") to fit thinner legs.

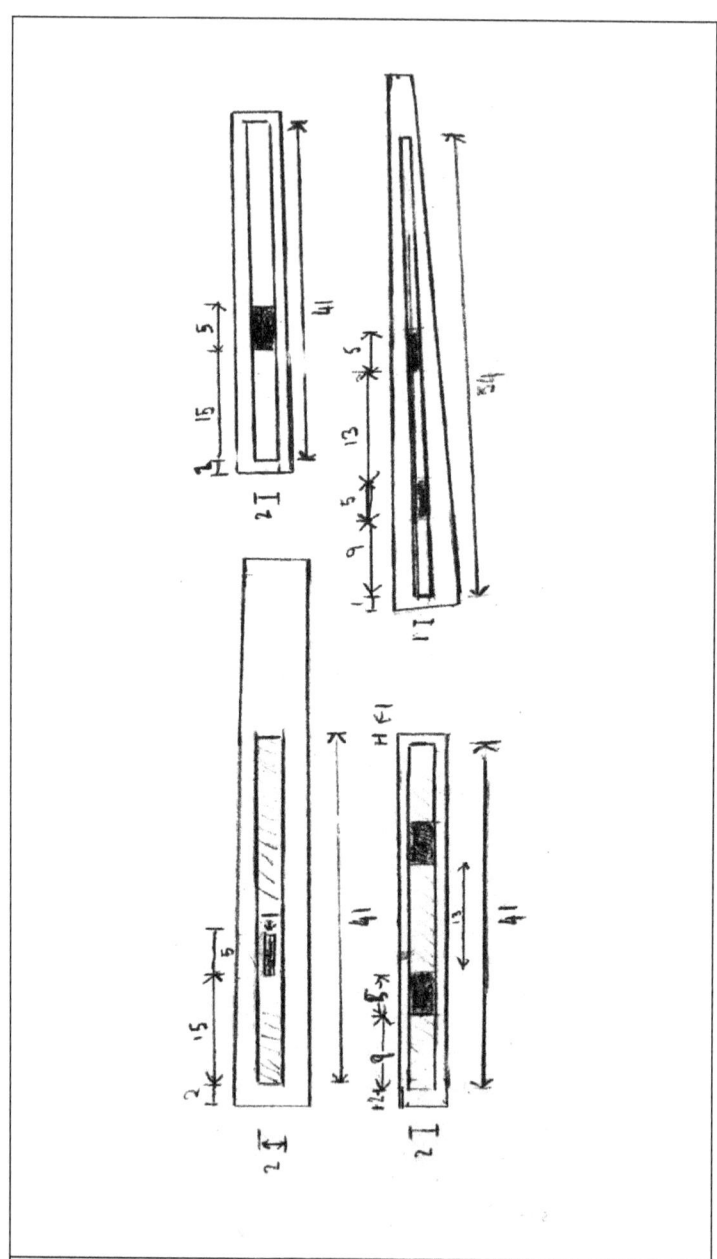

Drawing 15. The recesses in the back and front legs (cm), to the depth of 6mm (1/4").

Photo 36. The back connected to the back legs, showing the recesses.

Photo 37. All the parts connected, awaiting the rope woven seat.

Fitting together - Flat pack or not ?

You may decide to make this chair a flat packed item of furniture (i.e. *'Ikea'*) but you will need to re-weave the seat each time. For fewer pieces to carry as a flat pack I recommend that you glue and dowel the front piece to the front legs, and the back to the back legs, and have the sides separate.

If you are going to have the chair permanently fixed together you can apply glue to all the joins and dowel through legs and tenons.

Photo 38. The back connected to the back legs with dowels and glue, showing the recesses.

Doweling.

Drill holes the size of the dowels. Round end of dowel inserted into hole. Put some glue into the hole and onto the dowel. Slowly tap the dowel into place to avoid cracking the timber. Wipe off excess glue with a damp cloth. Apply Linseed oil or Danish oil to finish stool.

Note: timber will dry out over time; for a good leg fit I recommend soaking the top ends of the legs in water prior to use. I also recommend an annual coating of suitable oil for the preservation of the wood.

Write or carve your name, year made and group on the bottom of the seat.

Weaving the seat. (using between 15 -16 m (49' 2" – 62' 6") of wool, linen or hemp fibre).

1. Start at the bottom back corner running from back to front, front to back across the seat, and pull through as you weave.
2. In the opposite rear corner either tie off or continue around the corner post and enter the side rear hole and weave the cord under and over cords running back to front.
3. Tie off at the front side corner.
4. The tie off knot can just be a simple half hitch. The seat cords may need to be retightened over time.
5. A wooden wedge can be inserted in one of the outer loops to increase the weave tension.

See Photo 29 for vision of the woven seating.

Recommendation: use a cushion on the seat to avoid a chequered end.

The Hedeby chest.

By Stephen Wyley.

The Hedeby Chest	Find location: Hedeby (Haithabu) Harbour, Germany	**When**: Pre 982 CE
Stored: Viking Museum Haithabu	**Collection no.**: SH1919-4.4804	**Material**: Oak & Iron
Size: L (base 52cm (20 $^{15}/_{32}$")), top 42cm (16 $^{17}/_{32}$")), W (base 23cm (9 $^{1}/_{16}$"), top 22cm (8 $^{21}/_{32}$")), H 27cm (10 $^{5}/_{8}$").		

Introduction.

The chest was found in the harbour of Hedeby in Germany, dropped in clear water. Judging from the position of where it was found it was probably dropped over the side from a ship. Loaded down with a stone (granite, weighing 16.4kg (36 pound, 2.5 ounces)), lock plate missing, indicating that it had been stolen, broken into, emptied and disposed of into the waters of the harbour.

> "The chest was found under "*The royal longship "Hedeby wreck 1" dates from c. AD 982 (-0/+7) and lay in the so-called Hebekasten section of the cofferdam. During excavations here in 1979, a sea chest was found near the transition from the ship's bow to the midship, only 0.90 m from the keel. The chest lay c. 0.5 m deeper than the wreck itself, which seems to rule out any connection with the ship.*" Kalmring, 2010.

The chest is made of oak, trapezoid in shape, somewhat reminiscent of the Oseberg 178 chest, with a bottom mortised into the ends.

The tenons of the bottom are not centred on the end board and appear closer to the back of the chest, see Drawing 16 and 20. The planks themselves come in a range of thickness and thickness varies across the board, the original maker has taken this into consideration, whereas the plans are drawn for a standard 20mm (3/4") thick plank.

The lid is dished out on the inside and carved on the outside from front to back. See Table 8 - Trapezoid chest comparison, updated from Viking – Volume 1 (2021).

This chest is the **ONLY** currently extant[13] Viking chest with any form of carving on it, consisting of straight lines around the edges on the ends, front and back. See Drawings 22 and 23 for more details.

Since the lock is missing and a hole remains and there are two hasps on the lid (at different levels on the lid), we can deduce that the lock was a double hasp slide lock. The second part of this article details how to make a lock to fit the extant hole in the front of the chest. See Section 2 on the double hasp slide *'Winchester'* lock.

---

[13] Too many times I see a supposed *'Viking'* chest provided with a carving of a *'gripping best'*, this is wrong, it is not a replica, it's a bit of fantasy and has no part in re-enactment or a living history display.

Photo 39. Hedeby chest at the Viking Museum Hedeby (Haithabu.)

Photo 40. Hedeby Chest Replica in pine.

Materials.
Timber (oak preferably but Pinus radiata will do) 27cm (10 $^5/_8$") wide x 225cm (89") long. I recommend getting at least 3 metres (118") of the timber just in case. See Table 8 for the timber cutting list.

Other materials include:
- Linseed oil (diluted 1 part boiled linseed oil to 3 parts mineral turpentine;
- and wood glue (also known as PVA).

Table 8. Showing cutting list for an original Hedeby chest.	
Bottom	52 x 18cm (20 ½" x 7 ¼"")
End * 2	27 x 22cm (10 $^5/_8$" x 8 ¾"")
Front	52 x 27cm (20 ½" x10 $^5/_8$")
Back	52 x 27cm (20 ½" x 10 $^5/_8$")
Lid	42* 22cm (16 ½" x 8 ¾")

Nails (x26, get 30 just in case), glue, mild steel for fittings (hinges, hasp, lock plate and key), spring steel for the spring in the lock, see Table 9 below.

These measurements are based on the original chest but plans are available for larger and smaller versions, see Appendices 5 and 6.

Table 9. Metal requirements.			
Steel	*Hinges*	*Lock*	*Keys *2*
3mm Mild Flat bar (1/8")	750mm (29 1/2")	24 x 8mm (1" x 3/8")	150 * 5mm (6 x 3/16")
2mm Mild sheet (14GA)	-	240*70mm (9 ⅗" x 2 $^3/_4$")	-
Spring steel	-	60mm*10mm (2 ⅜" x ⅜")	-

Tools.

Rulers, eraser, set square, chisels (25mm & 7mm, plain edge), files (coarse - flat bastard, fine - square bastard), tenon saw, hand saw, plane, scraper, 'G' clamps, scrap wood (for holding work without damaging it), claw hammer, wooden mallet, bench vice, pencil, hand drill (with 4mm (11/64") bit).

Construction Instructions.

Bottom.

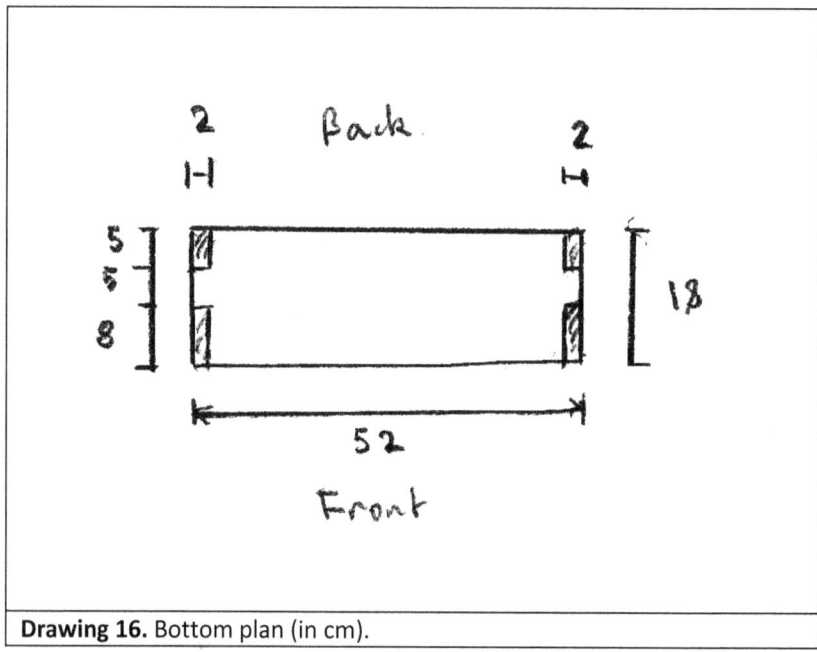

Drawing 16. Bottom plan (in cm).

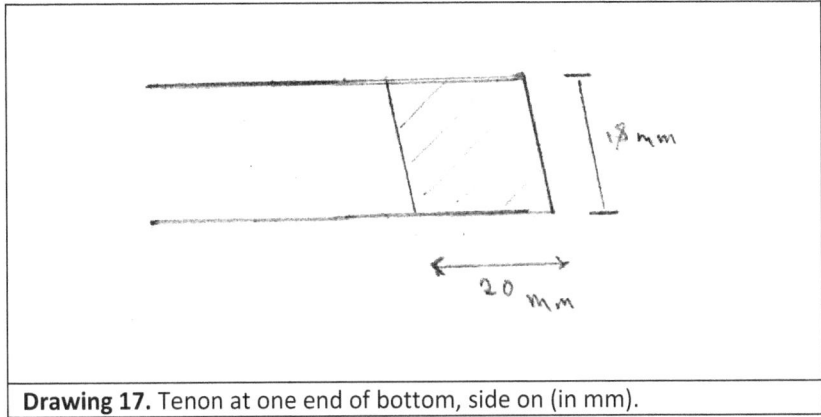

Drawing 17. Tenon at one end of bottom, side on (in mm).

1. Mark out the bottom with pencil, set square and ruler, including the angle of the tenons and ends.
2. Mark tenons 'A' and 'B'.
3. Cut the angled ends on either end.
    a. Place each end of the bottom in a bench vice and cut the end cuts on either side of the tenon, angle the cuts to match the angle of the end of the bottom.
    b. Turn the bottom on its side in the vice and cut down at an angle to meet the end cut on one side of the end.
    c. Check angle and modify if required.
    d. Erase pencil marks.

Carving the lines in ends, front and back.
- Prior to assembly of the chest.

Mark out the ends, front and back for the carved lines.
Carve lines with 'V' gouge, or you could use a sharp knife and a steady hand.

See Drawings 18 & 19. Note: the lines are based on the original lines but have been extended to make it symmetrical.

Drawing 18. Line decoration on front and back (in cm).

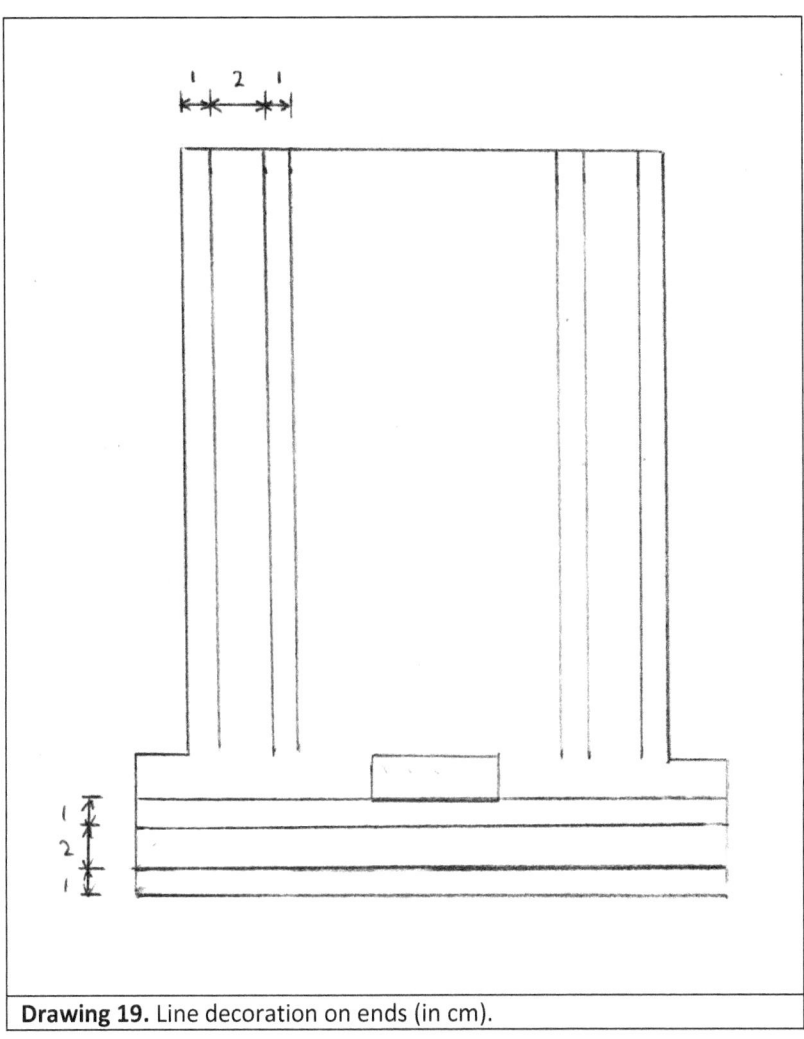

Drawing 19. Line decoration on ends (in cm).

Ends.

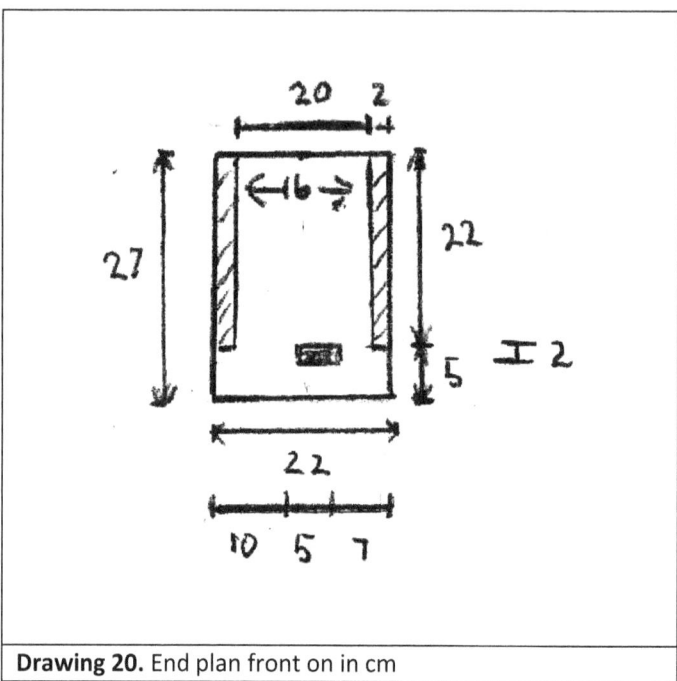

Drawing 20. End plan front on in cm

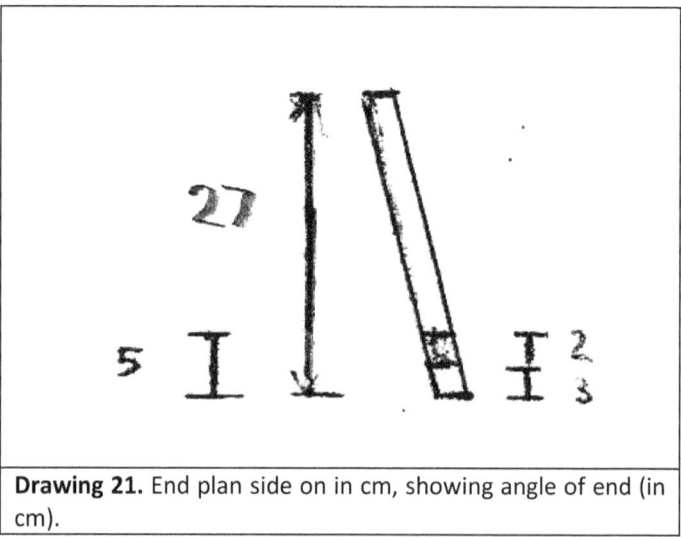

Drawing 21. End plan side on in cm, showing angle of end (in cm).

1. Mark out ends with pencil, set square and ruler.
2. Cut the ends.
3. Cut the angled ends on both ends.
4. Turn the end on its side and cut downwards at the angle to match the ends.
5. Turn the end on the bottom end and cut the side inserts.
6. Clean up joints.
7. Mark out the mortices. Mark (in pencil) on the end of mortice 'A' and the other end mortice 'B' so it matches with the bottom.
    a. using a sharp knife (Stanley/ box cutter) to make the outside of the mortice.
    b. clamp the end to the bench
    c. chisel or drill out tenon from either side.
8. Fit ends to the bottom, matching 'A's and 'B's.
    a. this may entail modifying the tenon or the mortice to fit snugly. A large squared section rat tail file proved to be very effective in the corners of the mortice.

Note: *It is important to have a clean tenon on the outside because people will see any error.*

Front and back.

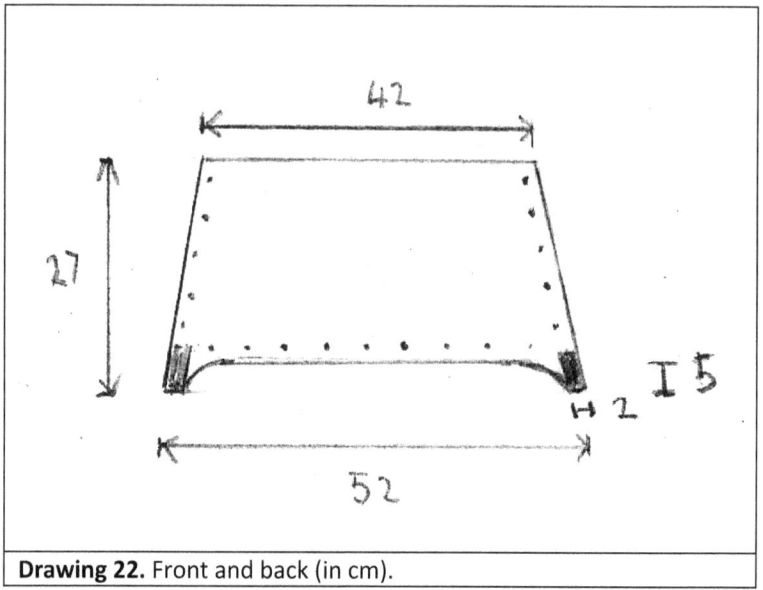

Drawing 22. Front and back (in cm).

8. Use the fitted bottom and ends to mark out the front and back.

    a. compare the angle of each end of the chest and modify the joints until they match.

    b. cut out the front and attach with nails, pre-drill nails holes with a drill bit a mm less than the width of the nails used (skew nails for better security) and apply glue to all the contact points. Clean up excess glue with a wet cloth.

    c. Set pieces in place, drill the first nail hole in the top corner, drill through the front just into the end, which leaves something for the nail to bite into. Then nail the other corner, the bottom corners, don't drive all the nails into the wood until you are sure all is, leave enough space to pull the nail out if it needs to be reset. Then hammer all the other nails in, skewing the nails in opposite directions as you go.

d. repeat for the back of the chest.

9. There is a single nail hole securing the end on the right side (*as you face the front of the chest*), see Photo 41. You may want to replicate the single nailing or repeat for all four corners for stability. So the process would look like: Mark and drill the nail holes in the bottom corners of each end so the nail goes through the end and into the edges of both the front and back boards.

Photo 41. Front right corner of chest.

Lid.

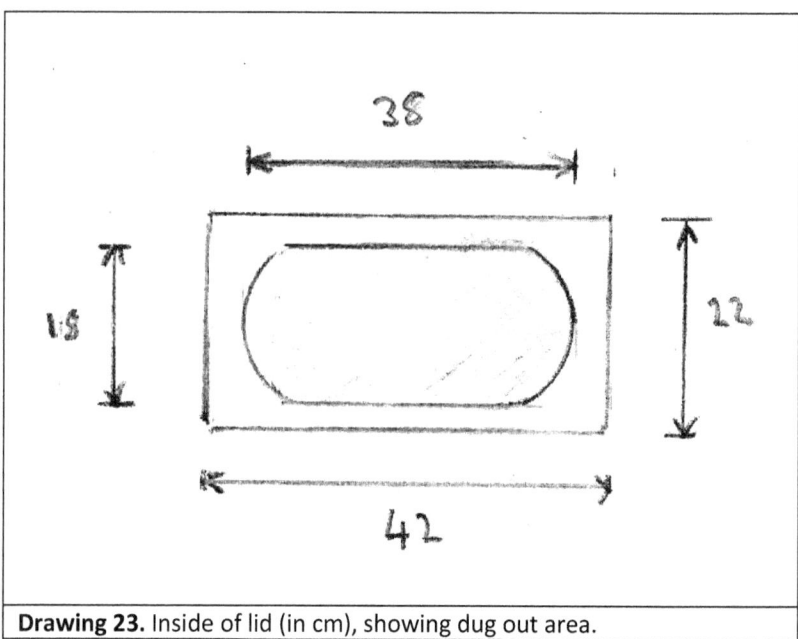

Drawing 23. Inside of lid (in cm), showing dug out area.

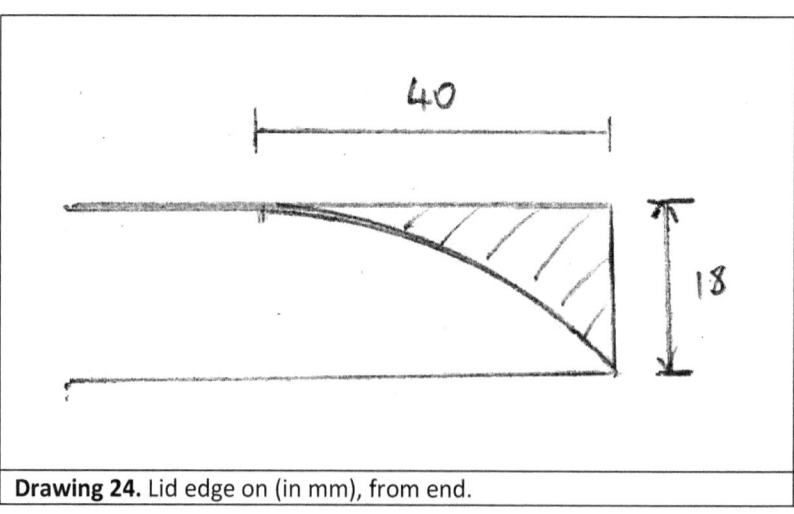

Drawing 24. Lid edge on (in mm), from end.

Photo 42. Replica chest with lid open

1. Place the box upside down onto the timber for the lid.
    a. Mark out the box outline on the timber using a pencil.
    b. Cut the angled ends to match the angled ends of the chest.
    c. Cut the lid to the required width.

Dishing out the lid.

1. Mark out rounded ended shape on the inside of the chest.
2. Secure lid to bench with clamps.
3. Using a curved adze or gouges to remove half the thickness of the board, shallower at the ends and sides (for a 18mm (¾") board you can take it down a 10mm (⅜") in centre of dug out. See Drawings 23 and 24, and Photos 40 & 42.
4. Use a flatter gouge to trim off ridges.
5. Smooth with scraper.

Carved top.

1. Mark out curvature on the ends of the lid. Mark out a line 4cm (1 ½") from edge on either side of lid matching curvature marker on ends of lids;
2. Secure in vice and plane (spokeshave or drawknife) of edges of lid.

Clean up the chest.

1. Remove any parts that stick out (i.e. bottom end of end leg, or tenon out of ends).
2. Plane and scrape to clean up the chest. Apply linseed oil as a preservative.

Note: It is recommended that boiled linseed oil (1 part boiled linseed oil to 3 parts mineral turpentine) is used as raw linseed oil leaves the surface sticky.

Making the Hinges.

Material: Mild steel flat bar. 24mm x 3mm (1" x ⅛").

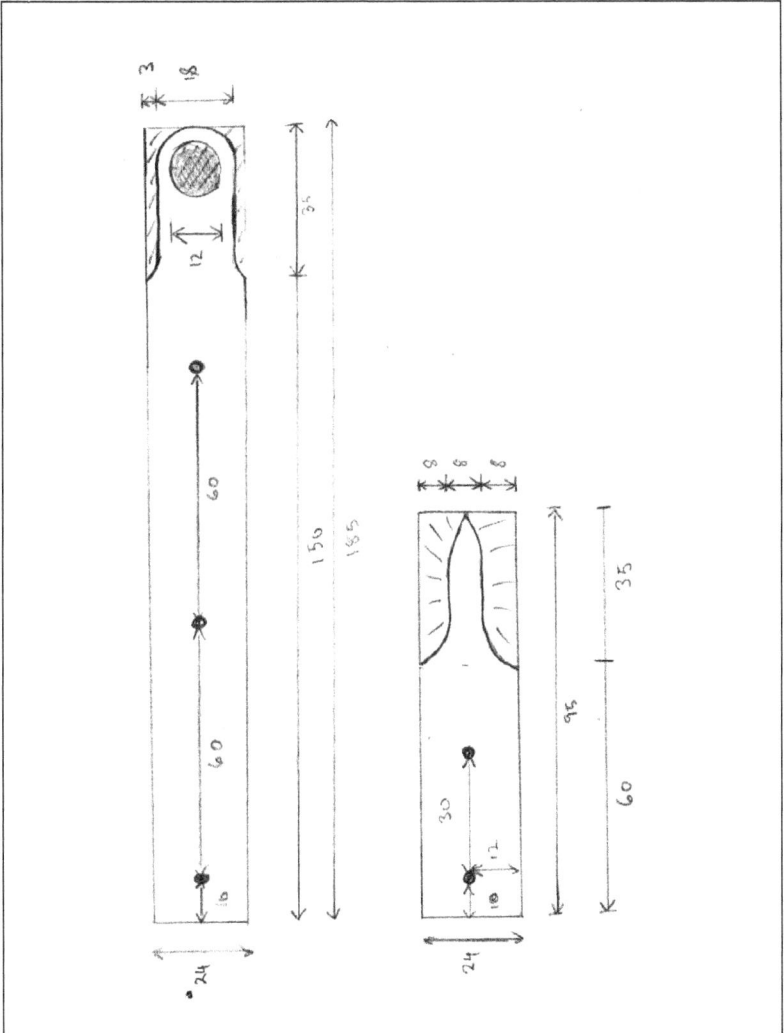

Drawing 25. Hook and eye hinges (in mm). The ring section is attached to the back of the chest. The top part of the hinge is bent to follow the curvature of the lid.

Blacksmithing.

Tools: Forge (gas, coal, charcoal), cut off, hammers (ball peen and cross peen), drift, tongs, anvil, hot punch.

1. Mark and use cut off to cut section of hinges to length;
2. Eye section, shape ring sections, drift hole for hook in ring section;
3. Hook section, reduce end to section down to point;
4. Bend point of hook end into a 'U' shape using hammer, tongs and horn of the anvil;
5. Pass hook end through eye and form loop with hammer, tongs and anvil, so it will swivel around eye without catching;
6. Shape hook section to curvature of chest;
7. Hot punch nail holes and clean up;
8. Blacken hinges to reduce rusting.

Cold.

Tools: Angle grinder with cut off disc or hacksaw, files, hammer, dishing block or anvil, drill and drill bits (size depends on the nails you use).

1. Mark and cut to length
2. Drill eye hole (15mm ($^{19}/_{32}$")) drill bit) in eye section;
3. Shape around outside of eye hole, clean up with files.
4. Cut and grind hook section, clean up with files;
5. Pass hook section through eye and form loop so it will swivel around eye without catching;
6. Shape hook section to curvature of chest using a hammer and a dishing block or the horn of an anvil;
7. Drill nail holes, clean up.
8. Blacken fittings to reduce rusting.

Adding fittings.

Add the **hinges** first.
1. Using a ruler and a set square mark out where the nail holes for the hinges are to sit, normally ¼ of the length of the chest from the ends, see Drawing 26 and 27.
2. Drill holes in the back of the chest for the back part of the hinge, using a drill bit slightly smaller than the thickness of the nail.
3. Nail back of hinge in places.
4. Repeat for the top part of hinges.
5. Turn the chest over and cleat the nails inside the front of the chest. Use a suitable lump of steel as an anvil to support the head of the nail, bend nails over the ends of the nails to form a staple and flatten.

Note: It appears that the hinges are inset into the chest.

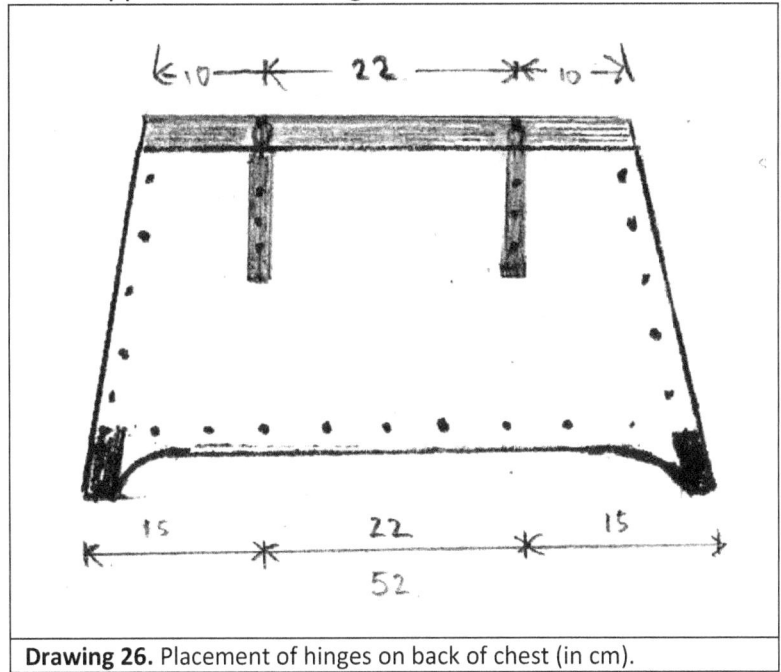

Drawing 26. Placement of hinges on back of chest (in cm).

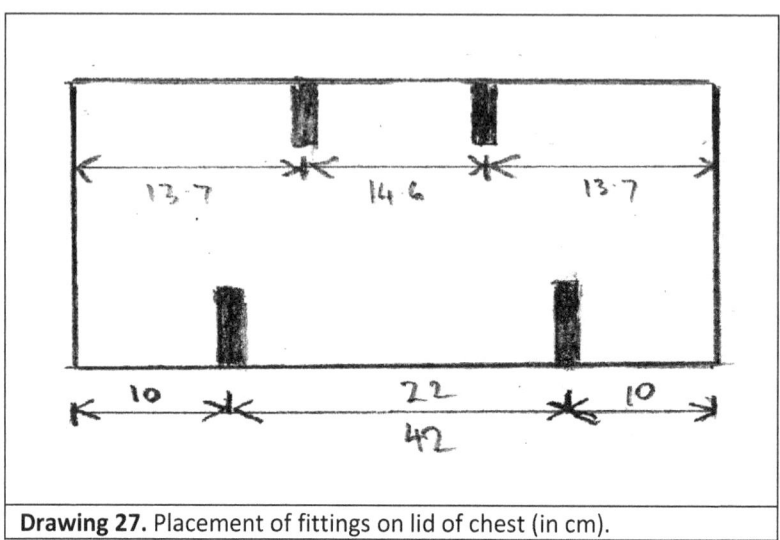

Drawing 27. Placement of fittings on lid of chest (in cm).

Adding the lock.

1. Centre placement of lock on front of chest.
2. Mark out outline of lock on front of chest.
3. Mark out features of lack on the front of the chest.
4. Chisel out wood to match the inside of the lock, test fit as you go. See Photo 39 for the shape of the hole left in the front of the chest by the lock.
5. Coat prominent features of lock with chalk (i.e. lugs, slide, spring and hasp) and bang into place, any high areas will be highlighted, remove high areas until the lock fits.
6. Nail in place but do not cleat lock plate in place, ensure lock works in situ, make modifications as necessary.
7. Apply grease to moving parts of the lock.
8. When happy that the lock works, cleat lock attachment nails to secure the lock.

Finishing.

1. Write or carve your name, year made and group on the bottom of the chest (it may help identifying the chest if it is lost or stolen).
2. Store in a clean, dry place, out of direct sunlight.
3. Timber will dry out over time, I recommend an annual coating of suitable oil for the preservation of the wood and joints.

Addenda.

On closer examination of Photo 39;
- it appears the lid hasp section is indented the lid,
- the hasp on the right is larger than the hasp on the left,
- the end of the hasp on the right hooks into the lid and there are two holes in the lid on either side of the hasp like the hinges of the Oseberg 178 chest,
- the top end of the left hasp is obscured by some sort of accretion (the remains of the end of the hasp),
- the accretion on the front of the chest on either end of the lock hole could be the remains of the lock plate.

Taking the above mentioned details into consideration and implementing them in a replica would make it even more accurate. I do look forward to closely examining the original chest when the opportunity arises.

The Winchester lock.

By Stephen Wyley.

The Winchester lock.	Find location: burial chest from The Old Minster Cemetery in Winchester, England.	**When**: 9th century CE.
Reference information: Winchester Cathedral, Green Cemetery (Goodall in Biddle 1990) 1003-5, 1016-17, Figs. 317-18, 3686).		**Material**: Iron (spring steel for spring)
Size: L. 25.3cm x W. 11cm (9 $^{61}/_{64}$" x 4 $^{21}/_{64}$") of lock plate		

Introduction.

The lock is missing from the Hedeby chest and this article is an instruction on how to make a working lock to cover the hole and secure the chest. As the hole left behind shows gaps for a double ended slide and the remains are the two hasps on the lid (at different levels on the lid), we can determine that the lock was a double hasp slide lock.

The Winchester Lock represents a clear example of lock type 2A, with two hasps on the left and right of the lock plate, with a central "L" shaped keyhole. From the drawings it appears that there is a metal border around the lock plate, I have chosen not to do this step, you may go the whole hog, I suggest you use 1mm mild steel strips for the border.

The thickness of the back end of the lock must fit inside the thickness of the front timber. The thickness of the timber of the Hedeby chest is unknown at this time (inquiries have been made). The assumption of 20mm (¾") timber is made and therefore the lock parts must fit inside that 20mm (¾"). The front of the chest is dug out to accommodate the thickness of the lock.

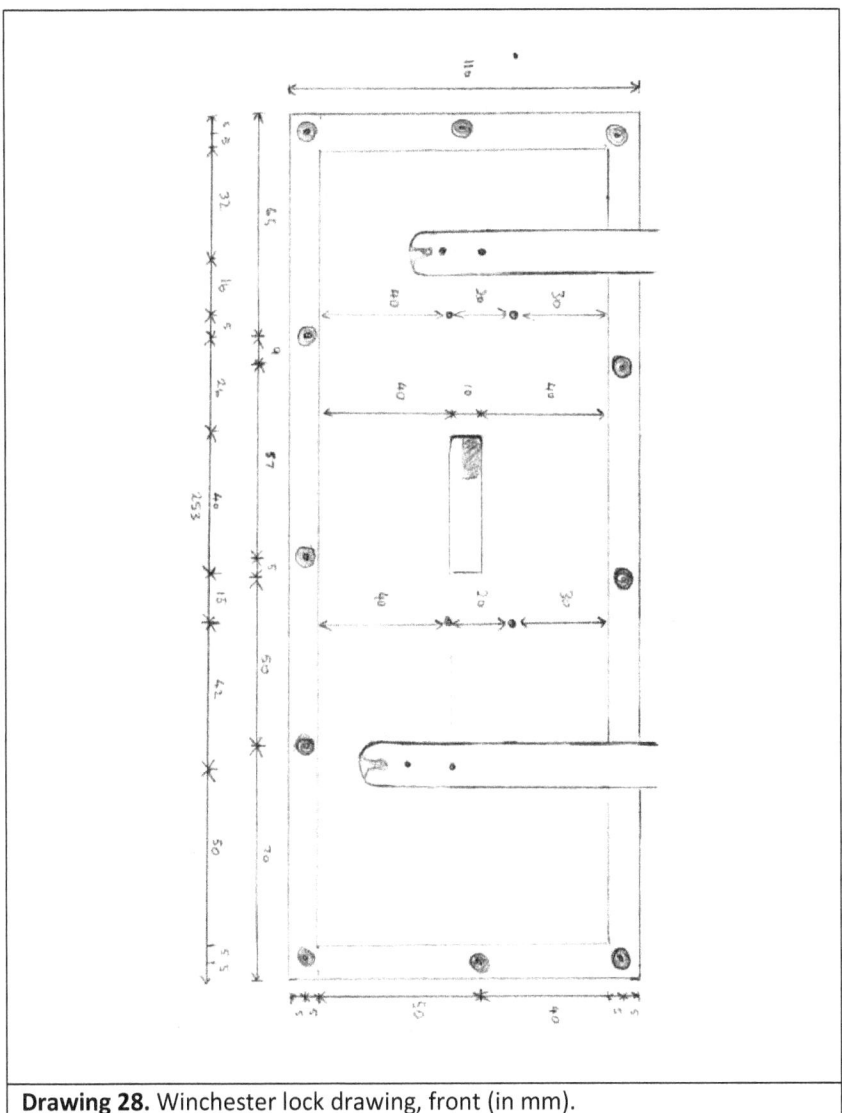

Drawing 28. Winchester lock drawing, front (in mm).

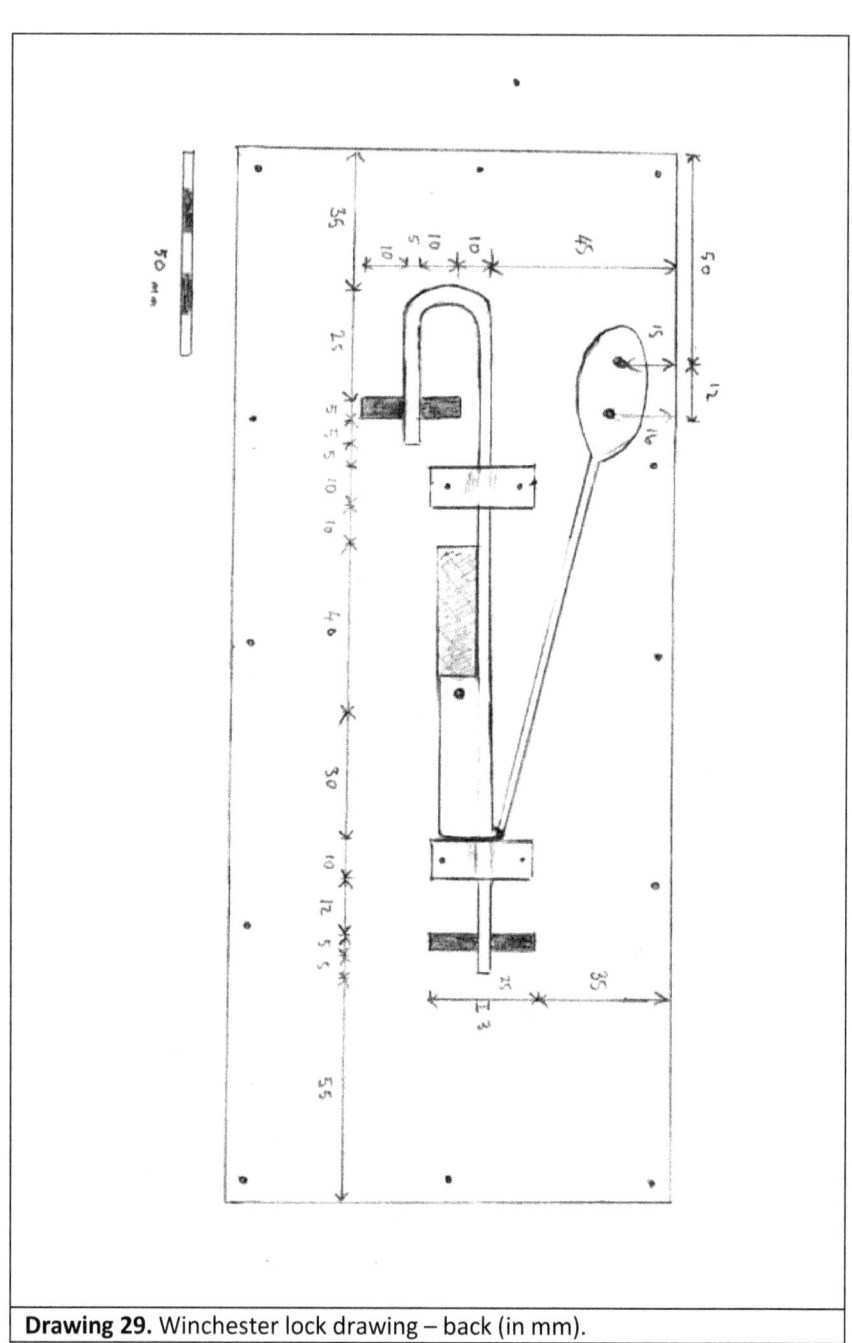

Drawing 29. Winchester lock drawing – back (in mm).

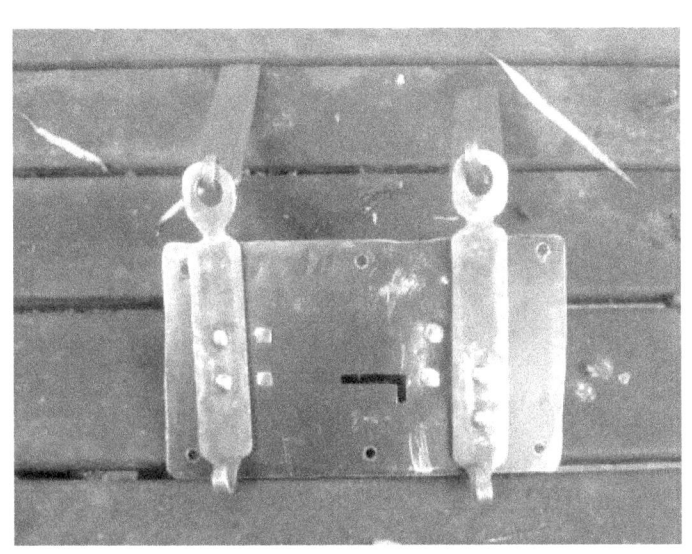

Photo 43. Lock based on the Winchester lock (front).

Photo 44. Lock based on the Winchester lock (back).

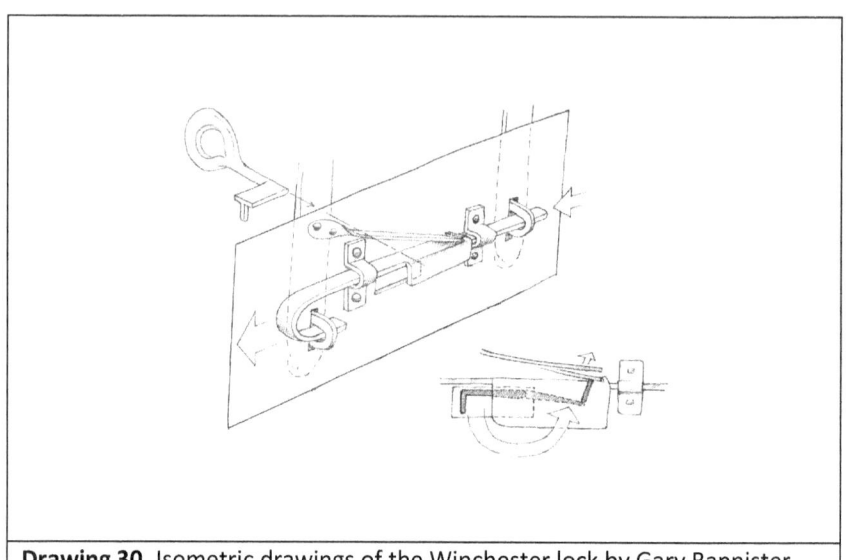

Drawing 30. Isometric drawings of the Winchester lock by Gary Bannister.

The following are basic instructions on how to make a replica of the '*Winchester*' lock.

Materials.

Mild steel is used for most of the lock, and spring steel for the spring.

Table 10. Metal requirements.

Number of pieces	Description of piece	Material required
1	Lock plate	Flat sheet 1mm (20GA) 253 x 110 mm (9 15/16" x 7/16"")
2	Lock hasps	Flat bar 3mm ($^1/_8$") 540 x 24 mm (21 ½"x 1")
4	Staples	Flat sheet 1mm (20GA)160 x 24 mm (6 5/16" x 1")
1	Slide	Flat bar 3mm ($^1/_8$") 225x25 mm (8 8 ⅞" x 1")
1	Spring	Flat sheet spring steel 1mm (20GA) 130 x 10 mm (5 ⅛" x 3/8")
2	Keys	Flat bar 3mm ($^1/_8$") 240 x 40 mm (9 ½"x 1 ½")

Total 3mm ($^1/_8$") (thick flat mild steel bar = 1005mm (39 ¾").

Equipment (Cold work).

Angle grinder with cutting disc or hacksaw (32 teeth per inch), or a hammer, cold chisel and a block of steel for cold cutting, bench grinder with a fine and coarse stones, files (various), anvil, bench vice, heat source (forge, gas torch).

PPE (Safety glasses, leather gloves, leather apron, safety boots, long sleeve shirt and trousers in non-flammable material).

Chalk or permanent marker and ruler.

Lock plate (See Drawings 28 and 29).

Method.

1. Mark out the lock plate.
2. Cut out the lock plate with a cold chisel, hammer and a block of steel, or hacksaw, or an angle grinder with a cutting disc.
3. Clean up edges with files.
4. Mark out and punch holes for attachment to the chest.

Hasp and hook (See Drawings 31 and 32).

Method.

1. Mark out mild steel to shape and size.
2. Cut to length with a cold chisel, hammer and anvil, hacksaw or an angle grinder with a cutting blade.
3. Grind to shape with a bench grinder, or an angle grinder with a grinding disc, or a set of files.
4. Grind pointed end, clean up with finer and finer files, beat point over anvil to form a loop.
5. Mark out centre of loop end, punch centre, drill out centre, file to shape with round files.
6. Punch and drill holes for staple.
7. File holes to fit ends of staple (mark with dots for each staple).

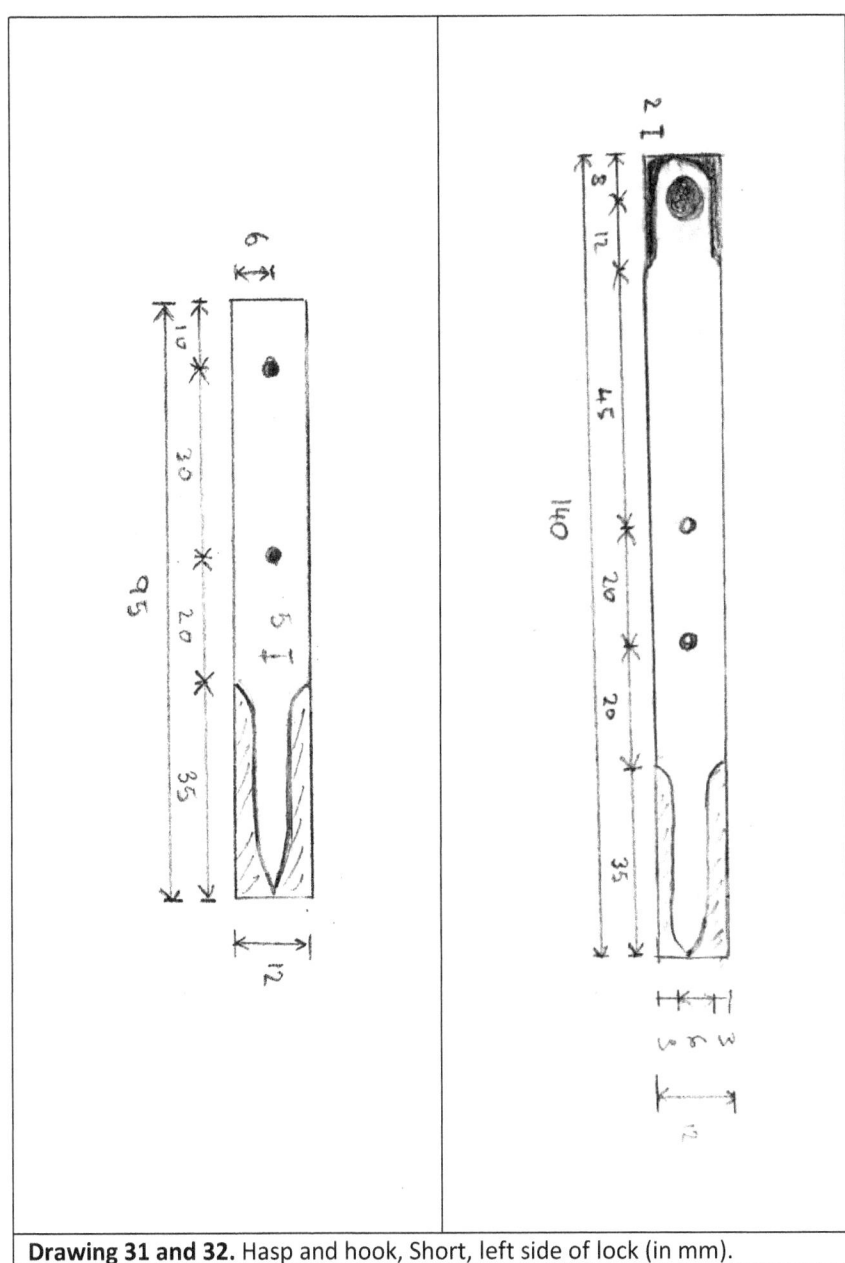

Drawing 31 and 32. Hasp and hook, Short, left side of lock (in mm).

Staples (See Drawings 33).

Method.

1. Mark out on mild steel.
2. Cut out the shape with a hacksaw or very slowly with an angle grinder with a cutting disc.
3. Clean up and adjust to the proper dimensions with a bastard file.

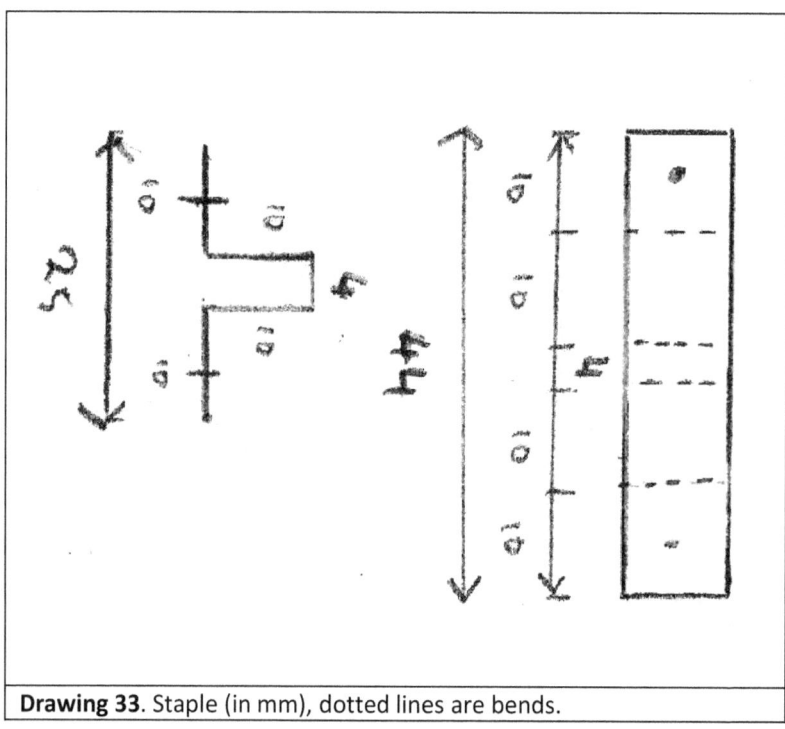

Drawing 33. Staple (in mm), dotted lines are bends.

Slide (See Drawings 34 and 35).

Method.

1. Mark out on mild steel.
2. Cut to shape with a hack saw or angle grinder with a cutting disc.
3. File the slide to the final dimensions and clean up.
4. Bend the hook end cold with a hammer (*left end when looking at back of lock*) over horn of anvil or a piece of round bar held in bench vice, to match shape of drawing no. 34. The bottom of the hook should be parallel to the top of the slide.
5. Bend side piece of slide cold while holding the slide in the bench vice with just the side piece above the jaws of the vice. Use a hammer to bend the side piece to a right angle to the top of the slide.
6. Drill a 3mm ($^1/_8$") hole in the end of the side piece of the slide to take the pivot point of the key. File the hole to fit the pivot point of the key.
7. Place keys pivot point into the hole of the slide, rotate key until the teeth of the key strikes the underside of the slide. Mark where the key's teeth come into contact, counterpunch the spot, drill out and file to take the key tooth. The tooth should pass through the hole in the slide and project above the level of the top of the slide.
8. Grind a slot in the top of the slide just past where the tooth exits the slide. This is the stop for the spring, the key's tooth pushes the spring up and over the slot so that the slide can slide. The slot should only be 2mm ($^5/_{64}$") deep.
9. Ensure the slide fits through the slot in the staples of the hasp and on the lock, and file to shape if required.

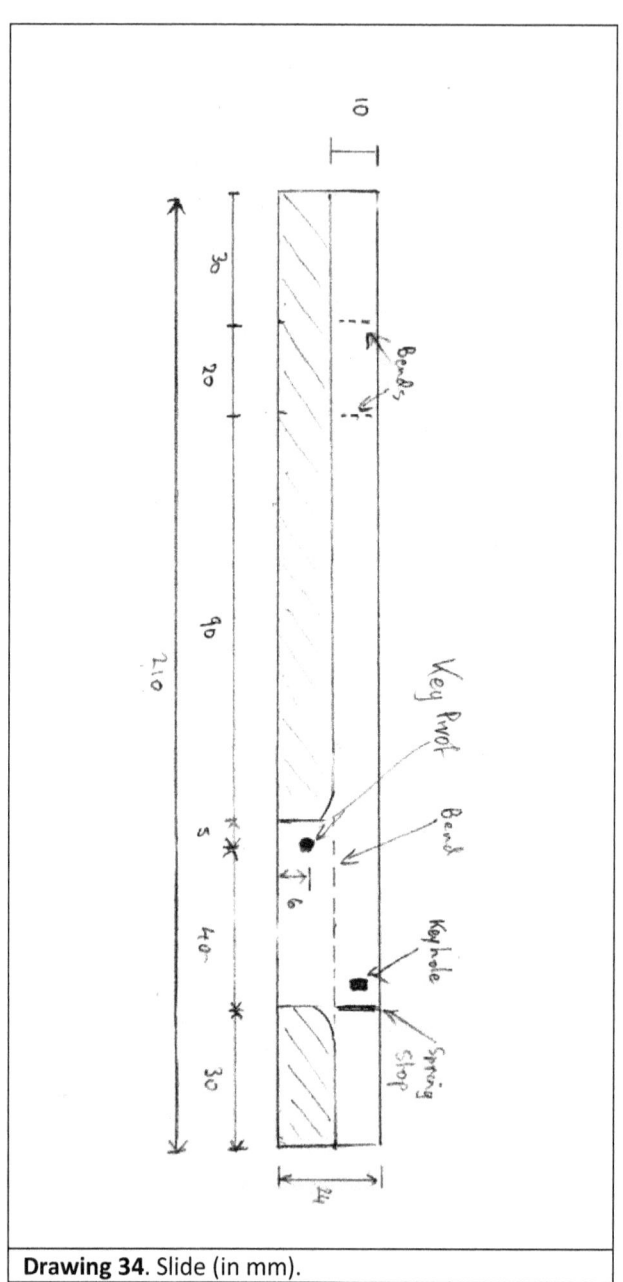

Drawing 34. Slide (in mm).

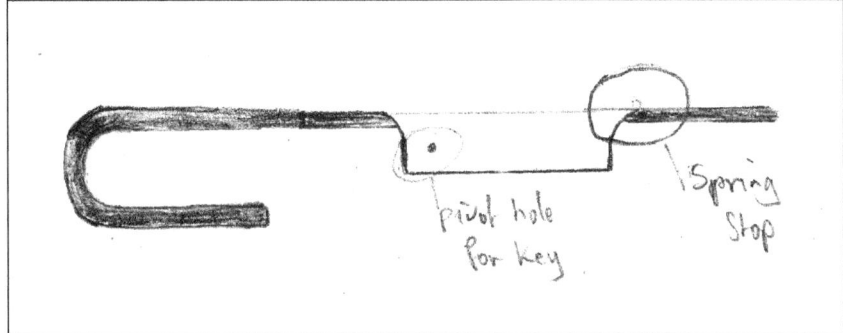

Drawing 35. Slide side on (mm), showing the hook and the key engagement area.

Spring (See Drawings 36).

Method.

1. Mark out to specifications on spring steel.
2. Cut with an angle grinder with a cutting disc, clean up with a bastard file.
3. Bifurcate the end of spring using a hacksaw.
4. Centre punch where attachment rivets will be located.
5. Drill attachment holes the size of the rivets to be used.

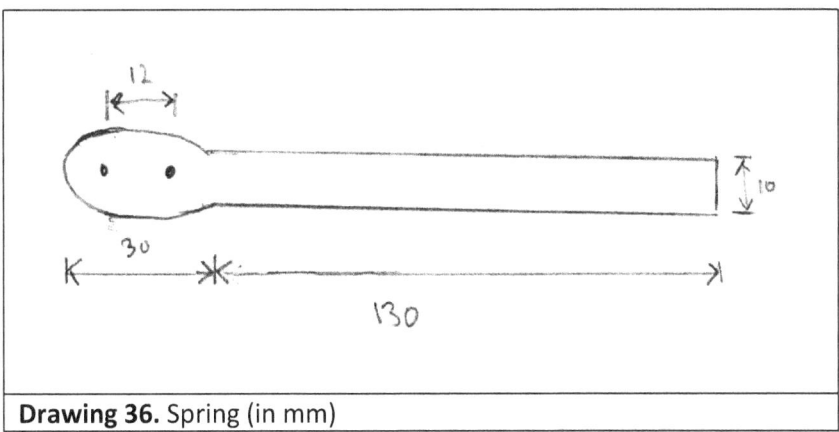

Drawing 36. Spring (in mm)

Keys (See Drawings 37).

The key for Winchester lock was not found so it is a matter of speculation as to the shape, size and appearance of the key. I recommend the lock from Winchester, Hampshire, c. 1065-1085, L. 117mm (4 ⅝"), with a pear shaped bow from Goodall, 1990-21, fig 325.3736.

Method.

1. Mark out and cut to length.
2. Cut out shape, grind and file to shape and size.
3. Bend the key tooth at right angles to the rest of the key.
4. Check against the key pivot hole and tooth hole in the slide so it fits. File to shape and size if necessary.

Crucial points.

- The pivot point needs to be snug but not too tight so the key can rotate 360 degrees;
- The tooth of the key must penetrate the hole in the slide and move the spring up and over the stop on the slide.
- I recommend making two keys because you are going to lose one, and never store the spare key in the chest that the lock is on.

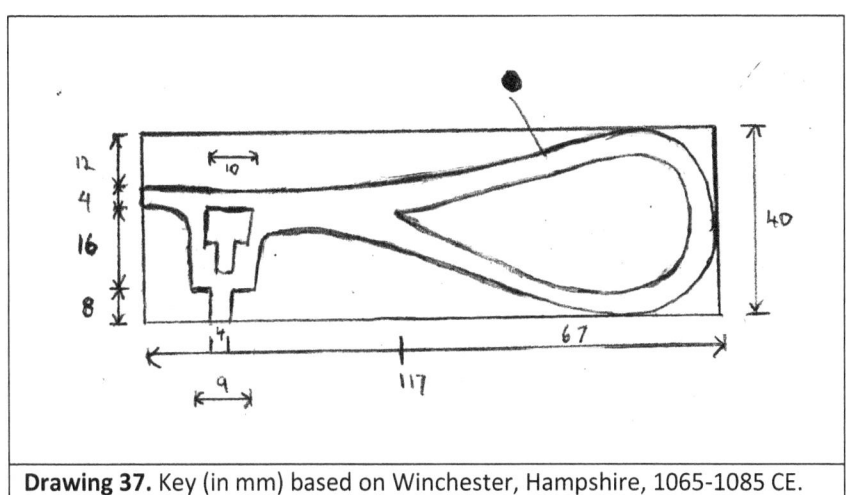

Drawing 37. Key (in mm) based on Winchester, Hampshire, 1065-1085 CE.

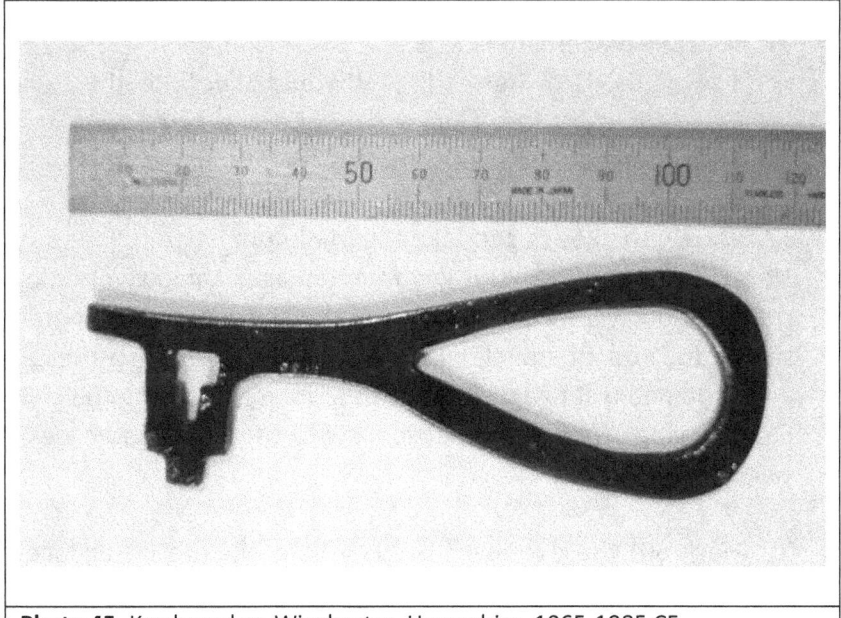

Photo 45. Key based on Winchester, Hampshire, 1065-1085 CE.

Assembly of Lock.

Slide attachment.

1) Mark and punch location of each lug on the lock plate.
2) Drill holes in lock plate for lugs, positions based on the slide and size of lug. Note: each lug may be different.
3) Secure the lock plate in the vice and drill holes.
4) File out holes for lug legs with a square rat file.
5) Insert lugs into holes, ensure slide moves freely.
6) Do **not** rivet lugs in place yet.

Key hole.

1) Key hole placement
    a. Line up where the key would slide into the *'swivel hole'* in the slide and where the key tooth would engage the slide, that gives you the length of the keyhole.
    b. The key has to take the minimum height of the key.

Note: The key enters the keyhole, engages the swivel hole, is rotated clockwise, and the tooth of the key goes up through the slot in the top of the slide, dislodging the spring, so the slide and slide and disengages the hasps staples, unlocking the chest. See Drawing 30 of an isometric view of the Winchester lock by Gary Bannister.

2) Mark out the extent of the key hole on the outer face of the lock plate;
3) Punch holes down the centre of the hole with a 6mm drill bit.
4) Cold chisel out the remainder of the key hole, file square.
5) Ensure key fits.

Slits for hasp lugs.

1) With the slide sitting in lugs mark '*Lock and unlock positions*'.
2) Mark out slits.
3) Punch mark down slit.
4) Drill slit – 3mm ($^1/_8$").
5) Cold chisel remaining pieces, using hammer, cold chisel and steel block (Do **not** use the anvil, it will damage the surface of the anvil).
6) File out the slit to fit the lugs of hasps.

Note: The hasps should not be impeded by the nails attaching the lock plate to the chest, nor the rivets holding the lock parts in place.

UNLOCK = the slide should pass to the left hand side of the lock.
LOCK = the slide should be just past the right of the slit.

Spring attachment.

1) Make the first hole for attachment of the spring (top left) – punch, drill, rivet.
2) Remove slide, rotate spring downwards until spring is 5mm ($^{13}/_{64}$") below the level of the slide.
3) Mark/punch drill second rivet hole
4) Rivet 2nd rivet in place.
5) Put the slide back in place, the spring should apply downwards pressure to slide.
6) Rivet lugs in place over the slide.
7) Ensure the slide slides, and both keys work.
8) Grease the lock.
9) Attach the lock to the chest.

The Hørning table.

By Stephen Wyley.

The Hørning table.	Find location: Hørning, Denmark.	**When**: 950 CE
Stored: National museets, Denmark	**Collection no.**: C31307	**Material**: Oak
Size: L. 50*W.50*20cm high (20" x 20"x 8")		

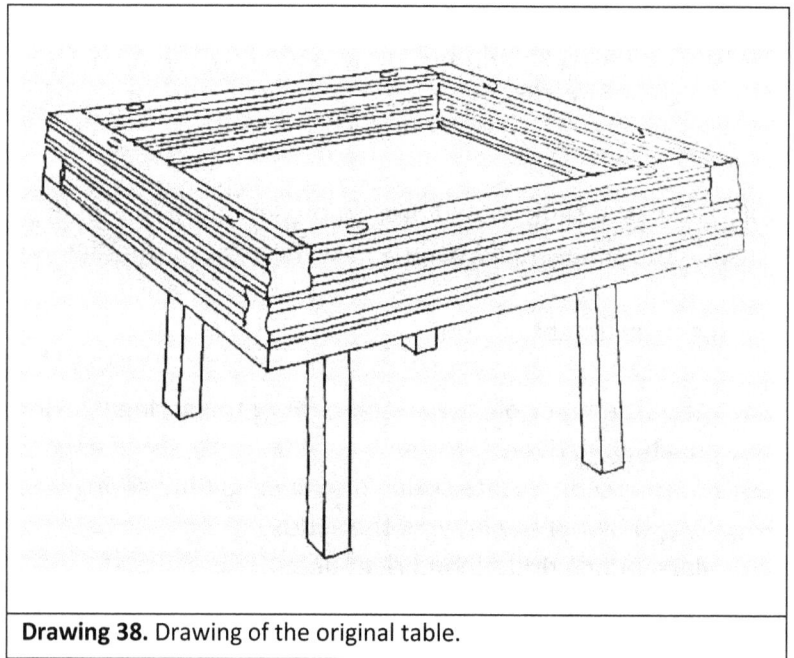

Drawing 38. Drawing of the original table.

Introduction.

The Hørning table was found in a wealthy women's chamber grave dating from 950 CE, the mound covering the chamber grave had been removed when a stave church was built on the site in 1060 CE. The chamber grave is similar to a grave found in the Bjerringhøj mound at Mammen near Viborg, Denmark.

Photo 46. The replica Horning table with brass bowl and wash cloth.

The women's grave goods consisted of: a carriage, five glass beads, a small knife, two small whetstones, a glass cup, a small casket, a wooden box, a pair of tubs, a wooden cask, and a small table with bronze bowl, unfortunately the items are too decayed to display. The purpose of the Hørning table was to hold the wash basin, a *'trapiza'* or a *'mundlaug'*, similar to the Sala Hytta table where the woman could undertake their ablutions.

Just a reminder that there are no extant large tables which have been found to date. However, it is interesting to note that the Bayeux tapestry (11th century CE) scene 43 shows Bishop Odo blessing the first banquet that Duke William and the Norman Barons held on English soil sitting around a large table.

The Hørning table top was 50 cm (20") square with raised sides, the sides were decorated on the inner and outer faces with three sets of three lines gouged or scratched into the surface, there were also two similar lines gouged or scratched into the top edge.

The Hørning table is unique amongst the Viking tables because of the addition of edging which would stop items like the bronze bowl falling off the edge. Other examples of Viking tables include the Oseberg table, which is the biggest at $0.30m^2$ (465 sq. inches), while the Birka table is the smallest at $0.09m^2$ (139 ½ sq. inches). See Table 11 for a comparison.

Table 11. Table comparison.				
Place	Dated CE	Collection	Material	Dimensions
Castleford, Yorkshire, England	1st century	Unknown	Timber	L. 61cm x W. 30cm x thickness 2.7cm (24 $1/64$ x 11 $13/16$" x 1 $1/16$") - only the top was found.
Oseberg farm, Tonsberg, Vestfold, Norway	800 – 850	Universitetets Oldsaksamling, Oslo, Norway.	Oak	L. 92.5cm W. 33cm, Legs from 28 to 29cm (36 $27/64$" x 12 $63/64$" x 11 $1/32$ - 11 $27/64$").

Hørning Church, 40 k east of Mammen, Denmark	950	Unknown	Unknown		Top 50cm square with edging, on 20cm high legs. (19 $^{11}/_{16}$") square with edging, (7 $^{7}/_{8}$") high legs.
Grave 4, Sala Hytta, Västmanland, Sweden	10 century	Statens historiska museer, Sweden. Collection no: SHM 11739		Timber	Table top: 45 x 20 x 2 cm (17 $^{23}/_{32}$" x 7 $^{7}/_{8}$" x $^{25}/_{32}$"), Height of table: 8.5cm (3 $^{11}/_{32}$").

The table found in the Roman fort at Castleford, made of ash, measuring 61*30cm (24" x 12") has four splayed holes for legs, however the legs did not survive.

The following are basic instructions on how to make a replica of the Hørning table parts and assembly.

Materials.

Timber (Oak if possible, see cutting lists), dowel, glue.

Table 12. Cutting list.	
Base	1 x 50 x 50cm (20" x 20") (or 2 50 x 25cm (20" x 10"))
Sides	1 x 200cm (80") x 2cm (3/4") x 4cm (1 1/2") (cut up into 4 x 50cm (20") pieces)
Legs	1 x 80cm (32") x 3cm (1 $^{1/4}$") x 3cm (1 $^{1/4}$") (cut up into 4 x 20cm (8") pieces)
Cross braces	1 x 80 x 3 x 2 cm (32 x 1 $^{1/4}$ x $^{3/4}$") (cut up into 2 x 40 x 2cm pieces (16" x ¾"))
Dowels	1 x 24cm (10") of 6mm (1/4") dowel

Equipment.

Saw, drill and drill bits (a drill bit to fit the dowels, and a drill bit for the tenon of the legs), scratch tool, mallet, draw knife, vice/clamps/hold downs, shaving horse, pencil and ruler.

Instruction.

Cross braces (to be fitted across the grain of the table)

1) Measure and cut to size.
2) Mark out for leg holes.

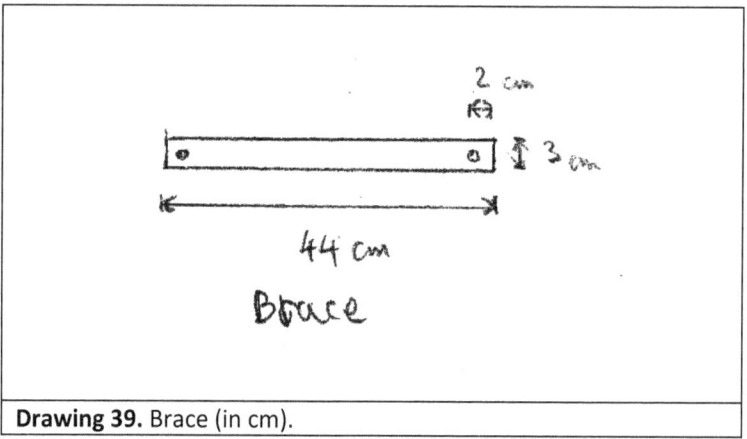

Drawing 39. Brace (in cm).

Table top.

The original table top was one piece of timber and if you do not have a piece of wood that big you will have to join two pieces of timber together.

3) Cut to size or if making up from smaller pieces – cut, dowel (three dowels) and glue.

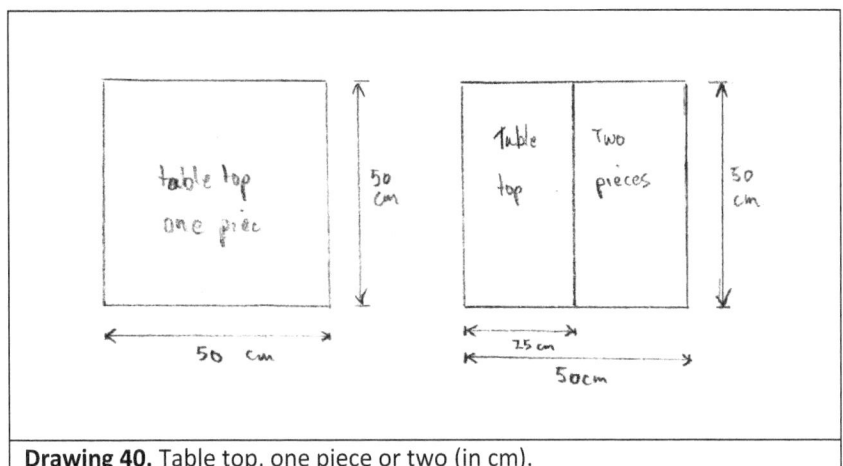

Drawing 40. Table top, one piece or two (in cm).

Photo 47. Gluing two boards together with sash clamps and an anvil (the anvil is an optional extra, it stops the boards bending upwards.

4) Mark location of braces.

5) Glue cross braces (they may need to be nailed or dowelled in place, there is no indication of how they were attached).

6) Drill holes for leg tenons through braces and table (ensure there is a waste piece of timber on the other side of the hole to stop the drill bit breaking or chipping the timber).

Photo 48. Braces glued and nailed in place.

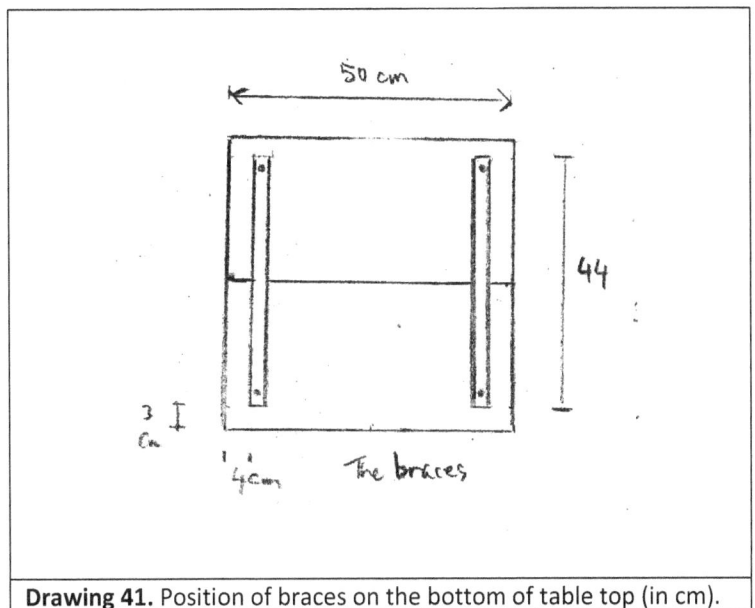

Drawing 41. Position of braces on the bottom of table top (in cm).

Photo 49. Using a spade bite on a drill to drill leg holes.

Legs.

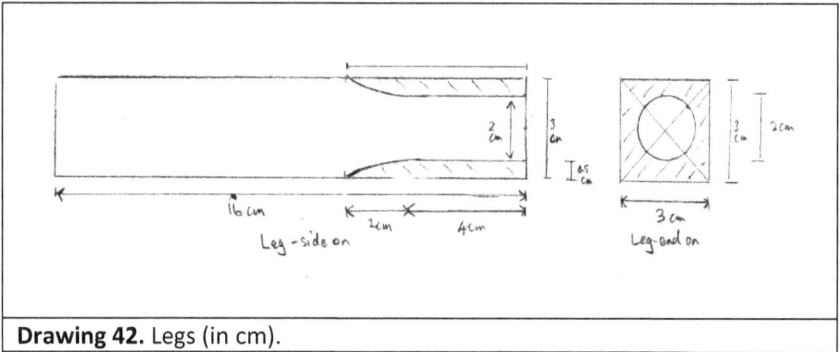

Drawing 42. Legs (in cm).

1) Mark a 2cm (¾") wide circle on the end of the leg and mark out the size of the tenon on all four sides of the leg. See Drawing 42.
2)   Using the drawknife carve tenon shape on two opposite sides of the legs, mark out the tenon shape on the flats and carve out tenons, turn the leg 90 degrees and start carving a curved shoulder, turn leg 90 degrees and repeat.
3)   Refine tenon shape with a sharp knife, cutting away from yourself, remove wood slowly, checking regularly to see how it fits in the leg hole.
4)   When you get a leg to fit, mark the leg and the hole that leg fits, it saves confusion when re-assembling.
5)   Using a knife, take off the corners of the legs, this helps to reduce the likelihood of splinters and damage to the legs.

Photo 50. Using a drawknife to carve down the leg from square to round.

Photo 51. Trimming down the leg with a knife to fit the leg hole.

6) Decide if the legs will be removable (for flat packing for transport and storage) or glue the legs into holes (for extra security you can cut top and add a wedge when the leg is in place). Then clean up glue with a damp cloth.

Photos 52. Nocking in the legs with a mallet.

Photos 53. Legs in place on the table top.

Providing the legs with a tapering shoulder allows for changes in the timbers moisture content and makes for a tighter joint between leg and table top. Gently tape the leg in position with a mallet, to remove, twist the leg and pull.

Sides.

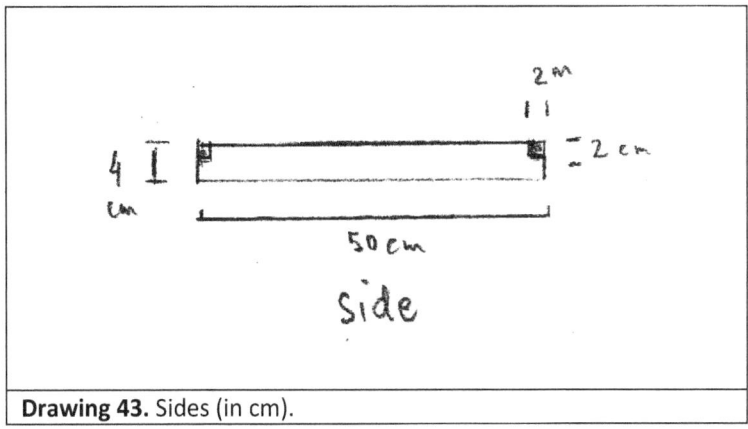

Drawing 43. Sides (in cm).

7)   Cut to length of the four sides (2 metres (80")).
8)   Scratch details with a scratch tool or a 'V' gouge with a straight edge (like a steel ruler) along 2 metre (80") in length.

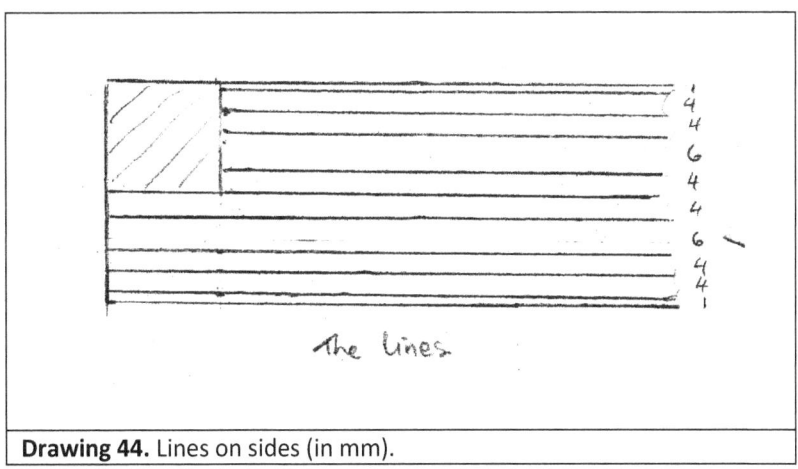

Drawing 44. Lines on sides (in mm).

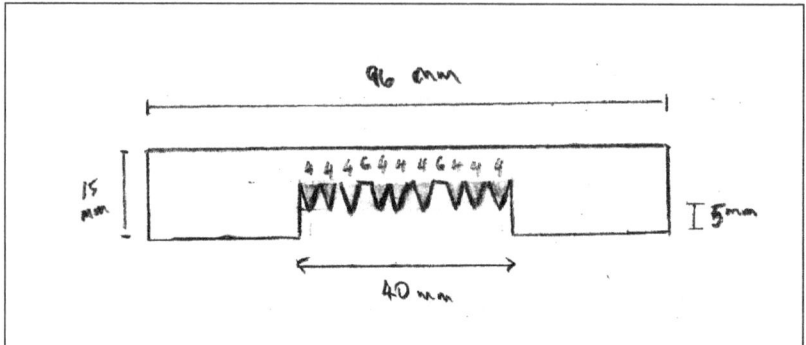

Drawing 45. Scratch tool (in mm), this could be put into a handle like a spokeshave for ergonomic use.

Photo 54. Cutting lines with 'V' gauge and a ruler as a straight edge.

9) Cut to 50cm (20") lengths, cut out corners, dry fit on table top.
10) Clamp edge section to the table to with the cut out up, drill holes for dowels.
11) Add glue to the dowel and insert into holes on top of edge pieces, allow to dry.
12) Repeat for the opposite edge piece, then the adjacent sides.
13) Clean up excess glue, light sand and a coat of linseed oil.

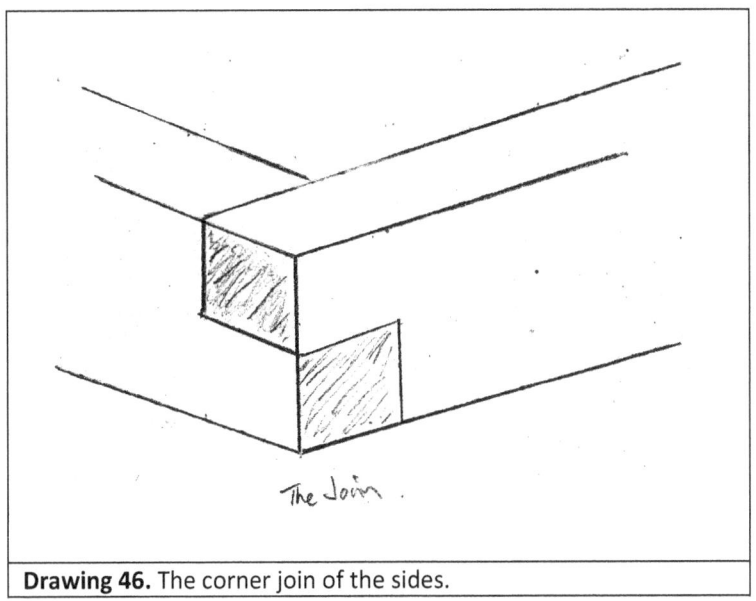

Drawing 46. The corner join of the sides.

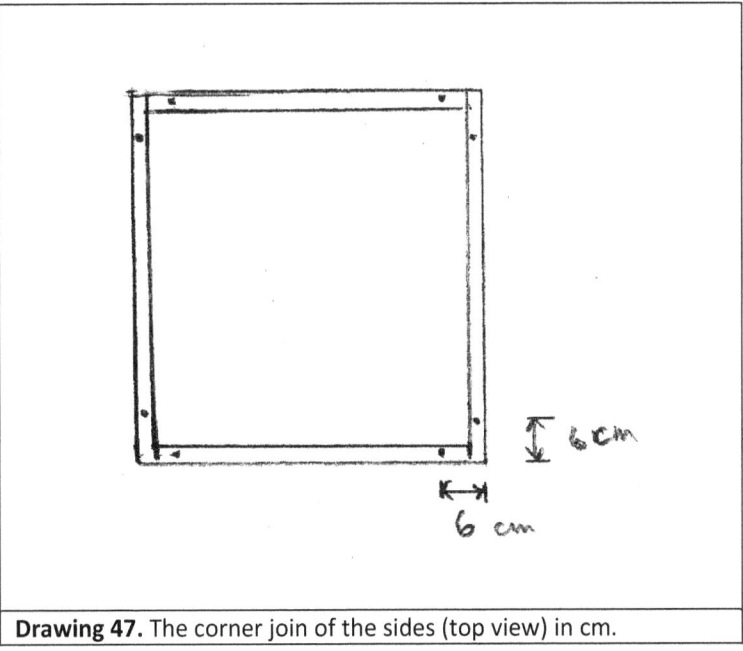

Drawing 47. The corner join of the sides (top view) in cm.

Photo 55. Dowels through the sides into the table top. The top of one of the legs through into the table top. And the corner halving joint of the sides.

The Gokstad Bed.

By Stephen Wyley and Brodie Henry.

The Gokstad bed.	Found: Gokstad Farm in Sandar, Sandefjord, Vestfold, Norway	**When**: 890 CE
Stored: Viking Ship Museum, Oslo, Norway.	**Collection no.**: C10410	**Material**: Oak
Size: 227cm (89 3/8 inches) *109cm (42 29/32 inches)* 70cm (27 9/16 inches).		

Photo 56. The original Gokstad plain bed.

Introduction.

The practice of high status burials including a bed includes of the Egyptians (Tomb number KV62, which is the burial place of Tutankhamun, a pharaoh of the Eighteenth Dynasty of ancient Egypt, 1334–1325 BCE), the Singer's Grave at Trossingen (Germany, 580 CE), the Saxon bed burial on Swallowcliffe Down from the 7th century CE, and the Vikings ship burials of Oseberg and Gokstad (9th century CE). See Table 13 for more information.

The Gokstad bed is part of the Gokstad ship burial find, similar to the Oseberg boat burial (800 - 850 CE). A skeleton of a 40-50 year old man was located on the bed under a wooden structure but the identity of the person is unknown. Aboard a 23.8m (78 foot) Viking longship the other finds included a grave chamber in the aft of the ship which was decorated with gold-embroidered tapestries, the other grave goods were eating and drinking utensils, a sleigh, six beds, a chest, a saddle, gilt harness, 64 shields, 12 horses, 8 dogs, 2 peacocks, a backpack and more. On the deck of the longship lay three boats which included a small, a medium and a large boat.

Photo 57. The replica of the bed, Legs in cedar, the rest is in pine. In this version all the slats are pegged.

The form and decoration of the bed is similar to the Oseberg bed no. 2 bed (see, Viking Volume 1, 2021).

Table 13. Bed comparison.

Place	Dated	Collection	Material	Dimensions
Gokstad Sandefjord, Vestfold, Norway	890 CE	Universitetets Oldsaksamling, Oslo, C10408.	Oak	Animal head board Height 140cm (55 1/8") x 23cm (9 1/16") width, 2.4cm (15/16")thick.
Gokstad Sandefjord, Vestfold, Norway (plain)	890 CE	Universitetets Oldsaksamling, Oslo. C10410.	Oak	Corner post 70-75cm (27 9/16"-29 17/32"). End boards 1.09mx 28-30cm (42 29/32"x11 1/32"-11 13/16"). Side board 2.27mx 28-30cm (89 3/8"x42 29/32"x11 1/32"-11 13/16").
Oseberg farm, Tonsberg, Vestfold, Norway (Horse Head)	800 – 850 CE	Universitetets Oldsaksamling, Oslo, Norway. No. 1 (K.69).[14]	Beech	L 175cm (68 57/64"), W 184 (72 7/16), H (Foot, 92cm x14cm (36 7/32"x 5 33/64"), H (Animal head, 168cm x45cm (66 9/64"x17 23/32").
Oseberg farm, Tonsberg, Vestfold, Norway (Plain)	800 – 850 CE	Universitetets Oldsaksamling, Oslo, Norway. No. 2	Timber	170cm long (66 59/64") 100cm (39 3/8") wide, 75 cm (29 17/32") high at the top of the side (and 100 cm (39 3/8") at the top of a leg).

---

[14] Roesdahl & Wilson (1992), provides a collection no. of K69 for the animal headed bed.

Materials.

Table 14. Material details.		
Oak, but Pine will do.	The size of the pieces.	The total length required.
2 sides	227x28x2cm (89 ½"[1] x 11 x ³/₄")	454 cm (179")
2 ends	109x28x2cm (43 x 11 x ¾")	218 cm (86")
4 legs	70 x 10 x 10cm (27 ½" x 4 x 4")	280 cm (110")
5 slats	92.4x16x2cm (36 ½" x 6 ½" x ³/₄")	462 cm (182 ½")
1 slat (centre)	109x16x2cm (43x 6 ½" x³/₄")	109 cm (43")
12 wedges	9.5x1x2cm (3 ¾" x ½"[1] x ³/₄")	114 cm (45")
2 dowels for centre slat	7x 2cm (2 ³/₄ x ³/₄ ")	14 cm (5 ½"")

Tools.

Rulers, Set square, chisels (25mm and 7mm (1" and ¼"), files (coarse - flat bastard, fine - square bastard), tenon saw, hand saw, plane, 'G' clamps, scrap wood (for holding work without damaging it), hold downs, claw hammer, wooden mallet, work bench, bench vice, pencil, drill (with 4mm ($^5/_{32}$") bit), spade drill bit (20mm (³/₄")).

Construction Instructions.

Head and foot boards.

1. Mark out and cut head and end boards to the length of your desired mattress (allow for expansion and contraction of the timbers).
2. Mark out and cut out end tenons.
3. Mark out and chisel out the mortise for wedges. Recommended that you cut the outside edges of the mortice on both sides to improve the edges of the mortice. Drilling out the mortice with a spade bit on a drill will also be faster.
4. Clean up edges with sandpaper.

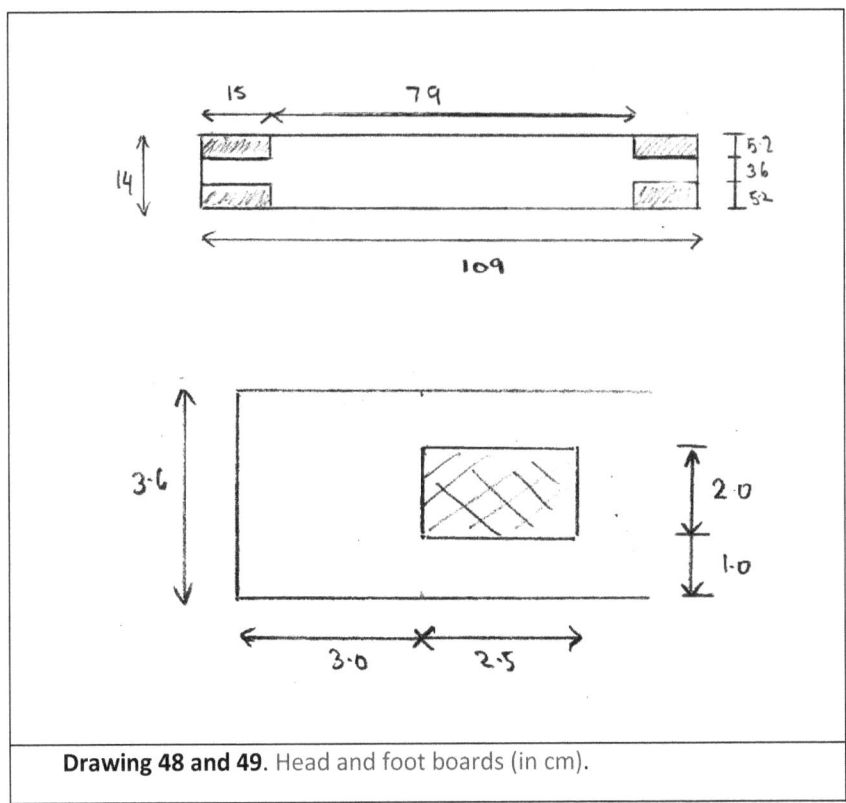

Drawing 48 and 49. Head and foot boards (in cm).

Photo 58. Tenon with mortice of head / foot board.

Legs.

1. Mark out and cut legs to length.

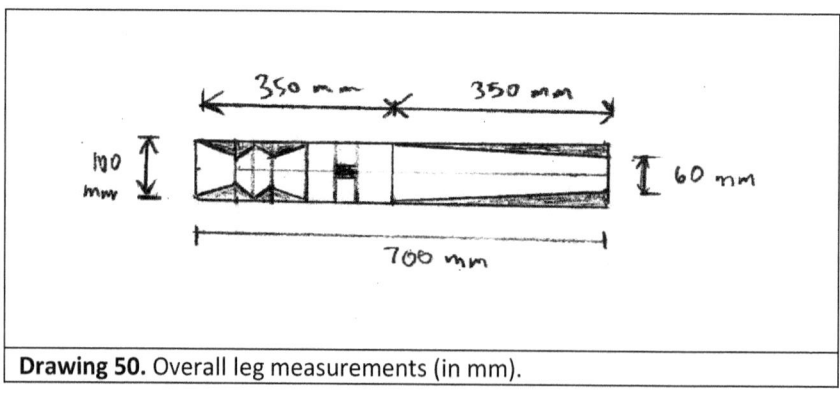

Drawing 50. Overall leg measurements (in mm).

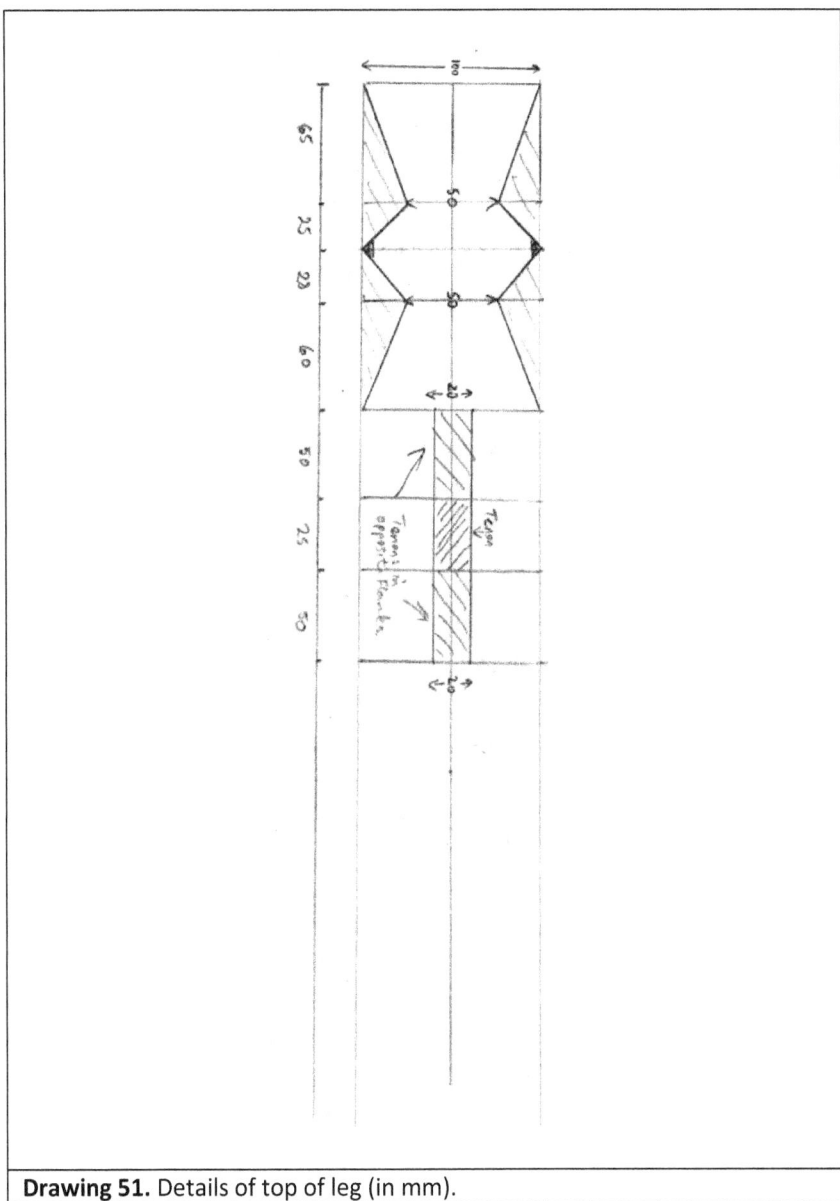

Drawing 51. Details of top of leg (in mm).

Top of legs.

2. Mark out leg cut outs on all four sides.
3. Secure leg in vice. Cut from top of leg down to first indent. See Photo 59.
4.

Photo 59. Sawing the top of the leg.

    a)   Turn the leg upside down. Cut down to the base of the first cut.

b) Turn back up right and repeat on all four sides.

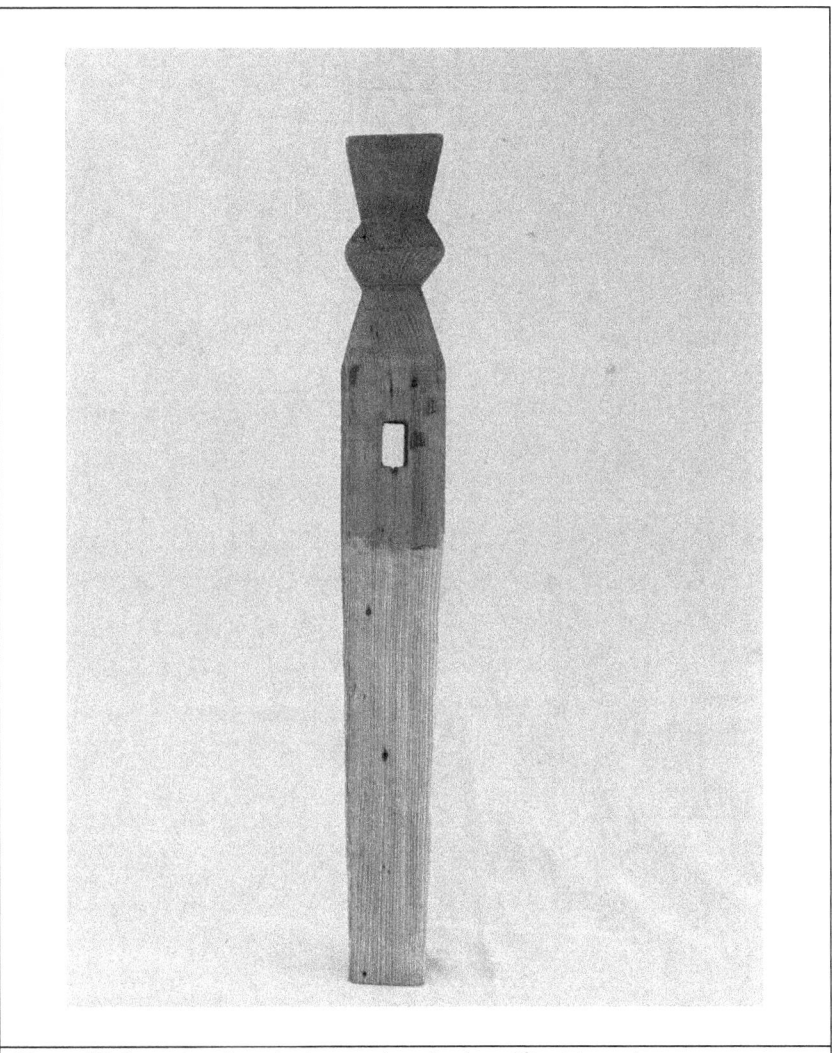

Photo 60. Leg, showing single mortices for head/foot board.

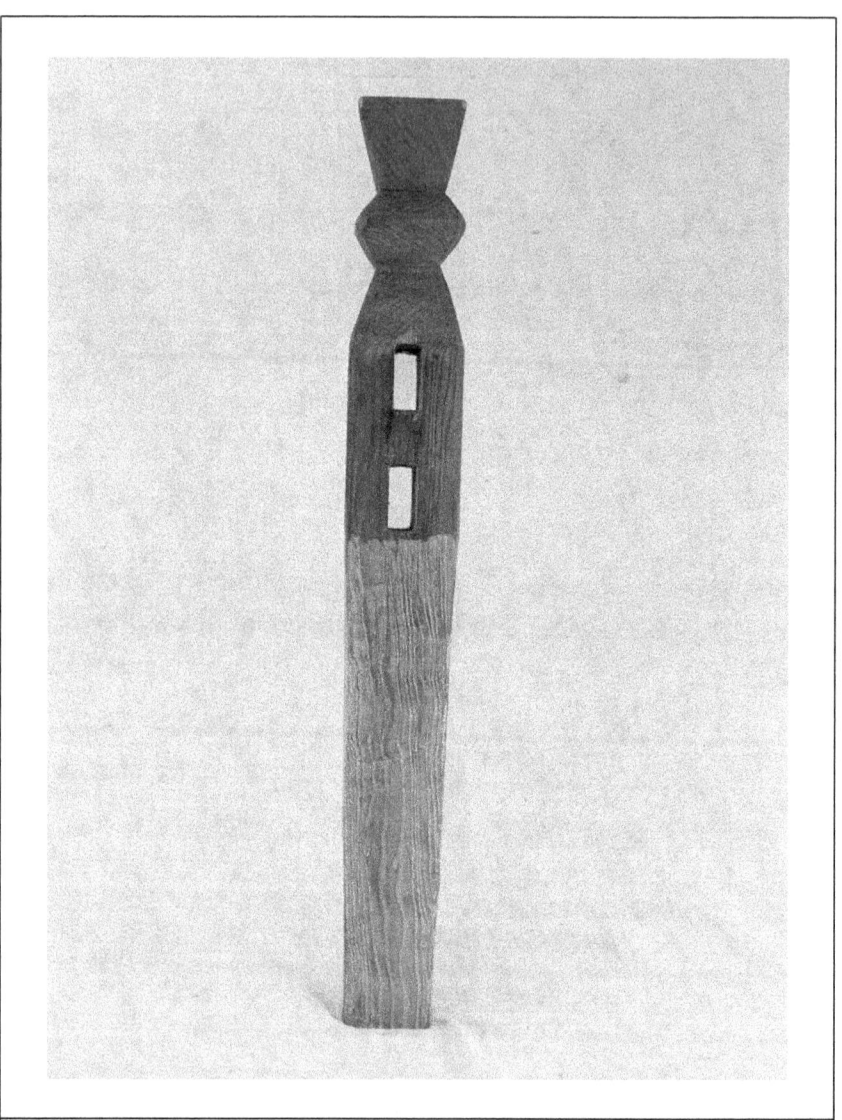

Photo 61. Leg, showing double mortices for the sideboard.

Lozenge.

4. Cut from apex of lozenge to first indent, then turn upside down and cut down to form lozenge shape.
5. Repeat on all four sides of each leg.

Mortices for head, foot and sides.

1. Mark out mortise on both sides of the leg. See Drawings 50 and 51.
2. Chisel or mark with a knife around each mortice, See Photo 62.
    a) Secure leg to work bench or in a bench vice.
    b) Drill out or chisel out the mortices.
    c) Clean up mortises with rasps and files.
    d) Ensure that there is a snug fit for the tenons. Make any adjustments to the mortices as required.
    e) Repeat for each leg.

Photo 62. Chiselling out the mortices.

Bottom of legs.

1. Mark out the tapering of the lower leg on opposite sides. See Photo 63.
2. Using a hand axe start lightly chipping away at the top of the tapper while holding top of leg in opposite hand, while rest the base of the leg on a waste piece of timber (for when the axe head skips off the leg, so the sacrifice board protects your bench top), a chopping block will do just as well. See Photos 64 and 65.

3. As the cuts come down the leg, increase the depth of cuts until you reach the base of the leg.
4. Ensure that both sides of the cut are straight.
5. Mark the taper of the two other faces and chop them down to size.

The same effect can be achieved using a bench vice and a drawknife or plane. See Photo 66.

5. If you use the axe, a smoother finish rounded corners can be done with a bench vice and a drawknife.

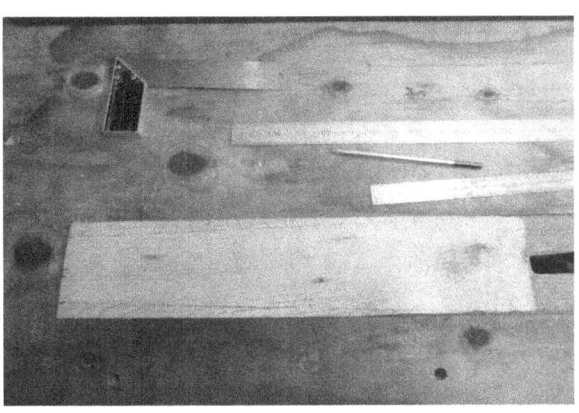

Photo 63. Leg taper marked out.

Photo 64. Tapered leg, sacrificial board held in place by a hold fast onto the workbench and bearded hand axe.

Photo 65 and 66. Using an axe and then a plane.

Photo 67. Legs cut down to size.

Fitting legs to sides and ends.

Snugly fit side and end tenons into mortices of the legs. This may include taking of material from the sides, ends and the mortices of the legs. Check fit on a regular basis. See Photo 68.

Photo 68. Legs fitted to end boards.

Slats.

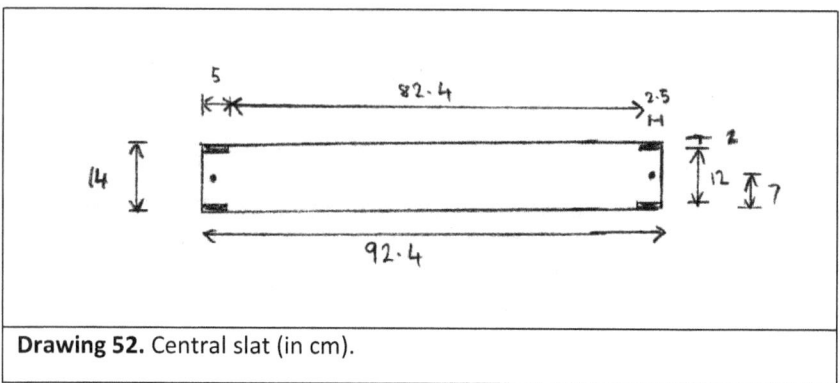

Drawing 52. Central slat (in cm).

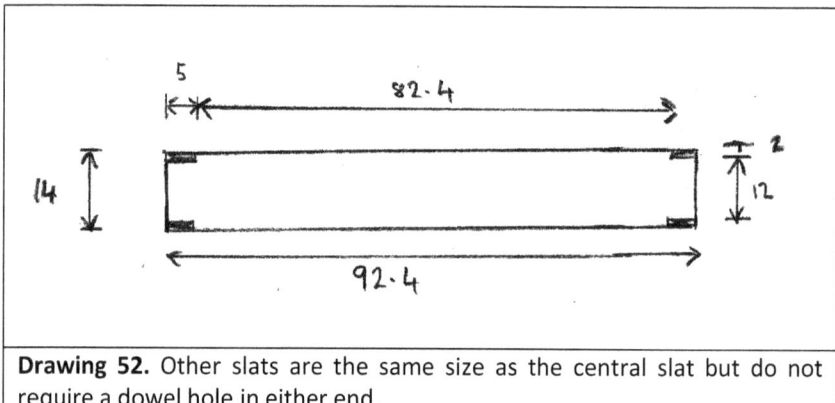

Drawing 52. Other slats are the same size as the central slat but do not require a dowel hole in either end.

For wider slats for more support see Appendix 7.

Side.

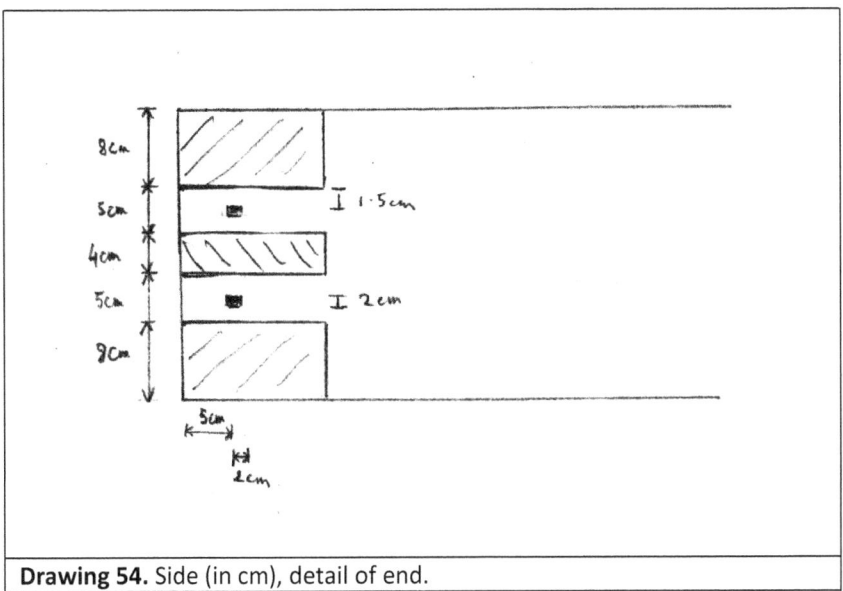

Drawing 54. Side (in cm), detail of end.

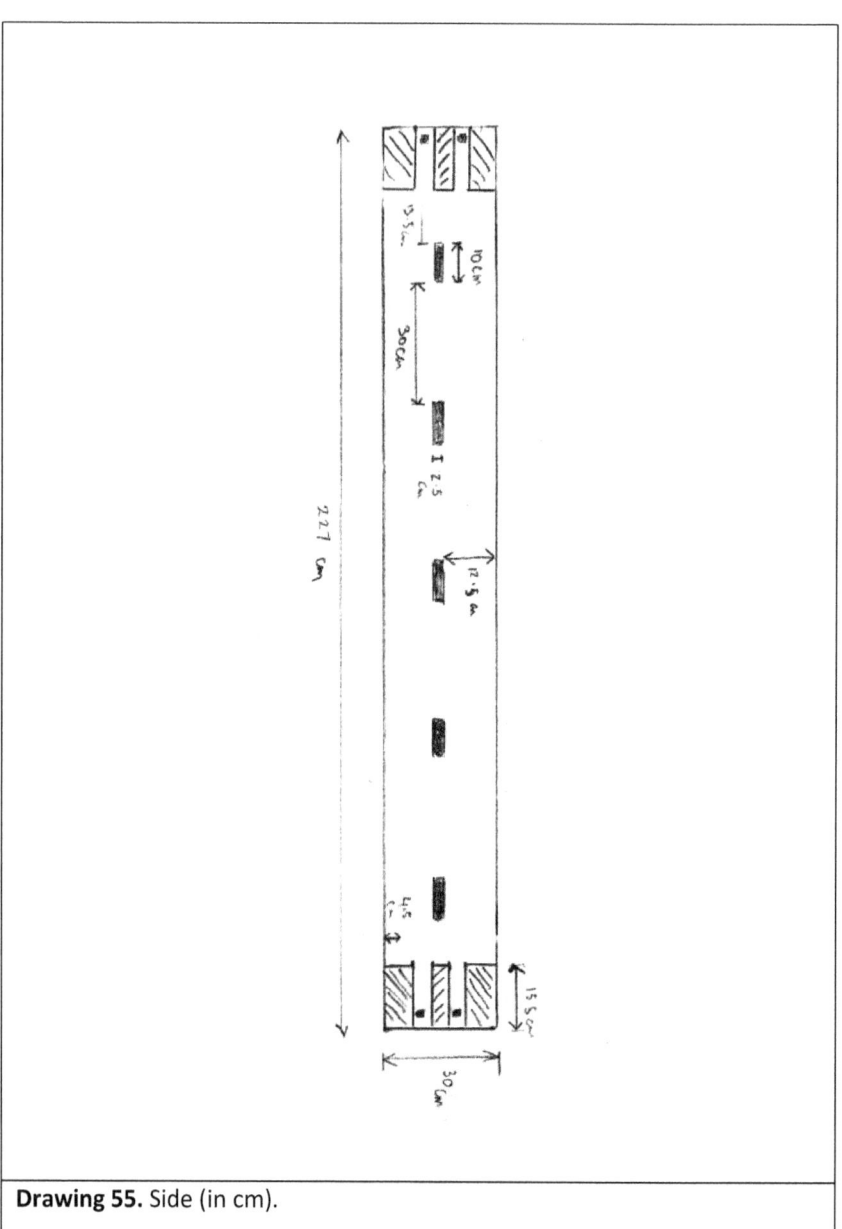

Drawing 55. Side (in cm).

Photo 69. One of the sides.

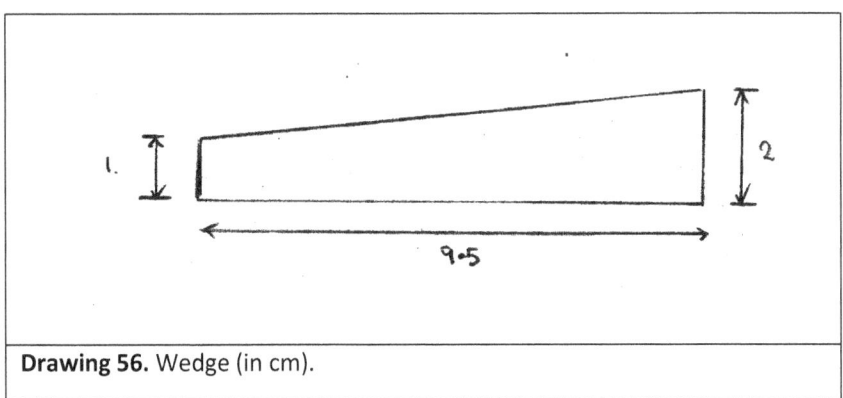
Drawing 56. Wedge (in cm).

Photo 70. Leg wedges.

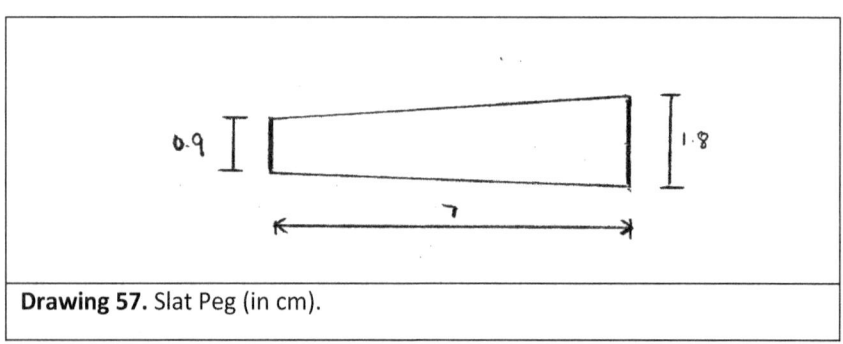

Drawing 57. Slat Peg (in cm).

Photo 71. The middle slat pegs.

Identify the parts.

6. Carve ("*marriage*") marks (i.e. Roman numerals) on the legs and the ends of the sides and ends so it is easier to match up when assembling the bed.

Bed Assembly.

1) Lay out sides on flat ground.
2) Lay out slats in between sides at 90 degrees.

Photo 72. The sides and slats are ready for assembly.

3) Insert the tenons of one side of the slats into one side.

4) Insert the tenons of the other side of the slats into the other side. (You may want to place the pegs in the holes in the tenons of the centre slat if attempting a solo assembly).

Photo 73. The sides and slats assembled.

5) Insert the tenons of the head and footboards into the legs.
6) Insert the tenons of the sides into the top legs.

Photo 74. The sides and slats inserted into head and leg board.

7) Repeat for bottom legs.

Photo 75. The bed assembled, nearly.

8) Set pegs and wedges in place.

Photo 76. The bed end and side is wedged in place.

Photo 77. The middle slat is pegged.

Note: You may need to use a persuader (wood mallet) to achieve this, however the mortise and tenons should only be a snug fit and pegs and wedges will hold it all in place.
Applying wax to tenons will help reduce friction.

Photo 78. Sven asleep on his Gokstad bed. Photo by Jonathon Lyon.

See Appendix 7. For wider slat plans Gokstad bed when you need more support.

Mattress.

If you have a mattress in mind you may want to modify the provided measurements to fit the mattress (allow for expansion and contraction of the timbers).

The Trondheim Hnefatafl board.

By Stephen Wyley.

The Trondheim Hnefatafl board.	Find location: Public Library site, Trondheim, Norway.	**When**: 1100 - 1150 CE
Stored: Vitenskaps Museet, Trondheim	**Collection no**: N29728/FH414	**Material**: Oak and iron nails.
Size: Length 25.6cm (10 $^5/_{64}$"), Border 8mm ($^5/_{16}$") high	**Other information**: 11 * 11 squares for the hnefatafl board and game of Nine man morris on the back.	

Photo 79. The remains of the original hnefatafl board.

Introduction.

The Trondheim hnefatafl board was found at the Public Library site (Trondheim, Norway), the board is damaged and one of the sides is gone, from the remains it appears the board is 11 * 11 squares, with '*X*' in the centre for the starting position of the king and two '*X's*' at the centre of each side for positioning the opposition. There is also a game of '*Nine man morris*' incised on the back, See Photo 91.

Photo 80. The replica of the hnefatafl board, complete.

A turned walrus ivory gaming piece (3.2cm (1¼") high, collection number N38256/FE1043) was found at the same site as the board, pear shaped with a flat base, a hole in the base, polished on the upper surface.

Hnefatafl is one of the games of strategy for the young and old in memoriam and is still played in this day and age. Tafl board games came in a range of sizes from: 7*7, 9*9, 11*11, 13*13, even 19*19 (which was probably used for a game called '*Alea Evangelis*'[15]). For more information on other hnefatafl boards see Table 15.

Hnefatafl = translation/meaning = "*fist table*," from the Old Norse (equivalently in modern Icelandic) hnef, '*fist*', and tafl, '*table*'.[16]

For this article a number of assumptions were made:
- That the missing part of the board mimics the extant part;
- That the top border is not appear to be nailed in place, thus if the top is glued in place why not the bottom piece (the glue must fit very snugly);
- The nails/nail holes in the sides are uniform in positioning, and nails have been add to the bottom end of the side edging;
- Nailing patterns on other hnefatafl boards vary in the number of nails used for attaching the edging. See Table 16.

Board pieces came in a number of different shapes and materials and there are more pieces extant than boards. Wood, ivory, amber[17], bone and glass[18]. See Table 17.

---

[15] Vimose, Næsby oved-Broby Parish, Denmark, dating from 160 CE.

[16] S. Hilbertsson and B. Gunnarsson, *Ensk-Islensk/Islensk-Ensk Ordabok* (Reykjavík: Ordabokautgafan, 1996).

[17] Rundkvist & Williams (2008).

[18] Vikings in the East Midlands - Glass Gaming Piece (LIN-C31CD7) https://emidsvikings.ac.uk/items/glass-gaming-piece-lin-c31cd7/ accessed 18 October 2021

Table 15. Examples of Hnefatafl Boards.

Date (CE)	Place	Collections details	Comments
Late 9th century	Gokstad[19]	Universitetets Oldsaksamling, Oslo	13 square cross section with a number of the squares are decorated, and a 9 man morris on the back.
Late 9th – Early 10th century	Ballinderry, County Westmeath, Ireland.	National Museum of Ireland (NMI), 1932:6533	7*7 with peg holes for pieces.
10th century	Coppergate, York[20]	Bulletin of York Archeological trust Interim volume 6, No.4.	16 rows, 3 columns, evidence of metal strip along surviving edge. See Morris (2000), p 2350-2351, 15 rows, 3 columns, L*481mm (18 $^{15}/_{16}$"), W*109mm (4 $^{19}/_{64}$"), T*23mm ($^{29}/_{32}$"), 20342 sf 6609 (PFB Fig 1158).
10th century	Toftans, Eysturoy, Faroes	Foroya Fornminnissavn in Torshavn, No. 4666/1762.	13*13, Oak (Quercus), Length 70.5cm (27 $^{3}/_{4}$"), in what appears to be a serving platter.
Viking era	Dublin, Ireland	Morris 1984a, M300, M398.	2 boards, part only, 10*7 rows, one in Fishamble, the second in Christchurch Place.
Late Viking era	Bergen, Norway	Bergen Museum.	2 boards, one has 9 man morris on the back, both are 13*13 squares.

---

[19] Nicolaysen, (1882), plate VIII.
[20] Vikings in the East Midlands - Reproduction Game Board https://emidsvikings.ac.uk/items/reproduction-game-board/ accessed 18 October 2021

Table 16. Nailing patterns

Origin of board	Nailing pattern description
160 CE, Vimose, Næsby oved-Broby Parish, Denmark	No nails indicated.
7th century CE Valsgarde, Sweden.	Small headed nails along all four sides, some are single nails, some in pairs perpendicular to the edging. Handle with loops on ends on one edge.
890 CE Sandar, Sandefjord, Vestfold, Bygdøy Gokstad, Norway.[21]	The edge survives to indicate small nail holes at regular space but are not uniform in spacing.
9-11th century CE Thumby-Bienebeck (Haithabu) Nth Germany. Game board from grave 37A.	Metal corner brackets on top of edging held in place by three nails. Nail at regular intervals along the top of the edging along all 4 edges. Circular ring used for the handle with loops on ends on one edge, placed at the centre of one of the side.
10-11th century CE. York, England. Fragment of game board.	Nails at either end and in the centre, nails have their ends cleated.
1100 1150 CE, Trondheim board Public Library site, Trondheim, Norway.	Multiple nails unevenly spaced on two of the existing sides.

---

[21] The World Tree Project - Wooden Gaming Board from the Gokstad Burial http://www.worldtreeproject.org/document/2221 Accessed 26/01/2022.

Table 17 – Examples of Gaming Pieces.

Dated CE	Place	Find details	Comments
800	Rogaland, Norway	Gunnarhaug, Torvastad, Karmøy, Rogaland, Norway. Historisk Museum, Bergan, B4438.	Glass * 16 (11 blue, 1 blue/yellow, and 4 yellow
850-900	Balnakeil, Scotland	Boys grave Balnakeil, Scotland.	14 antler pieces
9th century	Birka Sweden	Birka grave number 524.	15 amber pieces, King larger than the others, 3 red and 11 yellow
9th century	Östergotland, Sweden	Skamby boat grave, Östergotland, Sweden, County Museum Linköping	23 hemispherical amber pieces
10th century	Uppland, Sweden	Boat grave IX, Vendal Parish, Uppland, Sweden. Statens Historiska Museum, Stockholm, 7250	Bone*3
10th century	Baldursheimer, North Iceland	Islands Nationalmuseum, Reykjavik, 1 and 6.	24 Walrus ivory pieces and Whale bone king
10th to 11th century	Sjælland, Denmark	Roholte, Sjælland, Denmark. Danmarks Nationalmuseum, Copenhagen, C24292.	Amber male figure [a king piece?]
First half to mid 10th century	Morbihan, France	Ile de Groix, Morbihan, France. Musée des Antiquités nationales, St. Germainen-Laye, 86117.	Walrus Ivory*2, Antler * 12
11th century	Greenland	Sandnæs (Kilaarsafik), Ameralla, Ruin Group 64V2-111-511(V51), Greenland. Grønlands Nationalmuseum og Arkiv,	Walrus Ivory*2

Table 17 – Examples of Gaming Pieces.

Dated CE	Place	Find details	Comments
11th century	Dublin, Ireland	Nuuk, KNK4x400-401. Dublin (Fishable Street), Ireland. National Museum of Ireland, Dublin.	Walrus Ivory*2
11th century	Lund, Sweden	Lund (Kv Kulturen 25), Sweden. Kulturen, Lund, KM 38.252.	Walrus Ivory*1 [King?]

The following are basic instructions on how to make a replica of the Trondheim hnefatafl board.

Materials.

Timber (Oak is preferable) (wide plank or two not so wide planks joined together two make the board), and some thin strips for the edging
- Board 25.6cm² x 2cm (10" 10 x ³/₄"),
- Border 120cm x 2cm x 8mm (47 ¹/₄"x ¾" x ⅜"),
- Nails (x9) and wood glue.

Equipment.

Ruler, pencil, eraser, set square, bench chisels (6mm. 10mm and 24mm wide (¼", ⅜" and 1")), 6mm (¼") 'V' gouge, saw, rasp, hammer, drill, drill bit 4mm (5/32"), drill countersink, mitre box.

Construction.

1) Board.
    a) Mark out and cut to length, clean up the edges.
    b) If not wide enough join two boards together with glue and dowel. Allow to dry and set.
    c) Mark out board lines, See Drawing 58.
        a. Mark out the grid first, then mark out internal squares, mark out squares with crosses. See Photos 81 and 82.

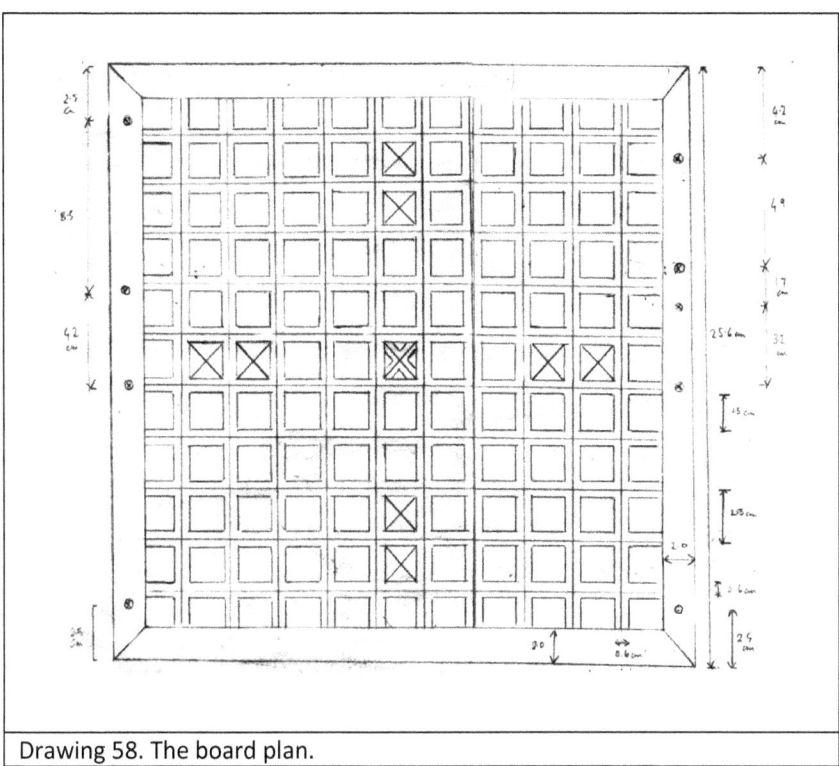
Drawing 58. The board plan.

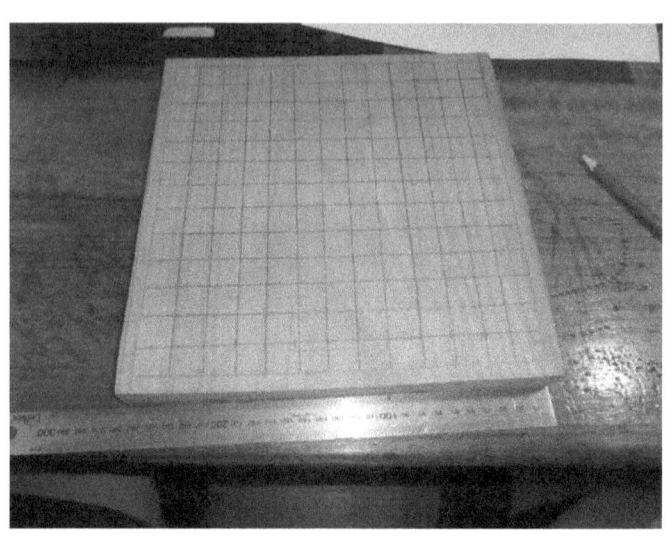

Photo 81. The Main grid marked out.

Photo 82. The inner squares are marked out.

d) Gouge out the "X's" with 'V' gouge. See Photos 83 and 84, including the extra detail for the centre 'X'.

Photo 83. The two of the XX's.

Drawing 59. Centre square detail.

Photo 84. The Centre X, the 'x' is still to be gouged out.

    e) Use the 24mm (1") bench chisel to cut the outside of the main lanes.
    f) Chisel down 1mm (1/32") along the lanes with the grain. Turn the board around and complete the lanes.
    g) Chisel out the gaps between the squares across the grain down 1mm. See Photo 85.

Photo 85. Lanes chiselled out and gaps between the squares on the right are underway.

h) Mark out the main frame, and gouge with 'V' gouge.

Photo 86. Gouge out the main lines with 'V' gouge

i) Clean up board. Rub out any pencil marks.
2) Edging.
   a) Cut to length with angled join for corners. A mitre box makes it more consistent.
   b) Dry fit test.
   c) Glue and clamp in place. See Photos 87 and 88.

Photo 87 Gluing and clamping the sides in place.

Photo 88. Gluing and clamping the sides in place.

3) Mark out 'Nine man morris' on the back of the board.
d) Use a ruler or straight edge to provide a guide to running 'V' gouge along lines of game or use a knife running to parallel cuts in a 'V' shape. See Photo 89 and 90.

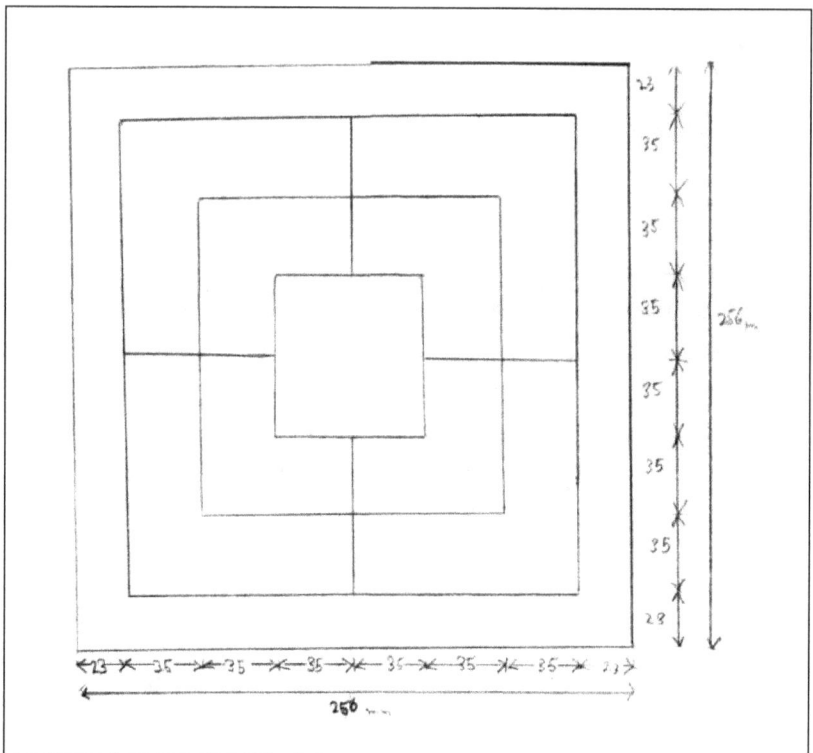

Drawing 60. The underside of the replica shows the Nine man morris game.

Photo 89. Nine man Morris gouged out.

    e) Erase pencil markings and sand.

3) Nails,
   - Mark out locations of nail holes through edging, drill with 4mm (5/32") bit. See Photo 90.
   - Use a countersink on the nail holes.
   - Hammer nails in place, cleat ends over flat with the surface of the bottom, with their heads supported by an anvil or similar lump of metal.
4) Clean up, sand off rough corners with sandpaper and linseed oil.

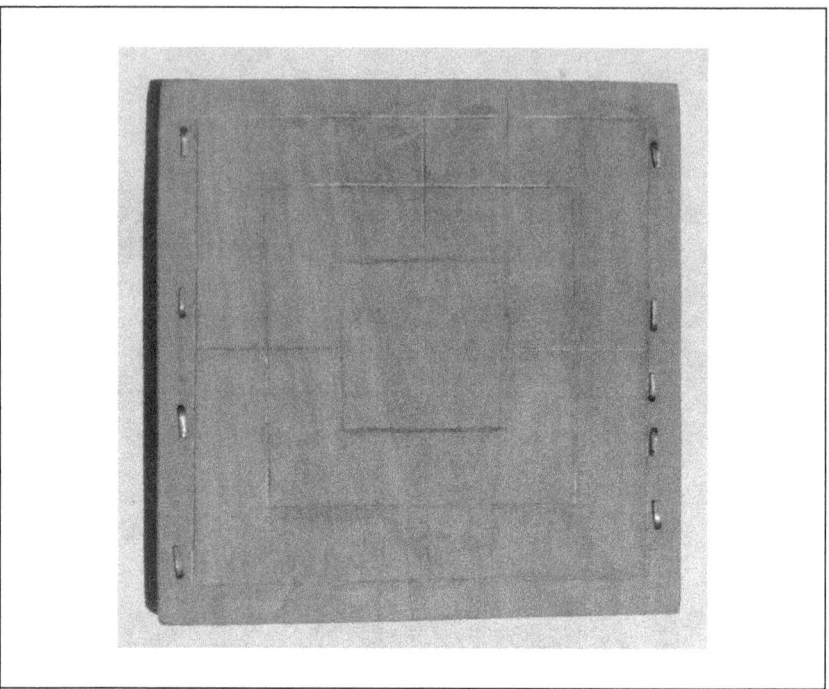
Photo 90. Nail cleated over on back with Nine man Morris board.

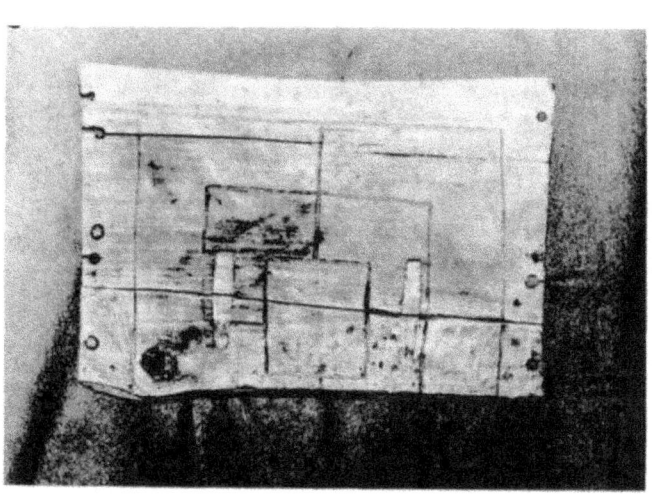

Photo 91. Showing the underside of the board, including repairs with wooden keys on either side of the central rectangle. [22]

The production of game pieces is up to you, there may be an article on making glass pieces in the planned third volume for making Viking gear. [23]

---

[22] When the wooden keys were added is unknown and appears to be polygon in shape, with the widest section at the crack, which is opposite in shape to the Butterfly key which would add better resistance to the crack widening.
[23] Vikings in the East Midlands - Reproduction Glass Gaming Pieces
https://emidsvikings.ac.uk/items/reproduction-glass-gaming-pieces/ accessed 18 October 2021

Photo 92. Game board with glass blue and clear playing pieces, and red agate king. The gaming pieces are based on the Rogaland, Norway extant pieces.

The Grytøy Whalebone Plaque (Smoothing Board).

By Shannon Joyce.

Grytøy Whalebone Plaque.	Grytøy, Trondenes, Norway.	**When**: 8th-9th century CE
Stored: Bergen Historisk Museum	**Collection no.**B.272	**Material**: Whalebone
Size: L34.5cm (13 $^{37}/_{64}$") x W 29cm (11 $^{27}/_{64}$") x Thickness 1.6cm ($^{5}/_{8}$")		

Introduction.

The Grytøy plaque is a flat rectangle of whalebone with incised and cut-out decoration on its upper surface consisting of a pair of animal heads facing each other and geometric line work around the perimeter and along the bottom edge. It was found along with a weaving batten in a chance find (Graham-Campbell, 1980).

The plaque is an example of many similar plaques found in predominantly female Viking Age burials (Photo 93). There has been much speculation regarding their function and Owen and Dalland (1999) contains an in depth discussion of this if you'd like to find out more. Generally, however these objects are considered to be smoothing boards used with a glass smoother such as the find from Namsos, Trøndelag (Photo 95) for the *'smoothing'* or pleating of linen.

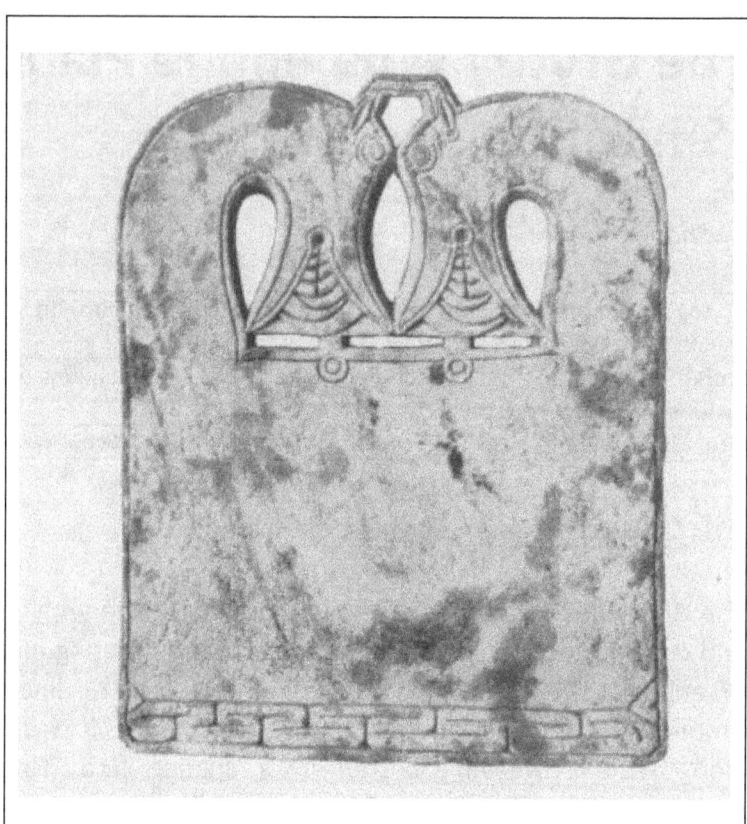

Photo 93. Whalebone plaque. Grytoy, Trondenes, Norway. Bergen (HM) B.272. Photo: Petersen, J, 1951.

Photo 94. The completed replica.

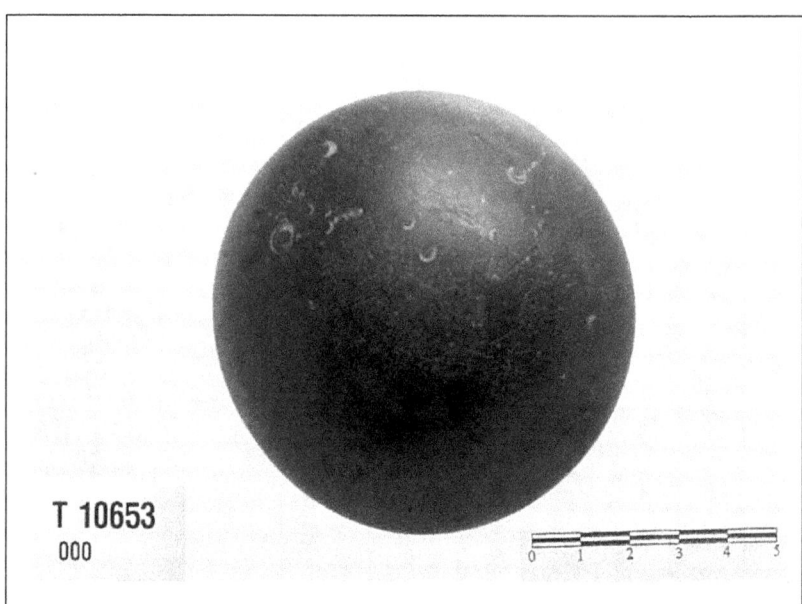

Photo 95. Smoothing stone made from glass from the Viking age, Namsos, Trøndelag (T10653).Photo by Ole Bjørn Pedersen, NTNU Vitenskapsmuseet, CC BY-SA 4.0.

Over 60 whalebone plaques have been found as detailed in Owen & Dalland (1999)[24]. Table 18 below details a few extant finds.

Table 18. Selection of extant whalebone plaques from the Viking Age.		
Place	*Collection*	*Size (LxWxTh)*
Scar, Orkney, Scotland	Tankerness House, Kirkwall, Orkney	26.6 x 21 x 1.0 – 1.7cm (10 $^{15}/_{32}$ x 8 $^{17}/_{64}$ x$^{25}/_{64}$")
Meløy, Nordland, Norway	Bergen Museum, B5393h	32.5 x 23.3cm (12 $^{51}/_{64}$ x 9 $^{11}/_{64}$")
Lilleberge, Namdalen,Nord-Trondelag	British Museum 1891.1021.67	23 x 20 x 0.9cm (9 $^{1}/_{16}$ x 7 $^{7}/_{8}$ x $^{23}/_{64}$")

---

[24] Appendix 4, pg.202.

| Gåre, Kvæfjord, Troms, Norway | Tromsø Museum | 18.8 x 13.3cm (7 $^{13}/_{32}$ x 7 $^{13}/_{32}$") |

Materials.

Obtaining whalebone was not an option for this project as it is illegal to collect bones from washed up marine animals in Australia.[25] I had been given a thick piece of maple measuring approximately the correct size. Maple or a similar hardwood would do the job.

Tools.

Ruler, pencil, eraser, saw, square, jig saw, wood carving tools, rasp, sandpaper.

Method.

1) Measure and draw a line 34.5cm (13 ½") from the bottom edge of the piece of maple to show the upper limit of the board.
2) Draw the design freehand onto the piece of maple trying to maintain the proportions of the original design (Photo 96). An alternative to this would be to enlarge a good quality image of the original board to the size of the extant piece and then trace this onto the piece of timber.
3) Use a variety of small curved and flat carving chisels to carve the design. Incise the line first and then hollow out the line or interior of the shape. This will help to keep the edges neat and design clean. Be careful doing this and **ALWAYS** carve away from yourself!

---

[25] Illegality: https://www.smh.com.au/environment/conservation/two-face-charges-over-alleged-removal-of-whale-bones-20100513-uzfz.html Downloaded 8 July 2022

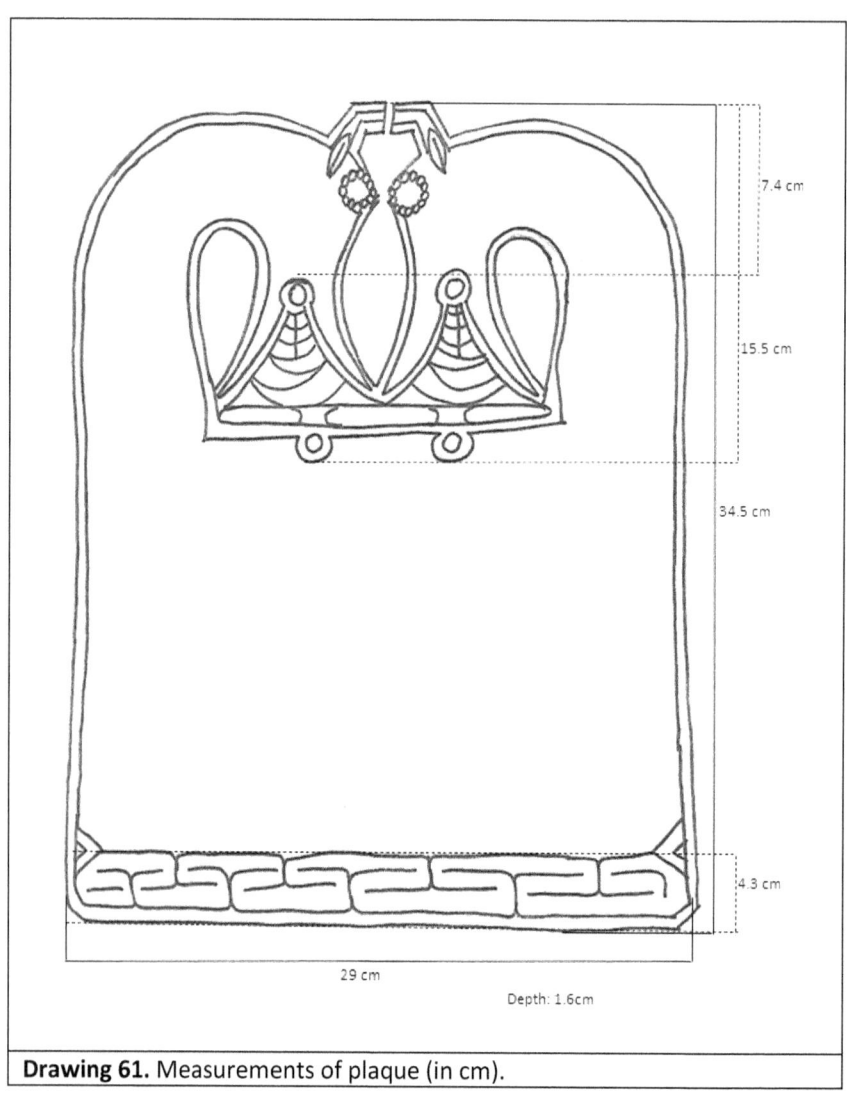
Drawing 61. Measurements of plaque (in cm).

Photo 96. Design drawn on a piece of timber. Carving of design at bottom has been started.

5) Trim the timber at the upper edge using a jigsaw following the curved line across the top of the board. To remove timber in the insert shapes use a combination of drill, jigsaw and chisels (Photo 97).

Photo 97. Top edge and inserts cut.

6) Continue to carve the remaining features and finish the raw edges with a rasp and sandpaper until smooth (Photo 98).

Photo 98. Finished board. Note: Board surface treatment: No treatment, such as linseed oil is required, as it would adversely affect the linen.

Living History Experiment.

I had finished the smoothing plaque and my friend and fellow author, Stephen Wyley, gave me a glass '*paperweight*' that he had made when he was learning glass blowing that was perfect as a smoother.

I decided to test the effectiveness of these objects for both smoothing and pleating linen fabric I had on hand. I determined that I would try the glass at both room temperature and heated in boiling water on dry and damp linen for both smoothing and pleating effectiveness.

My hypothesis was that the combination of heat and slightly damp linen would give the best results.

Method.

I lightly crumpled the dry linen in my hand and for the damp examples misted them with water from a spray bottle. See Photo 99.

Photo 99. Crumpled linen as a starting point.

I then methodically worked my way through the samples using the glass smoother to smooth one sample and pleat the other for each of the following conditions:
- dry linen with a cold smoother;
- dry linen with a heated smoother;
- damp linen with a cold smoother;
- damp linen with a heated smoother.

The smoother was heated in a pan of boiling water and held by the aid of a cloth to protect my fingers from burning.

Photo 100. Heating of the smoother in boiling water in a bowl.

Table 19. Results of Smoothing Experiment. **Photo 101 - 108.**

Conditions	Result Smoothing	Result Pleating
Fabric Dry Smoother Cold	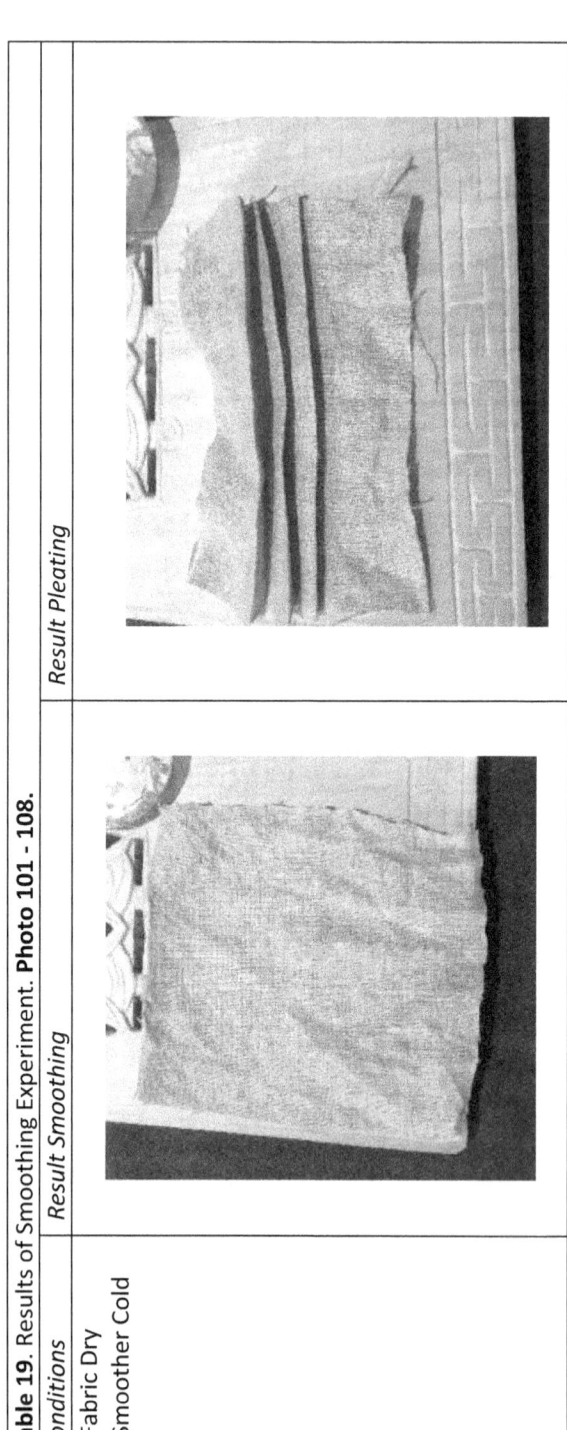	

| Fabric Dry Smoother Warm |  |  |

| Fabric Damp Smoother Cold | 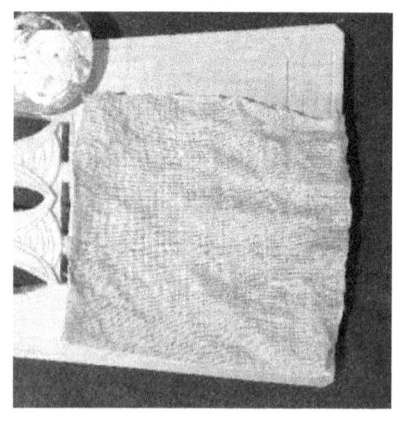 |  |

| Fabric Damp Smoother Warm | 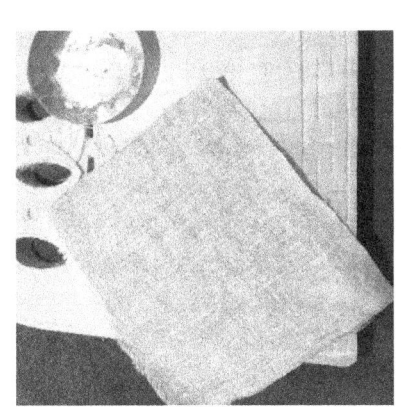 |  |

Table 19 visually details the results of smoothing under the different conditions. As I hypothesised the damp linen with a heated stone gave the best results both for smoothing and pleating.

Other things worth noting were that the glass smoother had the effect of creating a sheen on the linen where it had been rubbed which may have been a desired effect in this period. Also the damp linen 'caught' the smoother so the process was harder as the fabric would scrunch up under the smoother and create wrinkles. Finally, the practice of using a cloth to hold the heated stone meant that the fabric of the holder got in the way of the sample being smoothed. This may not have been an issue if I had a smaller cloth to hold the stone as the tea-towel I used had to be folded several times and became bulky. Once the stone had cooled slightly, I found that I was able to hold it in my bare hands and it was still effective.

Conclusion.

It is possible that the smoothing board may have been used for the smoothing and pleating of linen much like we use an iron today. This may well have been a high-status possession given the time involved in the manufacture of the board, the necessity of importing the glass smoother and the likelihood of ironed or pleated linen being a conspicuous display of wealth and status in period, as someone would have to be wealth to have the labour required to perform this task.

Coopering – a brief overview.

By Stephen Sinclair.

At the outset it may appear that the preamble and introductions in this article are a bit long winded at times, possibly so, however, let me assure you that it isn't this way because I am assuming everyone to be idiots, it is simply because I am assuming most people to not be Coopers, possessing little to no practical experience or working knowledge of this trade!!

Background:
I am a Master Cooper with 49 years' experience and still counting. I have done an official apprenticeship and spent my total working life as a Cooper, both overseas but the majority in South Australia. I have a strong interest in history in general, but these days, a specific focus on the traditions and history of Coopering. I have learnt my lessons well and, with a logical approach to safety, I can proudly say that I am one of a very few real Coopers, on a world scale, that can still count to ten on my fingers. Most I know would be lucky to get to 7½ and, sadly for some, they couldn't reach that number even if they removed their shoes!!!

So this is a warning!! As simple as Coopering may appear, it is fraught with many inherent hazards. Even when being performed correctly, you will find yourself or your hands/fingers in some reasonably precarious positions, this is where many years of experience counts. You will discover pretty quickly that numerous parts of your body are in the direct *'firing line'* at times, however, your hands/fingers will sadly be your primary target if you FAIL to think your objectives through carefully before you commence.[26]

Coopering is a standalone trade, albeit working predominantly with *'real'* timber, it shares very few similarities with other timber crafts. Consequently, tools and rules may vary significantly from the more common timber trades. I have been asked many times during my time – 'How do I perform a certain task or achieve a specific result?' The answer is quite simple, *'I have the correct tool and years of experience!'* Sadly this answer is somewhat irrelevant! The real question should have been – *'How do they achieve a similar result?'* and, unfortunately, the answer to that is – *'I have no idea!'*

The fact that this question has been asked would generally indicate to me that the appropriate tools and knowledge are not possessed by that person. Therefore, they will be required to improvise, adapt and use a fair degree of ingenuity based totally on their own personal circumstances, their own abilities and what other tools and facilities they have at their disposal. Obviously, I have no insight into anyone's personal situation! Hence, an area that I don't wish to give either specific or general advice about, nor take responsibility for!!

Based on this statement I recommend, as a minimum prerequisite, an existing sound and safe knowledge of working with solid timber from both a modern/mechanised perspective as well as some experience with the historical handcrafting of timber. Another useful skill to have for this project would be a basic knowledge and practical understanding of the principles, maths and geometry of circles.

---

[26] *** Please heed my warning ***

Accepting this situation, where steps or processes appear in the following '*Viking Bucket Instructions*' and I consider them to be either very Cooper specific or requiring of a very specific cooper's tool I will provide an '*Objective*' description. Hopefully this will provide you with sufficient information enabling you to make a safe and intelligent decision as to how, and with what, you will attempt to achieve this desired result.

Tools.
If you have been lucky enough to inherit your ancestors' coopering tools you may well have a great collection of reasonably valuable and highly interesting tools. Realistically, I doubt that too many of them will be of any real use to you in the execution of this project. Coopers tools in general are totally unique and very specific when compared to most other timber trades. Interestingly, in addition to this fact, they are also very specific to the actual size and diameter of the task being undertaken. Coopers tools are not universal, one size does not fit all, in fact they are quite the opposite in application. In other words, a tool designed to cut/shape a 30cm (12") diameter may, with a high degree of difficulty, be encouraged to create a vessel with a 60cm (24") diameter but, never in a million years, will it work the other way round. Therefore, you will find that most practicing cooper's tool chests are filled with handmade tools, built specifically to suit their own circumstances and production requirements – not necessarily yours!!!

Coopers' tools are basically all designed to cut curves, circles and angles on some pretty strangely shaped lengths of real timbers. Most typical modern and easily obtained hand tools/machines, although well made and precise, are designed to create perfectly straight, square and smooth finishes, features that are not strictly common in coopering. Useful exceptions are bandsaws (and other derivatives), lathes and routers. These modern alternatives can usually be substituted successfully without modification for performing certain coopering operations. Sadly, over the years, I have witnessed some absolutely horrifying modifications made to modern tools and machines in a naive attempt to *'force'* them to do what they were never intended to do. Please do not go down this path!!

In summary, the following process description is not intended to explain in either detail or clarity the intricacies of coopering, the whys and wherefores of the tools used daily by a cooper, nor to detail the skills and techniques developed through a lifetime of experience. It will simply assume that you have the basic prerequisites as mentioned. This project is actually the simplest of the coopering styles but, sadly, I am already aware that it will, no doubt, raise more questions for you than it can ever answer!

The Oseberg Bucket.

By Stephen Sinclair.

The Oseberg *'Buddha'* Bucket.	Find location: Oseberg Viking Ship Burial Oseberg.	When: 800 – 850 CE.
Stored: Viking Ship Museum Oslo	**Collection no.**: C55000/156	**Material**: Yew, bronze
Size: Diameter 26.5cm (10 $^7/_{16}$") to 32 cm (12 $^{19}/_{32}$"), Height 36 cm (14 $^{11}/_{64}$").		

Photo 109. The original *'Buddha'* Bucket of Oseberg.

Photo 110. A bucket based on the Oseberg bucket. The bucket has been Shaved Off, had the Finish Hoops fitted and has a light coat of Tung Oil applied. It also has a triple spliced natural fibre rope handle fitted.

Introduction.

Although several authentic surviving buckets have been discovered throughout Norway and surrounding Norse colonies dating from the Viking Era, no two are necessarily the same in either components used or specific dimension. The only common feature unique to them all is that they are all 'Coopered' using the same principles. See Table 20 for some examples.

Table 20 – Examples of Buckets.			
Date (CE)	Place	Collections details	Comments
Viking age (After 734)	Vorbasse, Jutland, Denmark	Fejle Museum, No. VT:GN83, 24.	Ash, the osier loops are joined with catches of willow. Height 21cm (8 $^{17}/_{64}$").
8th century	Birka, Grave 507, Uppland, Sweden	Statens Historiska Museum, Stockholm, Sweden, Bj507.	Birch with bronze fittings, height 18.5 cm (7 $^{9}/_{32}$"), diameter at rim 19.5 cm (7 $^{43}/_{64}$").
800 – 850	Oseberg, Sem, Vestfold, Norway	Universitetets Oldsaksamling, Oslo, Oseberg 303	Yew with brass fittings, height 17.5cm (6 $^{57}/_{64}$").

This fact is actually quite logical given the reality that a bucket usually served a very mundane and practical, albeit extremely important, function in everyday life. A specific bucket found within the Oseberg Ship Burial site in Norway known as the 'Buddha' Bucket was very unique and unusual. Highly unlikely to have been christened this by the Vikings themselves, it became known as this because of the resemblance to a seated

Buddha that some of its decorative castings took. Made from white oak, it features an iron handle and has a slightly taller body dimension than most buckets. It is bound with three bronze hoops adorned with several highly decorative and intricately cast fittings. Being included in a royal burial, it is my personal conclusion that this bucket is of a greater ceremonial appearance and purpose rather than any real representation of a practical and personal possession used daily. Of other examples found, it is reasonable to conclude that they are in fact much more representative of a simple and mundane daily Viking life.

Albeit, the history and story behind these discoveries is the prime motivation for my article, the simple fact that they are all traditionally coopered will become my main focus.

All the following coopering methods/instructions and requirements described herein will apply equally to all, regardless of any assumed status or functional mundanity, physical size, orientation or adornment and, as such, should be interpreted as cross-sectional and all encompassing rather than referring to only one, single stand alone bucket.

Design Rationale.

Although most buckets are identical in their constructional design (coopered) and, regardless of their actual place in history, may all vary slightly in their aesthetic interpretation and the particular materials used. This has led to much conjecture between latter day enthusiasts and experts as to *'what is and what is not'* authentically acceptable when making a modern replica of these items.

As a practicing cooper, in my opinion, these discussions are always interesting but serve little purpose. It is obvious to me that, not only did they have the skills and ability required, access and knowledge to both source and work a great variety of raw materials and, ultimately, the necessary life experiences to know how to put it all together in a manner that not only advantaged themselves but also their community around them. They sure as heck wouldn't have restricted themselves to one style, one size and one timber – and obviously didn't.

Evidence is an interesting subject, logically how much genuine evidence will really survive? Certain metals and other materials may survive longer than others, consequently interpreted as being more commonly used or the only used. Not necessarily so, they just survived better!! So, in essence, it comes down to three simple and very basic criteria that would have had the major influence on timber used and what size and form a simple bucket would take. Definitely not a legal and binding specification decided by bureaucrats.

In general terms, the three deciding criteria for individual bucket design are:
- Practicality & Function: What will the buckets purpose be?;
- The physical size/volume, material choice, orientation and general appearance would all be influential in this matter. A final consideration may have been – who was intended to carry and handle the bucket – Adult/Child/Male/Female;
- Material Selection: What timber quality will be used? What strength hoops are required and accessible? What style handle is suitable?
  Timber   Species – Hardwood / Softwood – Porous / Non Porous,
  Hoops – Iron / Bronze (Brass) / Wooden / Cane / Rope.

Handle - Iron / Rope / Timber.

Obviously, practicality & function would have some influence towards this choice. However, the more likely and significant factor would have been – what materials and skills are locally available and more easily sourced.

Life Expectancy: How long is it realistically expected to perform its duty for?

This aspect, in equal amounts, will have both influence and be in itself, influenced by the two previous criteria. So, in all honesty, if it was accepted or intended that this vessel would have a short and hard life, honourable but replaceable, then it would be built accordingly. However, in making this statement I do personally believe that it still would have been built as sturdily and accurately within those parameters as was realistically possible for the cooper at that particular moment.

Therefore, in my opinion, regardless of the final timber, size, orientation and general appearance of the bucket you choose to make, it will basically be as historically relevant as any other bucket providing the coopering principles are adhered to.

If you follow my specifications closely you are not necessarily reproducing any one specific existing historical bucket, however, the dimensions, orientation and overall style will closely match many. These specifications have been agreed upon by several amateur researchers and enthusiasts (including myself) to satisfactorily represent a basic and mundanely functional coopered bucket from the general Viking Period. Orientation with its low centre of gravity and inwardly sloping staves is totally logical and practical for seafaring people. Iron hoops provided superior strength for a water container and a rope handle ergonomically more likely. Timbers used would have ranged from oak (hardwood) to spruce, fir or pine (softwoods).

BEFORE YOU BEGIN.

Specification, Tools and Preliminary Requirements.

Table 21. Overall Bucket Specifications	
Top Diameter	215 mm (8 $^{15}/_{32}$")
Circumference	675 mm (26 $^{37}/_{64}$")
Bottom Diameter	255 mm (10 $^{3}/_{64}$")
Circumference	800 mm (31 $^{1}/_{2}$")
Body Stave Length	215 mm (8 $^{15}/_{32}$")
Handle Stave Length	250 mm (9 $^{27}/_{32}$")
Stave & Head Thickness	14 -16mm ($^{35}/_{64}$ - $^{5}/_{8}$")
Approximate Volume	8 Litres (2.11338 USA gallon)
Orientation	Inverted

Table 22. Material requirements.		
Item	Quantity	Description
Stave Blanks	14	215mm (8 ½") (long) x 52mm (2 1/16"") (wide) x 14 - 16mm (9/16 - $^{5}/_{8}$") (thick)
	2	255mm (10 1/16") (long) x 52mm (2 1/16") (wide) x 14 – 16mm (9/16 - $^{5}/_{8}$") (thick)
Heading Pieces	2 - 5	270mm (11") (long) x 255mm (10 ½") coverage x 14 mm (9/16"") (thick)
Hoops	2	1 meter (40") x 30mm (1 $^{3}/_{16}$") +/- x 2.5mm ($^{3}/_{32}$"/10GA) +/- Mild Steel
Handle	1	1 meter (39 $^{3}/_{8}$") x 10 -12mm (⅜" - ½") Diam. Natural Fibre Rope
Dowels	??	6mm (¼") x 25mm (1") timber dowels (Timber variety optional)
Rivets	20 +/-	6mm (¼") O/D x 12mm (½"") Shank, Steel Flat Head

Other requirements.

Linseed meal or plain flour, PVA glue, tung / nut oil (food safe) and 4 x brass retaining pins 2mm x 14mm ($^5/_{64}$ x ½-9/16") +/- (optional).

Table 23. Tools Used. See photos 110 and 111.	
Hammer & driver	Coopers anvil (bick iron)
Jointer or plane	6 – 8" dividers
Chiv or jigger	Draw knife and side axe or adze
Croze	Spokeshave, pail shave, buzz or scraper
Bow saw/s	Hoop level marker, rising clips
Work horse	Brace & bits
Stave jointing guide (**to be explained in detail later)	

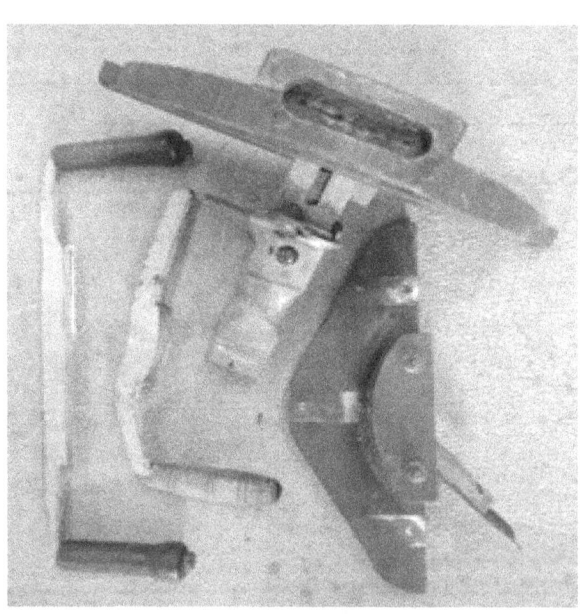

Photo 111. Tools used in Section A. (From LEFT to RIGHT); Heading knife / draw knife, jigger, hand croze with ¼" cutter, timber chiv.

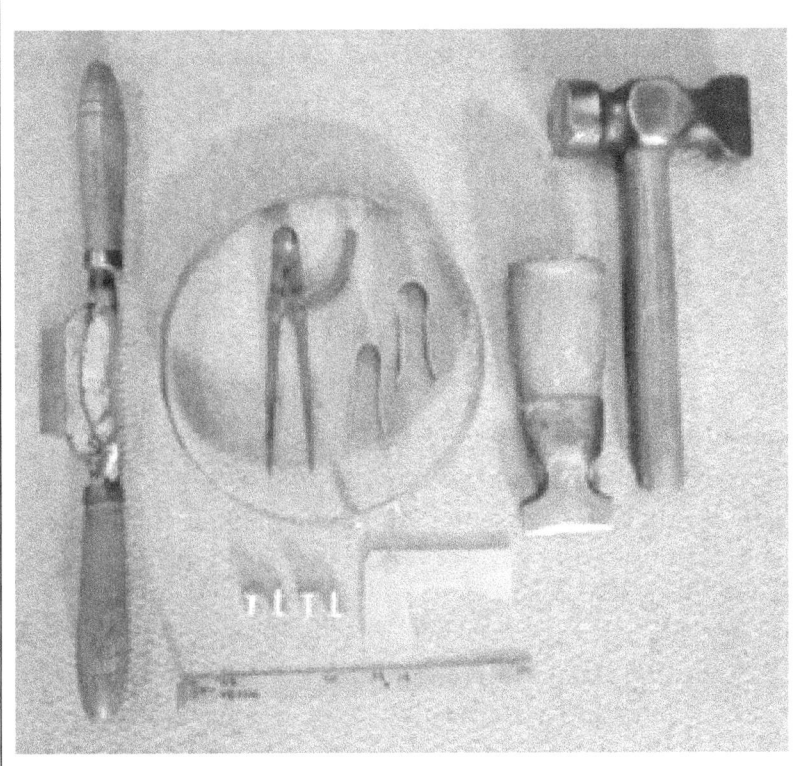

Photo 112. Tools used in Section B, C & D. Left: coopers spokeshave, Right: hammer & driver centre: (Top to Bottom); rising hoop, compass/dividers, rising clips (x 2), rivets (x 4), stave jointing guide, hoop level marker.

Footnote:
- These specifications and features are based on several authentic examples, realistically combined to create my own standard production '*Viking Water Bucket Replica*';
- I use clear coated, mild steel hoops because they provide superior strength;
- I use cooperage grade white oak because it is an authentic, sturdy and durable timber for this purpose;
- I fit a spliced fibre rope handle because I believe it to be the strongest and most practical for re-enactors;

- I apply a finish coat of Tung Oil simply to provide an extended protection/life to the aesthetics.

Pre-Commencement Build Requirements.

A. Stave and Head Pre-preparation.
B. Stave Jointing Guide Tool.
C. Working Hoops, Sizing and Riveting.
D. Hammer & Hoop Driving Tool.

As is the case with any project attempted, your forward planning and preparation will go a long way toward creating a flowing and successful outcome. So, it is well advised that you address these four essential requirements before you progress any further. Without them, any significant progress will be significantly hindered.

A: Stave and Head Pre-preparation.

Timber selection will be ultimately important. Always select clean and natural timber, critically ensuring that it has not previously been contaminated, coated, chemically treated or toxic in any way.

Stave Pre-prep Requirements.

You will require 16 stave blanks in total. (14 body staves and 2 handle staves)
14 cut at: 215mm (8 ½") (long) x 52mm (2 1/16") (wide) x 14 - 16mm (9/16 - $^5/_8$") (thick)
2 cut at: 255mm (10") (long) x 52mm (2 1/16") (wide) x 14 – 16mm (9/16 - $^5/_8$") (thick):- Handles

Head Pre-prep Requirements.

Avoid using a *'one piece'* head as the possibility of warping is high in some timbers. I personally aim for a 2 or 3 piece head but this will obviously depend on what widths are available at the time.

You will require sufficient pieces cut at about 280mm (11") in length x 14 – 16mm (9/16 - $^5/_8$") thick, that when jointed and *'laid u*p' side by side, will have a coverage of around 265mm (10 ½").

Note. This is the approximate slightly oversized diameter of the finished head).

Try to keep the two outer pieces as wide as possible when doing a multi piece head and ensure your compass diameter covers the majority of their width (remember the 265mm (10 ½") setting is already slightly oversized so don't allow too much more spare as the outer pieces may become quite narrow when actually cut to the finish diameter).

- Lay the pieces together, best face down and mark with chalk the circumference line, making sure the line falls within the length of each heading piece. Clearly highlight the centre point.
- Following the curve of your line but, importantly, about 40mm (1 ¾") clear inside - place a pencil line across each joint indicating where to locate the dowels, two dowels per joint is sufficient. In particular, ensure the dowel holes on the two outer pieces are well clear (inside) of the arc line and will not be exposed when finally cut round.
- Bore dowel holes to the depth required, minimise excess depth.

- Fit dowels to one joint on each piece, run a glue line along the opposing joint and knock the head together. Clean away any excess glue, then clamp securely with a sash clamp ensuring that all joints are compressed tightly (if they don't, check that your dowels are not too long). The glue will provide no structural integrity to the finished bucket, it simply will hold things in place when doing later processes, hopefully making it slightly easier for you!!
- Set aside both your pre-prepared stave blanks and head for the time being.

B: Stave Jointing Guide / Jig:

Objective: An easily made and very simple tool, based on the geometry of circles, that will allow you to quickly and accurately monitor and maintain the correct *'Coopers Angle'* during the process of jointing your staves.

This tool represents two essential features of your intended bucket: (1) – The outer circumference curve (shape) of the smallest diameter specification and, in relation to the widths of the staves being fitted, (2) – the angle created by the radius line as it extends out to that diameter. In all reality, a single radius line never changes angle, regardless of the diameter. However, when related to the potentially variable widths of staves being joined, this static tool is capable of precisely measuring an almost infinitely variable number of joint angles with no adjustment required.

For every different diameter vessel I have ever made I have also made the appropriate Jointing Guide. I have hundreds of them and would never part with any because they will always remain relevant for that diameter vessel.

How to make a Stave Jointing Guide;
- On a piece of 3mm ($1/8$") +/- ply and with your dividers set to a radius of 108mm (4 $1/4$") (½ the smallest outside diameter (O/D), scribe an arc section about 100mm (4") long and also clearly mark the divider centre point,
- Using a straight edge lined up radially from the centre point to a place on your arc close to one end (either end, it makes no difference), draw or scribe a sharp line that extends 30 – 40mm (1 ¼" - 1 ½") back (towards centre) from the arc. These two lines and how they intersect now become the critical features of this tool,
- To form the body of the tool, simply hand draw a line out from the bottom of the radius line at roughly 90º and then up and back around at a distance of 40mm (1 ½"") +/- from your original markings, finally dropping back down and meeting the other end of your arc,
- Cut this profile out making sure to cut the inner arc and radius line accurately, cleanly and true to the lines scribed.

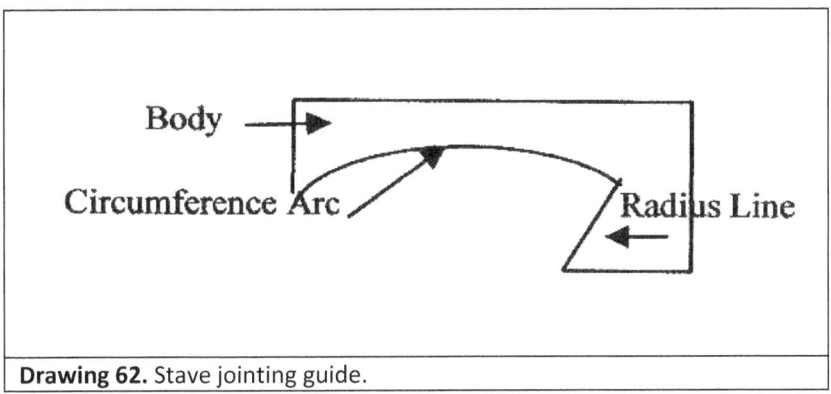

Drawing 62. Stave jointing guide.

How to Use this Guide.

One simple and basic rule in Coopering is: always measure and work from the smallest end (diameter) of the vessel, regardless of its type and size or the specific method or style of coopering employed at the time. Theoretically (if not a bit presumptuously), once you have the small end right and you have followed everything through correctly, the bigger diameter will automatically follow suit.

Remembering that this tool is designed for the smallest diameter, it will also only be accurate when used on the joint at the smallest end of each individual stave. This end, from here on in, will now be referred to as the '*Rise End*', the end that we will be working from more consistently.

- As you plane the joints on each stave the accuracy of the angle being produced can be monitored quickly and regularly by simply laying the '*arc*' section across the back of the stave (Rise End only) and the radial edge held against the joint. It will clearly indicate whether the angle being produced is correct or requires increasing or decreasing. Obviously, the aim is for it to match perfectly and, believe me, any misalignment or inconsistency allowed at the jointing stage, regardless of how minimal it may initially appear, will be magnified later, potentially causing significant handling and structural issues. Simply, bad joint angles are amplified x 2 when they appear on adjacent staves.

C: Working Hoops.

Objective: Again, for every different coopered item that I produce I have also made at least one set, in most cases several sets of Working Hoops. As implied, these hoops are simply used repeatedly to do the majority of the initial work required, continually receiving all the hammering, staining and abuse dished out during the production process and then replaced at the end with clean, new finish hoops. At the end of each individual production run, they are set aside ready for the next similar project. Interestingly, they do provide several advantages – always there and ready to go, however, the greatest bonus they offer is consistency. If you use exactly the same rising hoop every time almost guarantees a consistently sized product.

In all reality, having a dedicated set of Working Hoops for your project may well be considered total overkill, however, one way or the other, you will need a set of hoops at the beginning regardless. The fact is, sourcing two sets of hoops is no harder than for one and it will be good practice for making your Finish Hoops anyway. Whatever your decision, the following instruction is as relevant for both work or finish hoops equally once you get passed the initial sizing instruction.

**Hint: Getting a steel merchant to cut appropriate strips from a sheet is quite acceptable. Digging through your old Uncle's scrap pile may also reap potential reward but who knows what you will actually be getting. However, a good resource could be the discarded hoops from a second hand wine barrel. Preferably the narrowest/lightest hoops.

Hoop Requirement and Preparation.

2 per set mild steel @ 1 meter (40") x 30mm (1 ¼") +/- x 2.5mm ($^3/_{32}$"/10GA) +/-
6mm (¼") O/D x 12mm (½"), steel, flat head coopers rivets.

All hoops will need to be splayed to the taper angle of the bucket and also rolled to the average diameter of the bucket prior to any further processing.

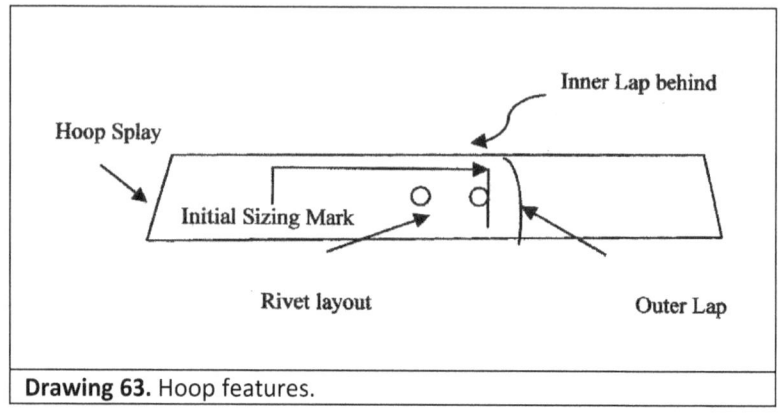

Drawing 63. Hoop features.

Size and Make Working Hoops.

Only proceed with your working hoops at this stage and, using the theoretical finish diameter of your bucket – top O/D: 215mm (8 ½") and bottom O/D: 255mm (10"), you will need to size this set purely by measurement due to the present absence of a physical bucket. This measurement must take into consideration that, for two reasons, your 'starting' bucket diameter will be slightly larger than the *'finish'* diameter.

- In the initial processes, presumably each individual stave back will be flatter and, hence, when raised together in the hoop will create a more geometric, multi-faceted shape rather than a smooth round shape. These *'corners'* will increase the initial diameter slightly.
- At a later stage of production, not only these *'corners'* but also any stains and markings created will be shaved/sanded off, obviously reducing the overall diameter to the finish size and the size the finish hoops will be made to.

Procedure:
- By eye and by hand shape the hoops to form, as accurately as possible, a consistent circle approximately 5 –

10mm (¼" - ⅜") larger than the Finish O/D. A clamp may be useful when doing this to keep it all under control.

Note: Importantly, with the top/small hoop take this measurement across the top edge (smallest diameter assuming the hoop is splayed correctly). With the bottom/larger hoop, do the opposite, take the measurement across the bottom edge (largest diameter). This should ensure that, when driven tight, both hoops sit within the parameters of the angled dimensions of the bucket.

- Once happy with the size, at a point about 25 – 30mm (1 - 1 ¼") back from the end of the outer lap, with chalk draw a mark up and across both the inner and outer lap clearly defining that position where they overlap. This marking is the location for the first rivet and, when the marks are realigned, dictates the size of the hoop.

- It is likely at this stage that you will have excess hoop length on the inside. Remove the clamp and allow the hoop to relax. On the inner lap measure along form the first overlap mark roughly 150mm (6") and make another mark (ensure you go in the right direction – towards the end of the inner hoop length), this will allow sufficient hoop for the location of the second rivet. On this mark, cut off and discard the excess hoop. With the excess removed, handling the hoop will become slightly easier, so it will pay to re-align the marks and confirm your original sizing – amend if necessary.

**Hint: If you sourced extra hoops in the beginning and at the same length, then take note of the excess removed from both hoops as this can be applied accordingly to your Finish Hoops which will make them easier to handle right from the start.

Riveting Hoops.

- Starting with the outer lap - drill an appropriate sized hole (your rivet size) in the centre of the hoop and directly on the 'line up' mark.
- 50mm (2") +/- back from this hole and again, centre hoop, drill another similar hole. This hole spacing now represents the rivet locations and should, for the purpose of aesthetics, be repeated at the same scale for all hoops.
- Now, on the inner lap - drill the same sized hole, again centre hoop, directly on the inner *'line up'* mark.
- Lining up the two sizing marks, punch/place a rivet through both holes. Invert the hoop on a Coopers Anvil and peen/dome the rivet over. Ensure that both laps are sandwiched tightly together.
- Ensure both laps now sit evenly along their length, and then complete drilling the second hole through the bottom lap.
- Insert a rivet and peen/dome over as before.
- Repeat this procedure for the other hoop/s.

**Hint: If you decide later that these hoops require modification or resizing due to either an initial error in sizing or they just simply have stretched through use (which they will), then just punch/drill the old rivets out and resize again re-using the existing holes in the outer lap as your line up marks. Drill and rivet as before.

Work hoops are intended to take the majority of the continuous battering of the production process, hence resizing and repairing them is quite a common practice.

D: Cooper's Hammer and Driver.

These are two of the most important tools in their kit. They will usually never let them out of their sight and would rarely lend them to another Cooper! They are both very specific to this trade but, more importantly, become very personalised and moulded to the style, strength and physical actions of the individual cooper using them, hence, usually difficult to source and, sometimes, variable in basic design.

The Cooper's Hammer:

This hammer is both weighted and shaped specifically to address several separate coopering requirements. It generally weighs in around 2 kilograms (4.4 pounds), has a broad circular face of around 50mm (2") diameter and usually has a rounded, vertical peened back.

The closest modern facsimile to this is probably a small sledge or block hammer, but let's be realistic now, for your purposes *'a hammer is a hammer'*. Get as close to these specs as you can but the important features are:
- Enough weight to encourage the steel hoops to stretch and be driven firmly down onto your bucket.
- A broad enough face to give you half a chance of actually hitting the target you are aiming at.

The Cooper's Driver.

Once again, a very unique and specific tool designed for one purpose only – when struck firmly with the hammer forces the hoops tightly down. It features a hardened steel working head which is shaped specifically to allow it to be located quickly, confidently and soundly on the top edge of a fitted hoop. It usually has a short, straight grained hardwood stock housed behind the working head to absorb the *'shock waves'* when struck. The wooden stock is usually also around the 50mm (2") diameter simply to give you a reasonable target to aim at. In reality, a skilled Cooper will rarely be looking at the driver, he is simply swinging the hammer and locating the driver as a matter of routine – so it is damn nice when the driver is actually where it should be.

That statement is intended to highlight the most important feature to be considered. That ability for the driver to be located soundly and with confidence, on to the hoop because, as mentioned much earlier if it slips off when being struck with intent - will happily amputate a toe after it ricochets off your shin and, the hammer on its follow through, once finished smashing the fingers that were previously holding said driver, will rather unceremoniously but, no doubt, to the total amusement of anyone watching, usually embed itself quite uncomfortably in your groin.
*** Please enjoy because, sadly, I'm not joking. ***

So YES, you are going to require a Driving Tool of some description. The principle is quite simple, the aesthetic design is open to interpretation, however, the working application and inherent hazards must be taken seriously, and considered in the design.

Having now achieved these four preliminary requirements you should be in a good position to commence with the actual project at hand. In some places you are going to be left to your own devices and ingenuity as to *'HOW'*. *** Think clearly, think logically and, most of all, think safety ***

BUILDING INSTRUCTIONS IN CHRONOLOGICAL ORDER.

1: Stave Jointing.

Traditional Tools Used: Most likely roughed out with either a draw knife, adze or side axe while held firmly on a cooper's work horse then accurately finished off on a large wooden jointing plane mounted diagonally to the floor.

Objective: To accurately plane both edges of all staves straight and smooth to the specified widths, while at the same time, producing the correct *'Coopers Angle'* per your Jointing Guide and, simultaneously developing the required stave taper which ultimately will dictate the size/diameter and shape/orientation of your finished bucket.

Process: For purely economic reasons, traditional coopering is based around the use of random width timbers. In particular, Cooperage Grade Oak, being of a very high quality and milled in a specific way (Quarter Cut and at times, hand split) by highly specialised millers – hence very expensive, motivated the individual Coopers to gain maximum value from random width timber supplies.

However, for ease of explanation and a slight degree of simplicity for you, I have chosen to approach the Stave Jointing process from a *'standard stave width'* perspective. **Hint: If you choose to use random width staves the physical Jointing Process will be basically the same, however, it will simply require more measuring, monitoring and balancing to keep the two halves of the bucket symmetrical.

Required Finish Dimensions.

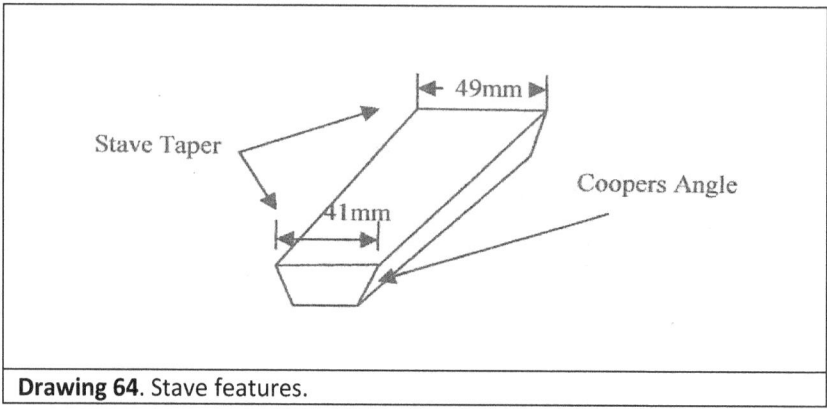

Drawing 64. Stave features.

Joint all your Staves to these specifications:
- Small End (Rise End): 41mm (1 $^{39}/_{64}$");
- Big End (Bottom): 49mm (1 $^{59}/_{64}$").

• Take the measurements accurately across the back of each stave.
• The two handle (longer) staves are jointed exactly the same but taking the smaller measurement at roughly 215mm (8 ½") up the stave.
• Once jointed, at the very top of the two Handle staves, with a compass set to that width, scribe an arc spanning from side to side and to the top, also mark the centre point.
• Bore a 13mm (5/8") +/- hole at the centre point and cut around the arc, creating the mounting holes for the rope handle. Smooth off and sand as required.

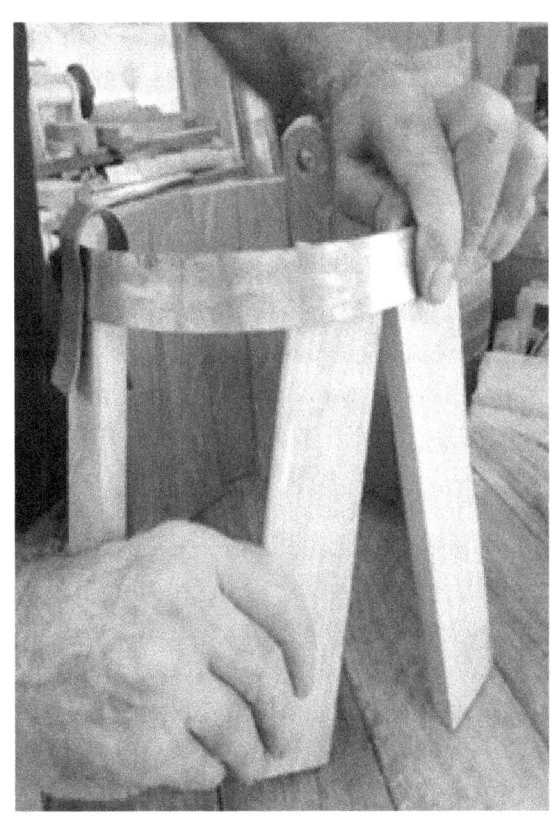

Photo 113. Raising a bucket. Raise Hoop & Clip, Staves.

2: Rising your Bucket.

Traditional Tools Used.

Hammer & driver, simple metal clips or clamp, rise hoop.

Objective: To assemble all the staves into the Rise Hoop in the correct position, with the same orientation and in a symmetrical and balanced layout.

Process: As you progress through this project it will become increasingly more important that the original order that the staves were raised in remains constant throughout. Therefore, as a precaution, once you have successfully risen your bucket and have the hoops tight, clearly number the staves consecutively so that it can be re-risen in the same order and direction should it happen to collapse at a later stage and, again YES, the odds of this happening are pretty good.

• First off, divide the staves into two stacks of seven body staves each, also keeping the two handle staves within easy reach. No specific order necessary at this time.
• Holding the Rise Hoop stave height from your flat work surface, clip/clamp one body stave at the Rise End onto the inside of this hoop (avoid the lap section). By keeping lateral pressure (at hoop level with your thumb) against the joint of each progressive stave as introduced, feed in and support the first seven body staves, then one handle stave followed by the remaining seven body staves. If the remaining gap is wide enough, then finally, slip the last stave in and up into position, remove the clip and allow the hoop to drop down and take up the pressure. It does require a reasonable amount of double handed coordination to achieve this, but if you can keep the hoop level and the staves firm at all times you shouldn't have too much trouble. If the gap is too small, follow the next instruction.
• Fitting the last stave can be the trickiest for beginners. If the gap is too small, in what space there is from the missing stave, scissor the fingers on one hand to support both the first and last stave fitted – applying pressure in both directions. Once you have achieved this control, remove the clip and, maintaining lateral pressure, carefully lift the hoop level up the staves. Because the hoop is splayed, as you lift it you will also be increasing the diameter you have to work with, ultimately increasing the gap wide enough to slip the last stave in. If still

having trouble, perhaps inter-change the stave being fitted for a shorter body stave, they may be easier to handle. If you still can't increase the gap sufficiently to fit the stave – maybe your hoop is undersized – resize if required and try again.

- Once successful, by eye - level the bucket vertically and upright, fit and drive both hoops down firmly but not over tight just yet.
- From the bottom edge, tap the staves into place, either up or down as required, to create a flat and level base. Also, from the inside, knock the staves out level with each other.
- Firmly tightening the hoops now, and number the staves as a precaution.

Photo 114. Working out the end. Forming the circular inner surface using a '*Jigger*' prior to cutting the groove.

3: Working Out the End.

Traditional Tools Used: Chiv: A handmade compound curved, wooden plane designed specifically to shave the end internal curve shape, and mounted to a flat timber working base. Jigger: A member of the draw knife family but specifically shaped for this purpose.

Objective: To level out any thickness and shape irregularities on the inside bottom 40mm (1 1/2") +/- of the staves, while at the same time, creating a smooth and circular inner base for the Croze (Groove Cutter) to run against.

*Although more specifically referring to the remaining section beyond the groove, when finished, this area of any coopered vessel is generally known as the Chime, the area at the end of the staves that is profiled to house the Head.

Process: Initially your bucket, both inside and out, will be slightly more *'multi-faceted'* rather than smooth and circular. When cut out, your Head will (or at least – should) be circular, so therefore you must now make that inner bottom level of the bucket staves (the big end only) circular so that, once grooved, the back shape of the groove provides a smooth, regular curve for the Head to bed against. This result must be achieved while still retaining as much physical thickness and strength to the staves at that level.

Note: In all honesty, this step is going to be one of the trickiest for you to achieve without the traditional tools, but if you want to make a half successful bucket, you will need to make some effort to achieve this requirement.

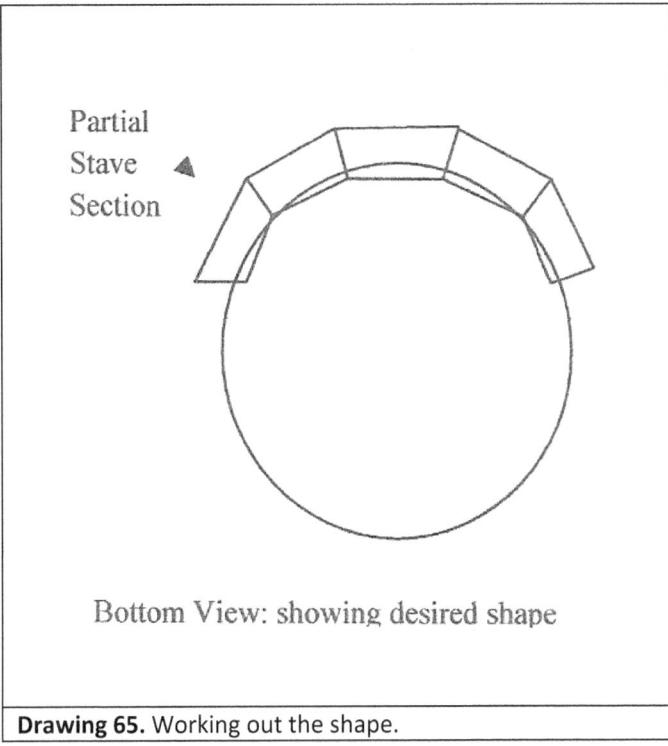

Drawing 65. Working out the shape.

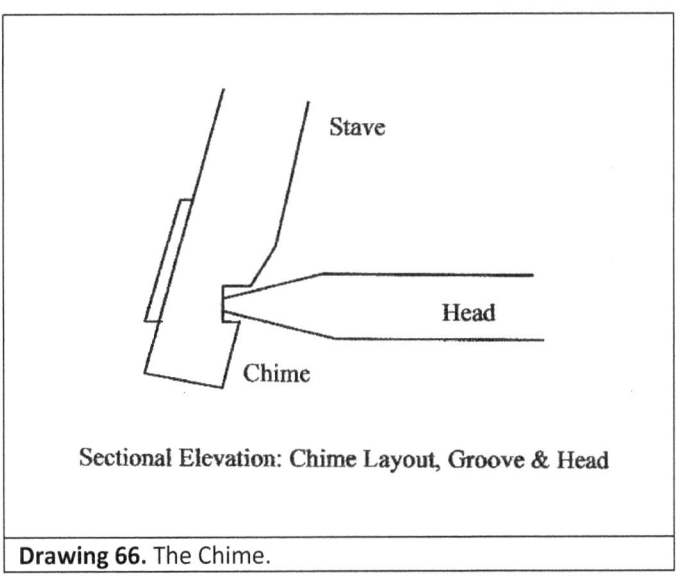

Drawing 66. The Chime.

Note: Hopefully these basic diagrams are sufficient to provide enough insight into what the desired outcomes are for this and the following step – Grooving. The diagrams are intended to highlight the Principle only; they are neither to scale or intended to show accurate detail of shape or fit.

4: Cutting the Groove

Traditional Tools Used: Croze: Again a specifically designed tool usually handmade from timber. The main feature being a height adjustable 'turret' which houses either a saw tooth cutter or chiselling style blades which have a fixed pre-set depth and width cutting action. This turret is mounted through a flat timber working base similar to the chiv.

Objective: To cut a clean, sharp, accurate and consistent groove, parallel to but approximately 20mm (¾"") +/- up from the bottom edge (large end) of the staves. At a constant depth, this groove is cut the full way around the inside of your bucket with the tool being guided by the previous Working Out shape produced.

This groove is obviously going to house the finished head and, as such, becomes one of the critical sealing points for your bucket, so accuracy and consistency are paramount.

Process: The precise depth and width of your groove will potentially be decided by the tooling you have available, however, a dimension of as close to: 5mm ($^{13}/_{64}$") wide x 5mm ($^{13}/_{64}$") deep should be your preferred target. So, within reason, this dimension isn't totally critical and the final Head profiling process will be done to fit your achieved dimensions, providing the following requirements are observed.

- Ensure the depth of your groove is not cut too deeply into the stave, limit it to no more than 1/3rd maximum of the stave thickness. If too deep, all staves will become significantly weaker at that level, reducing their ability to hold pressure against the head and, most likely, just simply breaking away. Also a deep groove will make shaping the head profile to allow it to reach the back of the groove comfortably basically impossible. Width and depth should always remain as relative as possible.
- Once again, try to keep the groove Width ideally ⅓ to ½ of the Head thickness. However, a slightly wider groove in relation to its depth is far less detrimental than a narrow and deep groove, providing the width does not exceed the actual thickness of the head to be fitted.
- When setting your tool to the height/level that the groove will be cut at, ensure that sufficient length of stave (Chime) remains below the lowest edge of the groove. I would suggest leaving about 20mm (¾") of chime (refer to Drawing 65).

An obvious modern alternative to the traditional croze is a Router with an appropriately sized '*Slotting Cutter*' fitted that has the correct bearing depth control. Depending on the router, a larger plywood base may need to be fitted to help keep the router level, any '*tilting*' during the journey will create inconsistency in groove width.

Invert the bucket onto a solid work surface that accommodates the handle extensions and, simply, run the cutter around at the specified setting, cutting the groove.

5: Measure and Mark Head.

Traditional Tools Used: Compass/dividers: double point with locking adjustment and an open span of 180mm (7 ¼") +/-.

Objective: To measure an accurate circumference length at the back of the groove and then transfer/apply this precise measurement to the Head, guaranteeing the correct sizing and ultimate fit.
Process: This step is reasonably simple to achieve but requires some close attention to detail to gain the accuracy required. Initially by eye, set your dividers to the estimated radius of the bucket at the back of the groove. Providing your estimation is vaguely close, either over or under size, this setting will be a 'close enough' starting point for you.

- Starting with this initial setting, clearly press one point of the dividers into the back of the groove at any place, clearly marking your start point. From this point step your dividers around the groove SIX times, hopefully ending somewhere reasonably close to your starting mark.

**Hint: As you make the progressive stepping avoid pressing too hard/deeply on the points as this may produce an inaccurate measurement and also create divots that may interfere with the fine tuning process. However, it is also imperative that the located point doesn't slip or change position – so therefore, use a happy medium pressure.

- Paying close attention to either the 'shortfall or overstep' of the divider point at the last (6th) step, estimate the gap/distance from the initial start point to where you finished. Now, estimate 1/6th of this distance and carefully re-adjust the dividers present setting by that amount (increase or decrease accordingly).

- Re-step the groove SIX times and, theoretically, you should have now finished much closer to the original start point. Again reset your dividers to 1/6th of the remaining difference and repeat (if required).
- The specific aim is: after the sixth step to actually finish as close to 2mm ($^5/_{64}$") short (before) your starting point, preferably not right on it and, definitely NEVER over (beyond) it. In other words, the best finish head size should be very slightly undersized – never oversized.
- Systematically readjusting your dividers accordingly after each attempt, repeat the process until the desired result is achieved.

**Hint: Sometimes this can be a very frustrating process – going from one side to the other but never where you want. Previous divots may be having an effect, if so, relocate your Start Point. However, the most likely reason is that the incremental adjustment required is simply too fine for your dividers to achieve.

If you can't actually finish closer than 3 - 6mm ($^1/_8$ - ¼"), don't stress!! Although not ideal, we can address this difference later – for now just remember what it is.

- Using the closest setting achieved, on the underside of your head and from the original centre point – scribe a clear/sharp circle of that exact diameter.

Photo 115. The finished groove. The finished Chime and Groove ready to Measure and fit the Head.

Cut Head Round.

Traditional Tool Used: Bow saw.

<u>Objective</u>: Simply to cut out a disc/head to the precise size required to match your bucket groove diameter.

Process: For modern purposes either a bandsaw or jigsaw will achieve the desired result with less effort and are usually reasonably common to find.

Note: Regardless of the saw used, remember that the blade will be designed/sharpened with '*set*'. This allows clearance for the blade and may prevent jamming, however, the timber removed or '*kerf*' also has a width value of usually around 2 – 3mm ($^5/_{64}$" - $^1/_8$") +/-. The scribing mark will also have some minimal width value of around 1mm, so the combined value of these can produce a potential 3 – 4mm ($^1/_8$ - $^5/_{32}$") area of discrepancy if not taken into consideration.

The accuracy of the finished head size is critical to the future ability of your bucket to seal and hold water. So, where and how you line the saw up in relation to the scribe line to make this cut is equally as critical. Hence, a badly cut head could quickly and easily become 3mm ($^1/_8$") in radius (6mm ($^1/_4$") in Diameter) smaller than intended and, sadly, it just ain't gonna fit.

**Hint: A simple philosophy worth remembering when working with timber is: *'It is much easier to recut timber shorter if it is too long than it is to cut it longer when it is too short!'* For coopering purposes just substitute the words - long & short for big & small.

Accepting the value of this observation, with a degree of skill and accuracy on your behalf, you can now use this knowledge to your advantage if required. Thinking back to the previous step, 5: Measuring for your Head and, where I said *'don't stress'* if you are having trouble achieving the exact result, this is why.
- Given the knowledge that you could easily influence the final head size, to your detriment, dramatically without even knowing it, then equally, with a bit of finesse and forethought, you can reverse this situation to benefit yourself.
- Remembering that the required *'adjustment'* is only 1/6th of the total discrepancy observed which, in fairness, probably represents less than 1mm+/- to the radius, then, by paying particular attention to where the relevant edge of your saw blade is cutting in relation to your scribed line (on it, under it, above it) you should be able to create the final adjustment

required. Also remember that it is preferable that your final head size is the proverbial *'bees dick'* undersized, not over.[27]

7: Cutting In the Head.

Traditional Tools Used: Heading knife/drawknife, (a side axe may have initially been used to *'rough out'* the desired profile depending on physical size and thickness of the head) and held firmly with a cooper's work horse.

<u>Objective</u>: To reduce the outer perimeter thickness of the head to create a central 3 – 4mm ($1/8$ - $5/32$") tapered *'Bead'*/ Basil via a 20mm (¾") +/- wide bevel cut onto both sides of the head. The profile formed must allow the head to enter and press firmly against the back of the groove all the way round while, at the same time, bite into the top and bottom leading edges of the groove creating a strong and secure seal.

Process: Again, a critical process that, if not achieved with a degree of accuracy, will dramatically influence the functional outcome of your bucket.

**Hint: If you have difficulty visualising the required partnering shape between Head and groove I suggest you first make a couple of simple guides (Drawing 67) that should help you understand the profile required and how you might go about producing it. With minimal force, the taper profile of guide B must touch the groove as indicated. As you physically cut in your Head, use guide A to constantly monitor the consistency and accuracy of the final profile you are producing. Cutting the

---

[27] **Author's Note: Yes, at this point I am happy to admit that I am an anal perfectionist. I work to an accuracy level of – left edge, right edge or down the centre of a very sharp pencil line – and proud of it.

underside bevel wider will help allow better penetration into the groove.

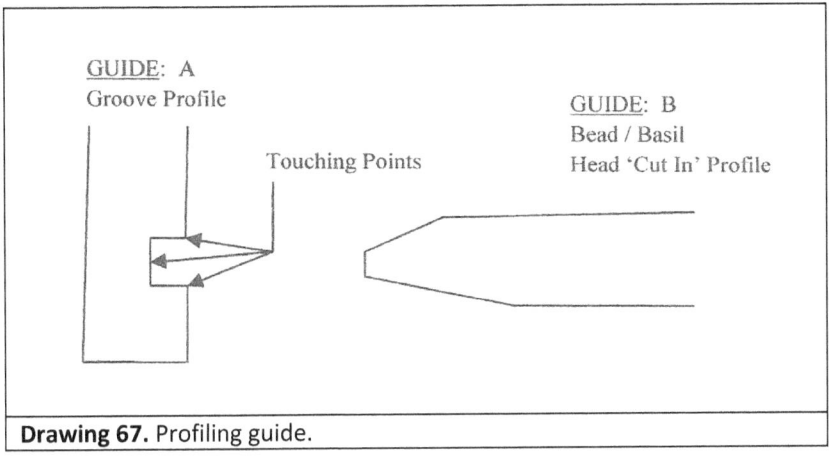

Drawing 67. Profiling guide.

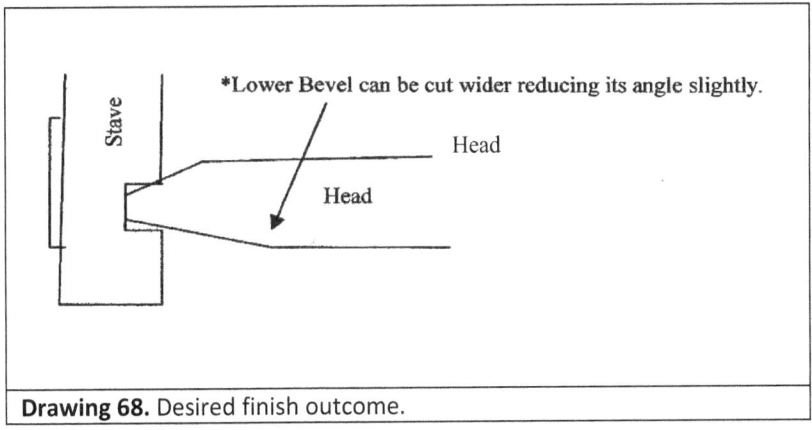

Drawing 68. Desired finish outcome.

8: Heading Up.

Traditional Tools Used: Hammer & driver, possibly flat metal levers.

Objective: Quite simply, to locate the Head into the bucket groove and tighten the hoops so that all components bed together as required.

In theory, this should be one of the more straightforward procedures addressed so far, sadly, it is also one of the riskier moments you will encounter. You will be required to remove one supporting hoop from the bucket totally and probably loosen the other. Nervously, your bucket will be in a very precarious situation during this time and, with no way of avoiding it, you will need to be prepared, be organised, be gentle and, finally, be quick.

If not already done – number the staves as previously suggested.

Several factors can contribute to the risk of collapse at this point, regardless of the fact that you have loosened the hoops.
- Badly jointed staves with inaccurate stave angles.
- Ill-fitting working hoops that don't match the bucket shape or taper angle.
- The position the hoops actually sit on the bucket (too high/too low)
- The working surface you have the bucket sitting on. Ensure that when inverted, the bucket is supported in a level and sound position with the extended handle staves, not only accommodated for, but also prevented from dropping clean out of the bucket.

If it does collapse, don't panic, you won't be the first person that this has happened to! Just re-organise your scattered staves per your numbers, re-rise the bucket, re-level the groove and simply have another go at it. You will eventually succeed if you can progressively recognise and counteract the issues that may be causing you concern.

Process.

- Firstly, although not totally essential but highly recommended, a mixture of either flour & water or linseed meal & water – mixed into a thin, putty-like consistency should NOW be applied into the groove. This food safe paste will provide a secondary seal in the groove, squeezing back out what isn't required as the hoops are retightened and, with what is retained, drying out and filling any irregularities that may exist between the marriage of the head and staves. **Hint: I personally use linseed meal/mater because it makes an easier and less messy mixture to use but, admittedly, isn't quite as readily available as flour. (French and European Coopers have traditionally used flour/water pastes, but if you have ever tried rolling out pizza dough, you will know it's like rolling out a tennis ball – it just doesn't do what you want it to).

- With the bucket now inverted, knock the Big End hoop off, allow it to drop down to the work surface but don't remove it from around the bucket.
- The stave joints should open up slightly at this time and allow for a degree of flexibility/movement at the open end but, depending on the location of the remaining small hoop, may not have allowed sufficient flex yet to allow comfortably fitting of the head. You will need to make a logical judgement as to your situation.

Place the head onto the open end and, simply, compare its size against the present opening. Ultimately, how much forcing will be required to persuade the head to slip inside the chime and be tapped down to the groove varies.

**Hint: Some minimal resistance is fine but excessive force or hammering has the potential to cause significant damage to the staves and, more likely, fatal damage to the head.

In some cases the staves will actually open up sufficiently without the need to loosen any more hoops, if so great – drop the head in and retighten the hoop.

- Sadly, the most likely scenario is that it will still be too tight, in which case the last hoop (small hoop) will need to be loosened slightly. This is the risky stage, loosen it gently, a tap or two at a time while checking the gained flex as you progress. At all cost avoid having the hoop drop off completely or becoming too loose that the groove/staves move out of alignment.
- Once you have achieved the desired *'Status Quo'*, align the head orientation however you want (grain running handle to handle or front to back) and the clean unmarked face to the inside of the bucket, slip the head inside the chime and then tap down into the groove.

**Hint: Thin metal strips/levers (like steel rulers) are useful when trying to get the head started. Systematically levering two staves at a time out and working your way around, gently tapping the head down until it is inside the chime and then finally tapped down into the groove.

- Achieving this objective may be a bit challenging, especially on a small bucket of this length as it is simply going to have the minimum of *'flex'* at the best of times. However, I suggest that you address one last task before re-tightening the hoops; although again not essential, I recommend that you run a bead of PVA glue down as much of the exposed stave joints as is conveniently possible. It may require you to *'scissor'* the joints slightly to gain access but don't go overboard, you don't want to collapse the bucket now! Simply attempt to get some glue into each joint, not necessarily the full length and control the amount. Gluing will add no structural integrity, it will simply make the next step much easier for you.
- When done, raise the missing hoop and firm up enough to allow you to re-invert the bucket and then fully drive both hoops down.

- As you tighten the bottom hoop you may need to 'box'/tap the staves in against the head to ensure a good seal is achieved and also, that all stave joints have now closed up tightly. Be careful when hitting against the chimes – don't break them.
- If successful, your head should give a sharp, ringing sound when tapped lightly.
- Clean away all excess sealant and glue. Set aside and allow glue to dry.

9: Shave off.

Traditional Tools Used.

Cross shave: Flat but with concave sole, wooden plane used to rough it into shape, cutting across the grain.
Spokeshave: Following grain direction, to clean it up.
Buzz/scraper: Create aesthetic finish.

Objective: To create desired finish shape by removing any visible external irregularities in thickness and shape. Also to remove *'witness marks'*, production marks, stains and bruising so as to present the bucket at the desired cosmetic level.

Process: If you succeeded in getting some glue into the joints and it is now dry then, simply remove both hoops from the bucket and either plane, shave, scrape or sand the exterior surface to achieve your desired finish level. Also round off the sharp *'aris'* from the top edges of the staves. Remember that timber has a *'grain direction'* so work in that direction if planning or shaving. Importantly, regardless of the gluing, handle and work the bucket gently and carefully to avoid breaking the glue lines.

If not glued, the objective is still achievable, albeit just a bit more awkward. Carefully remove one hoop (either) at a time and, ensuring the other remains tight:

- Address the exposed section of the staves - shave, scrape or sand as best you can.
- Following the next instruction (10: Make & Drive Hoops), complete those requirements for this exposed section and, when made, drive that hoop down into position.
- Now, remove the remaining *'work hoop'* and address the other half of the staves, try to blend the two sections together as best as you can.
- When completed, again referring to Instruction 10, complete the requirements for this hoop and drive it home.
- Fit the four retaining nails through the hoop, oil if desired and then move onto Instruction 11.

Photo 115. Driving the hoops. Hammer & driver, working hoops.

10: Make and Drive Hoops.

Traditional Tools Used.

Hammer & driver, Bick iron/coopers anvil, hoop level marker, flat head rivets.

<u>Objective</u>: To accurately measure and make the Finish Hoops that, when fitted, not only provide the strength and physical integrity for the bucket, also adding aesthetic character.
Process: The finish hoops will be made in exactly the same manner as the working hoops (Step C: Work Hoops) but, now

that you have a physical bucket, will be measured more accurately to you specific bucket size.

10.1: Preparatory Step.

With a sharp pencil, mark two parallel lines around the bucket, the first at a level of 20mm (¾") and the second at 150mm (6") from the bottom. These lines will indicate the finish level the hoops will be driven to.

**Hint: A simply made tool for this task is – a light piece of metal strip 240mm (9")+/- long with a 90º bend made at around 40mm (1 ½") from one end and 2 notches cut into one edge at distances from the bend of the previously mentioned hoop levels.

- With the foot of this tool held on the bottom of the staves and a pencil held in the notch, slide the tool around the base of the bucket marking the relevant lines.

10.2: Measure Hoops.

Ensure that the splay angle of both hoops match, as closely as possible, the taper angle of your bucket and are rolled to create an even circle close to the average bucket diameter.
Removal of excess hoop first will make handling much easier, so, assuming all sets of hoops were originally sourced at the same length, cut and discard the same length of excess from each hoop as you did when making your work hoops. If varying or you are re-using the work hoops simply remeasure. If re-using the work hoops check for, and remove, any burrs or sharp edges that may have developed.

- Using the marked level lines as a guide, wrap the appropriate hoop around the bucket with its bottom edge sitting approximately 10mm (⅜") above that line. In this position, keeping the hoop as snug and close fitting to the bucket as is possible all the way around and the laps lined up neatly, mark the *'overlap point'* the same as you did for your work hoops. It may take a bit of effort and re-shaping to *'fine tune'* the hoop shape to sit snugly, but the time taken is well worth it as your measurement will be way more accurate!!

- Obviously, repeat for the other hoop.

10.3: Rivet hoops.

Per the specific instructions: (Step C: Make Hoops and Riveting Hoops), layout and rivet your Finish Hoops using the same procedures. Pay attention to peen/dome your rivets as aesthetically as possible and ensure that they do not have burrs or sharp protrusions on or around them.

- At this point I usually drill two small holes in each hoop to hold retaining pins. So, assuming the lap section to be at 12 o'clock, at both the 3.00 and 9.00 o'clock position, the centre of the hoop drill a 2mm +/- (3/32") hole.
- I also usually coat my hoops with a Clear - Urethane coating prior to fitting. Although not strictly traditional, I will agree, it does slow down the natural rusting/patina that is eventually going to develop anyway. (again, your choice).

10.4: Drive Hoops.

With both laps aligned onto the middle stave of (either) body section, they can now be firmly driven down to their level as previously marked. It is desirable that, when tight, the bottom hoop finishes just at the level of the head and, if so, exerting the majority of its pressure against the head.
- Hammer retaining pins (I use brass) into your pre-drilled holes and ensure they are not going to penetrate the full thickness of the stave.

11: Oil the Bucket.

Totally your choice, but in reality, traditionally, most buckets probably did receive a protective coating of some type. Use a pure, food safe oil, don't add reducers or solvents.

**I apply a coat, inside and out, of pure Natural Tung Oil. However, it does take a minimum of 2 – 3 weeks to cure/harden sufficiently, so take this into consideration if applying it.

12: Fitting the Handle.

Your aim will be to create a strong, ergonomic and practical handle that will support the bucket weight comfortably when full.
- Using natural fibre 3 ply rope (Jute or Hemp) with a physical diameter of around 12mm and long enough that, when passed through both handle holes, forms a loop that arcs down to cover the top hoop. Remember to also allow 100 – 150mm (4 - 6") each end for either splicing or just tying a knot.
- I use a traditional, reinforced triple weave Spliced Joint on my handles. Sadly this would take me another six pages to explain *'badly'* and, in all honesty, is totally another subject. It is

actually simple enough to achieve with experience but I will leave it to you to research for yourself.

- The simple alternative is to tie a secure knot (i.e. Granny's Knot) at each end of the rope preventing it from pulling through the holes.

13: Using your Bucket.

If not used your bucket will simply dry out and possibly even collapse – use it!!!! Enjoy it and have fun!!

CONCLUSIONS.

It is my hope that this article has allowed you to experience and, perhaps, even ponder the intriguing history and amazing contribution that such a humble and relatively unknown trade, despite it being one of the largest and most common trades in its heyday, has had in the story of human achievements.

In reality, I have only served up the smallest slice of what Coopering has to offer. This article was never and could never explain the story in full. It is not designed to make you a Cooper, nor was it my intention to comprehensively describe in detail the tools, vocabulary and terms used that are totally unique to this trade.

Its simple purpose is to describe how to make a bucket – not how to be a Cooper!

The Gokstad Backpack.

By Brodie Henry & Stephen Wyley.

The Gokstad Backpack.	Find location: Gokstad, Norway	**When**: Pre 900 CE
Stored: Kulturhistorisk museum in Oslo (KHM)	**Collection no.**: C10412	**Material**: Oak & Leather
Size: Lid: L 47.9 cm (18 $^{55}/_{64}$"), W 18.7 cm (7 $^{23}/_{64}$"), thickness 1.3cm ($^{33}/_{64}$"). Bottom 47.4cm (18 $^{21}/_{32}$"), W 17.7cm (6 $^{31}/_{32}$"), thickness 1.0cm ($^{25}/_{64}$").		

Photo 116. The original, with decoration of a dog chasing a horse, and some geometric design. The bottom plank shows some damage but the shape is clear.

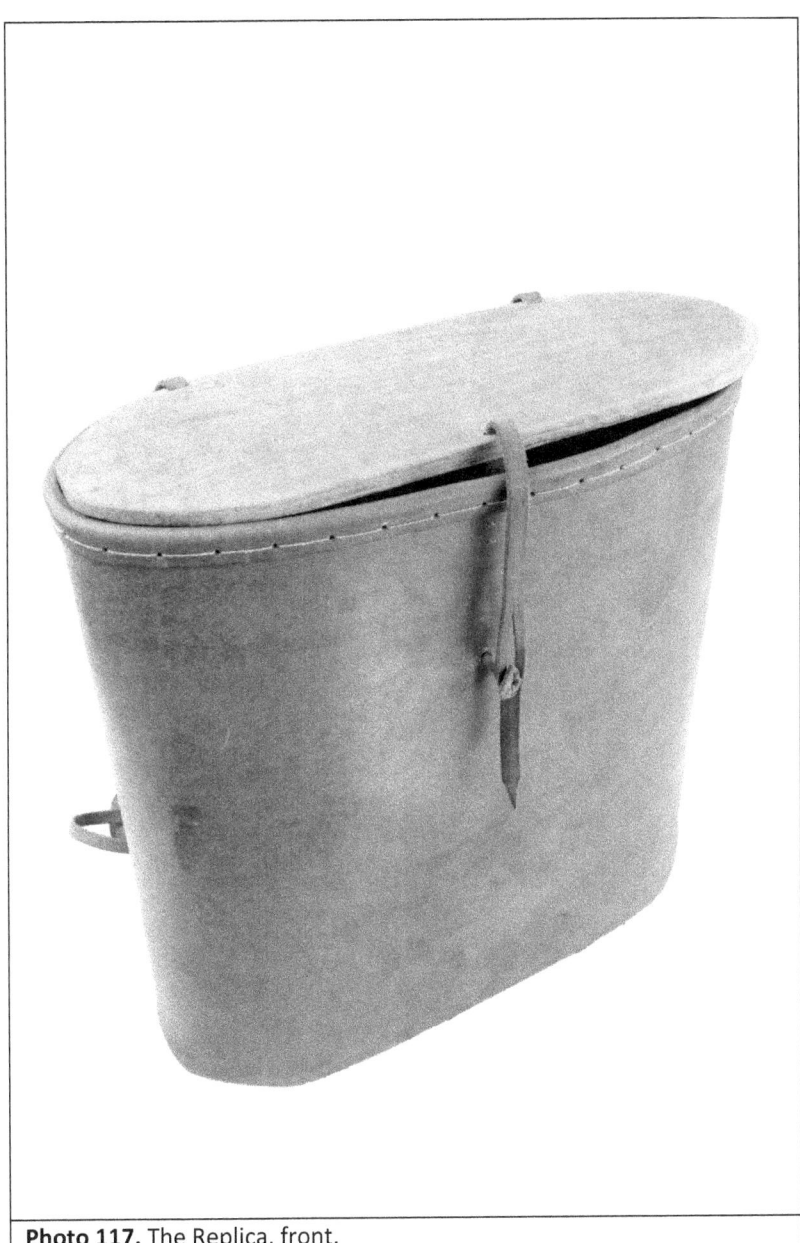

Photo 117. The Replica, front.

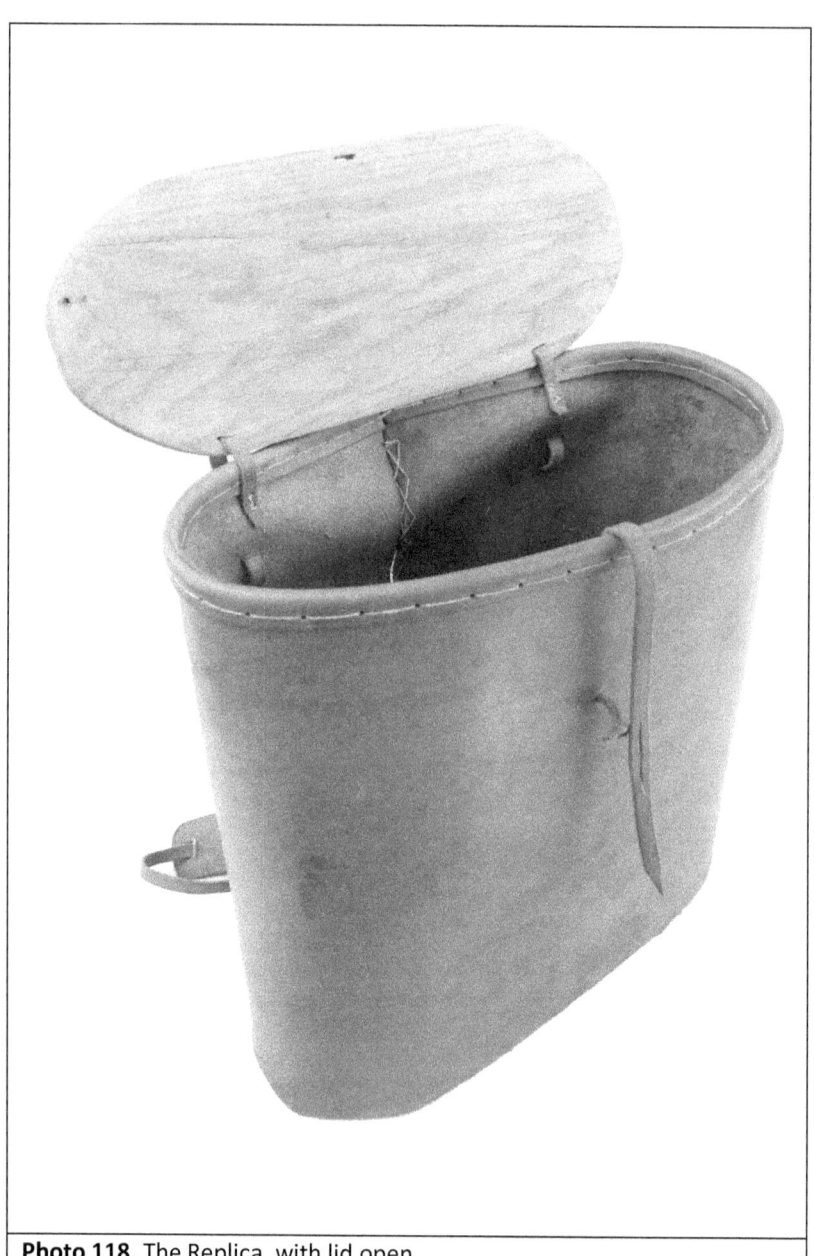

Photo 118. The Replica, with lid open.

Introduction.

The Gokstad Viking ship burial is one of a number of the Viking ship burials found with a range of extant equipment, including examples of beds, tents, three smaller boats, a sledge and riding equipment. Also found were two planks of oak which have been interpreted as being the top and bottom planks of a backpack used to transport gear and goods in an ergonomic fashion using 'Shank's pony'.

If the two planks, which are a similar shape and size, were to be used as a backpack the planks could be used as a base and a lid, with the body of the backpack made of leather or basketry. I am in favour of the leather body scenario because the two rows of holes around the base edge lends itself more to be attached to a piece leather, which can utilise the sets of two holes to attach the piece of leather, whereas basketry can only utilise one of the holes to hold the uprights in place.

The two sets of long holes in the base and in the back of the lid could represent attachment points for the shoulder straps in the base, and the hinges for the lid. Some people have had the top of the back pack straps attached to part of the back pack below the joint between the lid and the backpack, then again the backpack shoulder straps could also go through those holes in the lid.

The lid is slightly larger than the base (see measurements above) and could assist in diverting the elements away from finding their way into the back pack.

Of the reconstruction using the leather option a good stiff 3mm (8oz) veggie tanned leather works well for the body of the back pack, though it does not hurt to re-inforce the top edge of the body of the back pack with a gutter of leather inverted on the edge of the leather using a saddle stitch along the bottom edge of the gutter.

Table 24. Backpack comparison.

Place	Date (CE)	Collection	Material	Comments
Voll, Overhalla municipality, Nord-Trondelag county, Norway	850–950	Vitenskapsmuseet in Trondheim T1186	Wood	*"Boards seemed to be slightly concave and evenly cut. The finder interpreted this find as a backpack"* from Vlasaty 2017.
Gokstad, Norway	900	Kulturhistorisk museum in Oslo (KHM) no. C10412	Wood - Oak	Only top and bottom planks with rounded ends. Top plank had three holes (two on one side, one on the other), with carving of a hound chasing a horse and a geometric pattern. The bottom has a range of holes around its edge, mostly in pairs, there are two larger holes on one side.
Illuminated manuscript - Maciejowski Bible	1204	M638 - Folio 7r Piedmont Morgan Library, New York, USA	Reed	Woven basket with shoulder straps, being used to carrying building materials up a ladder of a tower.
Illuminated manuscript - Picture-book of saints	1275-1300	Fitzwilliam Museum MS 370, in England.	Leather	Leather backpack, with strap closure at top, one leather strap around centre used to hold back pack around shoulders, use of pointed base is unknown (musical instrument?)
Painting by Jheronimus Bosch – 'The Wayfarer,' another painting	1494	Museum Boijmans Van Beningen, Netherlands	Wood and reed.	Wooden lid and woven body which becomes more bulbous as it gets closer to the bottom. Strap in the centre of the lid to keep the lid closed. Shoulder strap across the top of the back of the back pack then hang over the shoulders.

| | | | by the same painting, 'The Pedlar', has a similar backpack. |

Part A – The Wooden boards.

The following are basic instructions on how to make a replica of the boards of the Gokstad backpack.

Materials.

Timber, Oak, Leather, 3 mm (8oz) veggie tanned leather, linseed oil (diluted 1:3 linseed oil to mineral turpentine).

> **Safety tip**: Rags used to wipe on linseed oil should be soaked in water afterwards because they can spontaneously combust and start fires.

The oak I had was 2.4 cm (1") thick and I planned it down to the appropriate thickness and added a bevel to the edges, using an electric plane (lots of shavings, don't do indoor because it makes such a mess).

Equipment; Pencil, ruler, clothing measuring tape, set square, plane/thicknesser/ electric plane, jigsaw/coping saw/ band saw, drill (hand/electric) but there are lots of holes to drill I recommend using a pedestal drill, 3mm ($1/_8$") drill bit, small flat bastard file, sand paper, scraping tool.

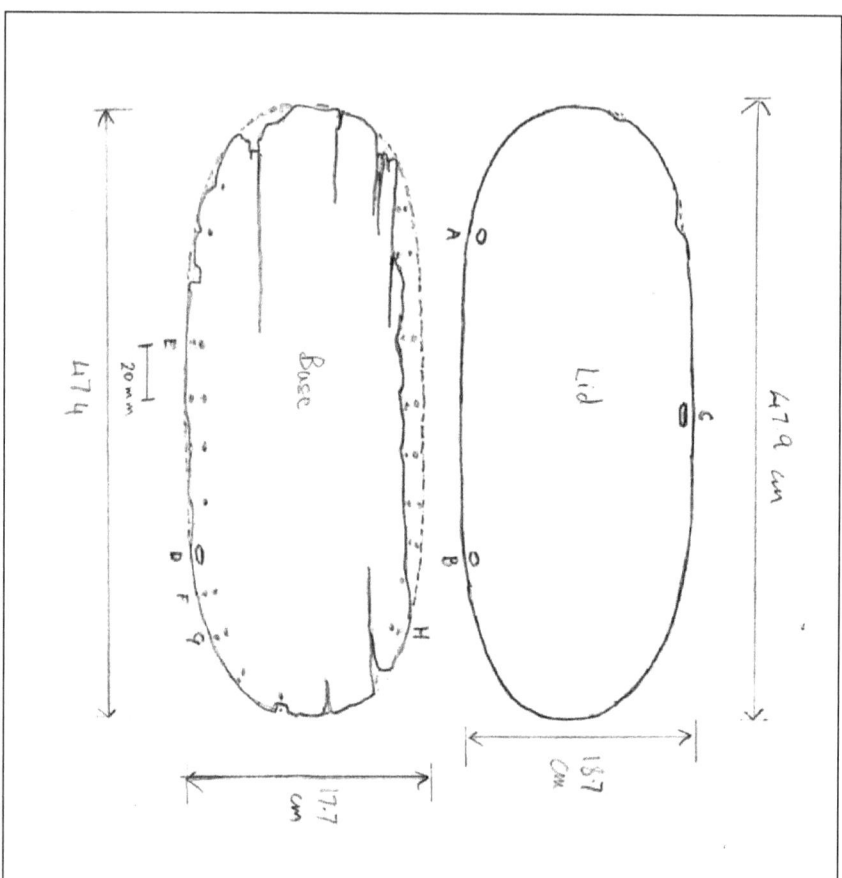

Drawing 69. The boards (in cm), the dotted lines suggest the original shape of the base, see Appendix 8 for a kids size version.

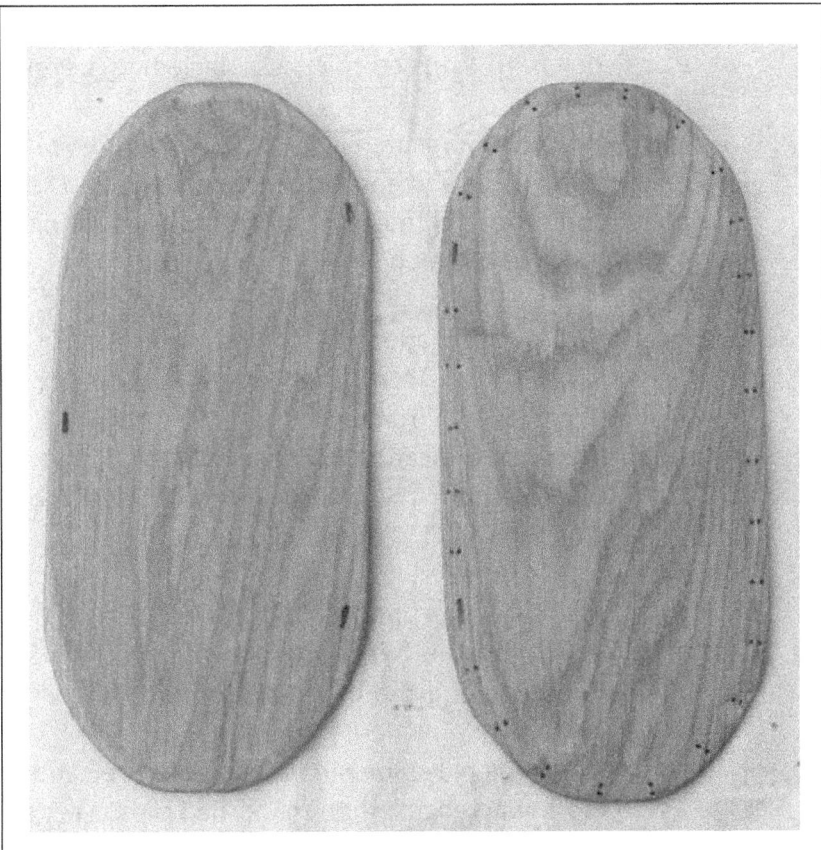

Photo 119. Boards for the top and bottom of the back pack.

Construction.

1) Cut planks to length and width.
2) Scale up plans using a photocopier (or other method).
3) Mark out outlines of planks.

Note: Use a pencil because it is easy to erase, but don't press too hard because you will put a dent in the timber. And erase pencil early so it comes off easier, as it definitely won't after a coat of linseed oil.

4) Cut out using a jigsaw/coping saw/band saw, clean up

shape with file or scraping tool.
5) Plane down to correct thickness including bevel on edges.
6) Mark out holes for stitching and straps as per plan. I recommend using a finger gauge to mark the two lots of holes, and a clothing measuring tape for measuring the gap around the edges.
7) Lid.
    a. Mark out location for front strap, centre of one edge of lid, 24cm (9 ½") from curve apex and 7mm (5/16") from edge.
    b. Mark out location for back straps, 17 cm (6 11/16") from the centre of the back edge of lid and 7mm (5/16") from edge.
8) Base.
    a. Use a finger gauge to mark out two lines encircling the base, one line a 6mm (¼") from the edge and the other at 12mm (½") from the edge.
    b. Mark the place for the two holes at the centre of both long edges, then mark the holes every 2cm (¾") from the initial centre holes.
    c. Mark the holes for the attachment of the shoulder straps on the back of the base board 6cm (2 ¼") from each side of the centre of the long edge, 1cm (⅜") long and 3mm (⅛") wide (depending on the thickness of the leather used.
9) Drill holes (I recommend using a drill press because of the large number of holes to be drilled) with a sacrificial wooden board on the back (to stop the board tearing out the back). For strap holes drill four holes close together, cut edges and join up the holes to make a slit, clean up the hole with a small flat file.
10) Clean up edges and holes with scraper / file / sandpaper.

11) Carve your name and date (normally just with a 'V' tool gouge.
12) Apply a coat of linseed oil, allow it to dry.
13) Trace designs of carving on plank(s), carve with 'V' gouge.

Part B – Carving on plates.

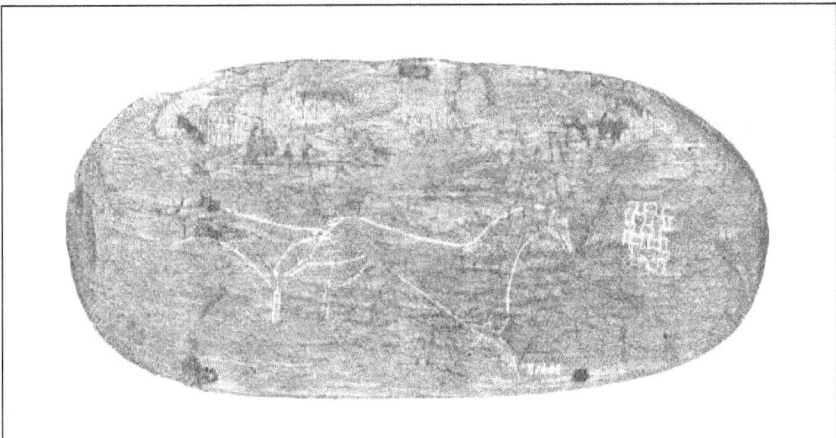

Photo 120. Deer and a hound, and a geometrical figure.

Photo 121. Another geometrical drawing on the bottom plate.

Material. Tracing paper.

Tools. Pencil, eraser, 'V' gouge, mallet.

Scale up photocopy of the plates to fit, transfer to tracing paper, transfer to planks (if you have not used tracing paper before see below), carve, clean up, seal with linseed oil. Sounds simple but I recommend you practice on some scrap timber before you carve the designs on the plates.

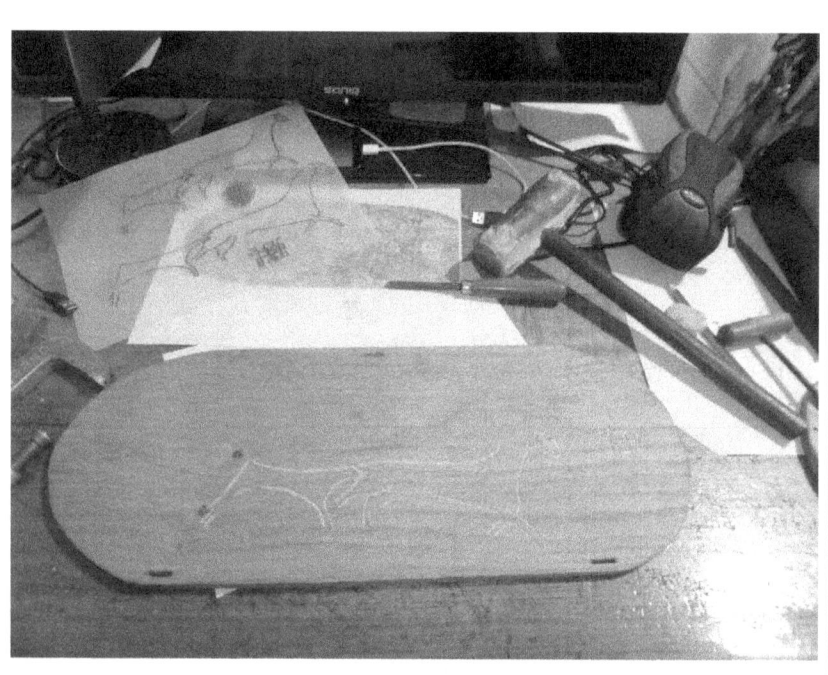

Photo 122. The dog chasing the horse and woven design carved onto the top plate of the back pack.

Using tracing paper to transfer design details.

1. Place the tracing paper over the drawing/photo/picture and trace the design onto the tracing paper with a

pencil.
2. Flip the tracing paper over and draw over the design so there is pencil over the whole design.
3. Flip the tracing paper back over, orientate on the piece you are going to put the design on and draw over the tracing to transfer the pencil on the other side to the wood.
4. Check the design has transferred. Redo or fill in the gaps.

Photo 123. Mail ring design carved on the bottom plank.

Part C – The Leather work.

Tools: Straight edge (ruler), pencil, knife (Stanley or some other retractable bladed knife), strap cutter, awl (or hole punch), needles (lots, because they break) or a speedy stitcher sewing awl, pliers (for pulling out stuck needles).

Cutting surface / Cutting mat.

Materials.

3mm (8oz) veggie tanned hide - half shoulder of cow hide.
Waxed linen thread – about 24 metres (about 26 yards)

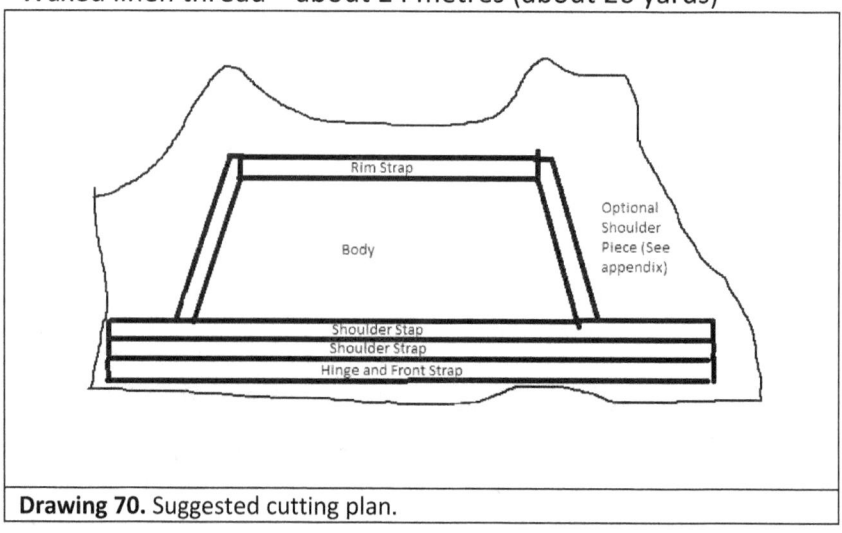

Drawing 70. Suggested cutting plan.

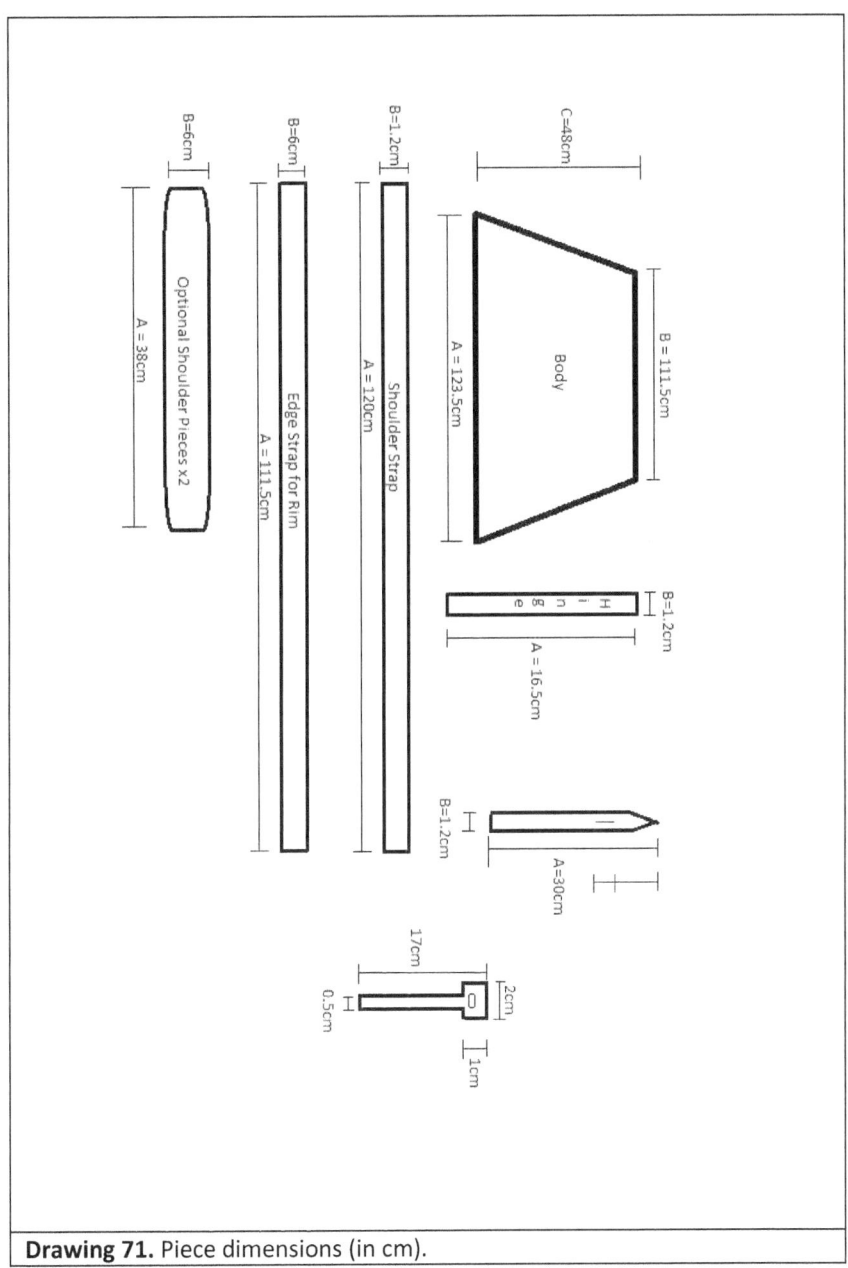

Drawing 71. Piece dimensions (in cm).

Body.

A: Measure the circumference of the lower board then add 4cm (1 ½") for the overlap. In this instance 119.5cm + 4cm = 123.5cm (47" + 1 ⅜" = 48 ⅝").
B: To create a tapered bag, make this measurement shorter than A. For example 123.5cm − 12cm = 111.5cm (47" - 4 ⅜"" = 43 ⅞"").
C: This can be tailored to suit the body of the wearer. In this instance it will be created for a tall wearer, and we will use 48cm (18 ⅞").

Edge Strap for rim
A: Same as the B part of the body, 111.5cm (44")
B: 6cm (2 ½")

Shoulder strap:
A: Use the strap cutter to cut the entire length of the shoulder (see placement image). These can be cut to desired length later.
B: 1.2cm (½") to match the holes in the wooden board.

Hinge Straps:
A: 16cm (6 ¼")
B: 1.2cm (½") to match the holes in the wooden boards.

Front Strap:
A: 30cm (12") (cut to desired length later).
B: 1.2cm (½"")

Optional Shoulder Pieces (See Appendix 11).
A: 38cm (15")
B: 6cm (2 ½")

Toggle:
T shape. 2cm x 1cm (¾" x ⅜") for the head of the T. 17cm x 0.5cm (6 ¾" x 3/16") for the tail of the T. See Drawing 70.

Glossary.

Cutting surface.
The tip of the blade will penetrate the hide and could damage the surface below that should be protected. Never use the kitchen table because cutting the table would elicit unending negative consequences which are too horrible to list here. The cutting surface can be a cutting mat or simply a sheet of plywood.

Reef knot.
Is a knot consisting of two half hitches on top of each other.

Saddle stitch.
Is a stitch using two needles on either end of a piece of thread that pass each other through a set of holes.

Straight edge and knife.
A straight edge can be a metal ruler or a piece of metal flat bark.
1)   Line up the cut and hold firmly in place and run the blade along the straight edge, the cut may take more than one pass of the blade.
2)   Avoid putting your hand, fingers or any other part of your body in the path of the blade.

Strap cutter.
A leather strap cutter can take a number of forms, the most common form consists of a handle with an adjustable cross arm with marking for the width of the strap and an inserted blade.

1) Modify the width of the strap by undoing the release nut and slid the cross arm to the desired width.
2) The edge of the hide will need to be cut straight (using a straightedge and a knife).
3) You may want to pre-cut the hide at the desired width or push the leather at the blade in the strap cutter.
4) Draw the cut strap out of the strap cutter, ensuring the edge of the leather remains in contact with the handle of the strap cutter. This produces another straight edge for cutting more straps.

Construction instructions.

Cutting out.

1) Select hide (ensure that there are no faults, cuts, tears, discolouration).
2) Mark out pieces on the hide with pencil (not pen or texture) on the inside of the hide.
3) Cut straight edge on one side of hide using straight edge and a knife. Cut straps and edging from long edge of hide using straight edge and knife or a *'strap cutter'*.

Bottom edge.

1) Wet bottom edge of the body of the back pack and mould around the edge of the bottom board.

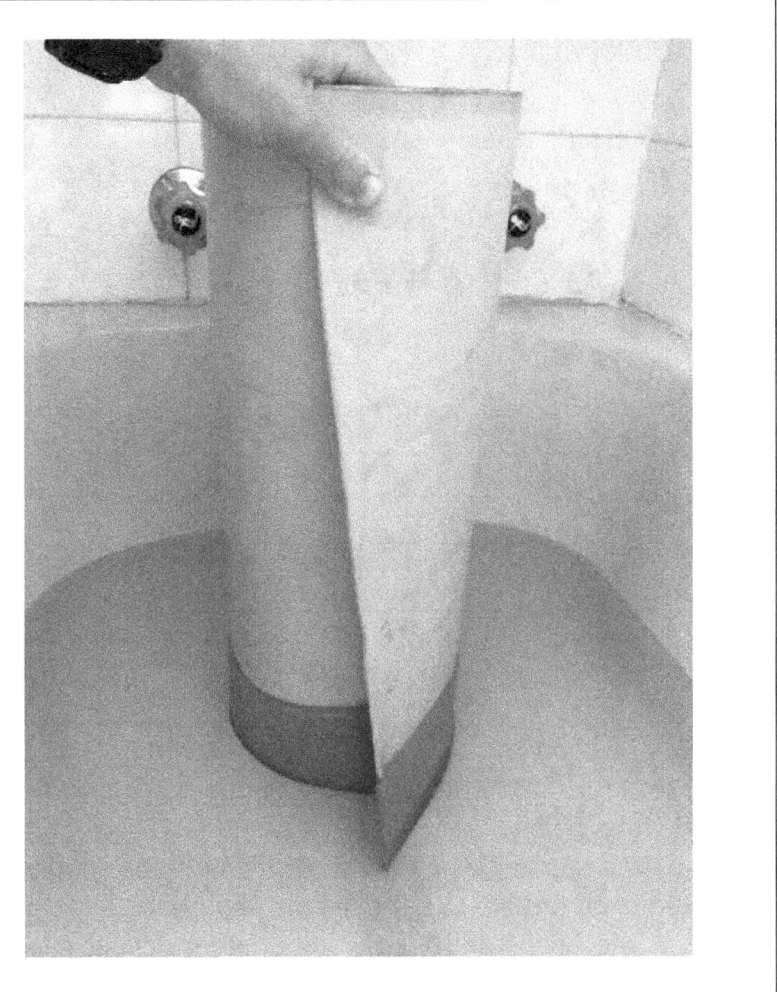
Photo 124. Wet moulding the body.

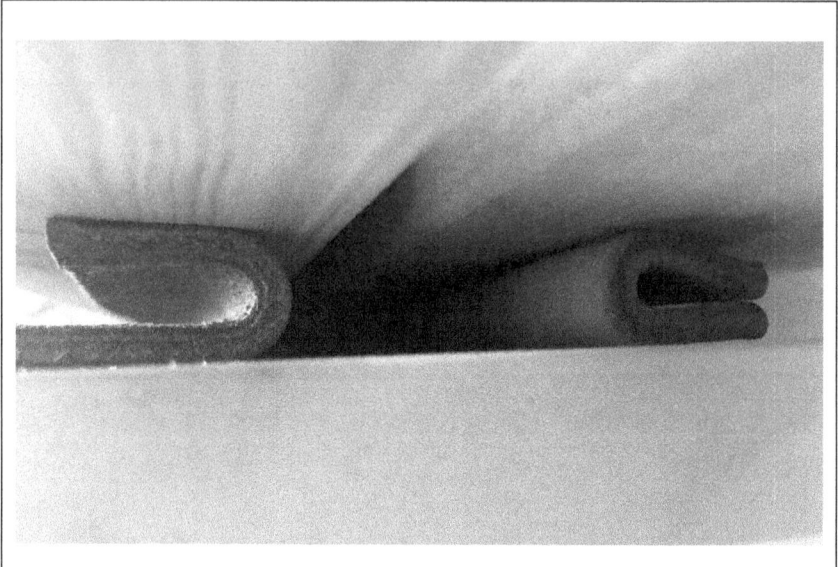

Photo 125. Folding the body and the rim. They are weighed down with boards.

Stitching onto the bottom board.

1)   Position the backpack on a wooden board and use an awl to push through the holes in the board to punch holes in the leather below.

2)   Use a needle of any size with an eye big enough for the waxed linen thread. Use the needle and waxed linen thread to fasten the board and leather together, stitching each set of holes separately.

3)   Using a *'saddle stitch'* pass the thread up through the outer hole, and down the inner hole. This can be very tedious to get the holes to line up for the needle to pass through. Leather shrinks from the heat of your hands as you work it. If you are having difficulty, use an awl or poker to widen the hole. A head lamp and pliers can be handy for this. Be careful not to snap your needle. Repeat stitch three times of each set of two holes for strength.

4)

Photo 126. Tape used to hold one of the thread while sewing the other end.

5) Pull each end to outside, tie a *'reef knot'* and pass thread ends back inside the backpack.

Photo 127. Tying a reef knot in the top of the bottom, inside the backpack.

6) To help the leather around the corners of the bottom you will need to cut slits in the bottom edge of the body of the back pack. See Photos 128 -132.

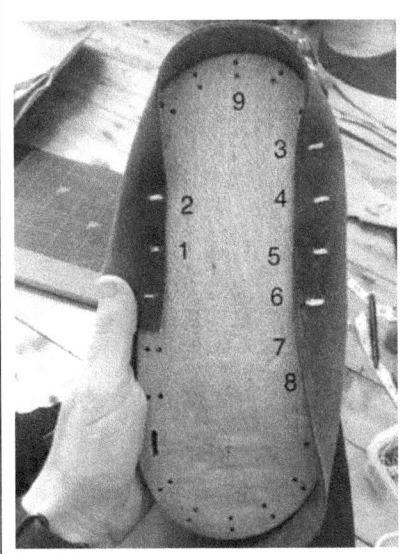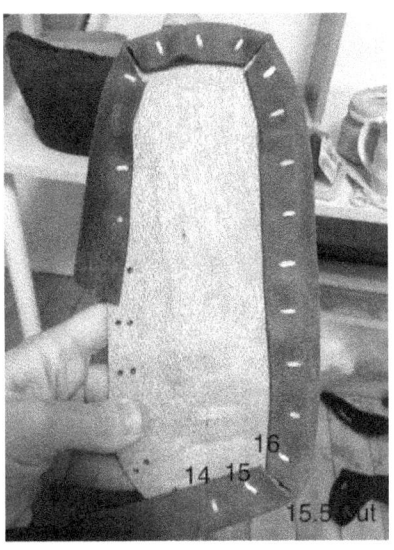

Photos 128 & 129. Sequence of stitching leather to bottom board, showing the cut outs/darts in the corners. Note: these are photos of a kids size version.

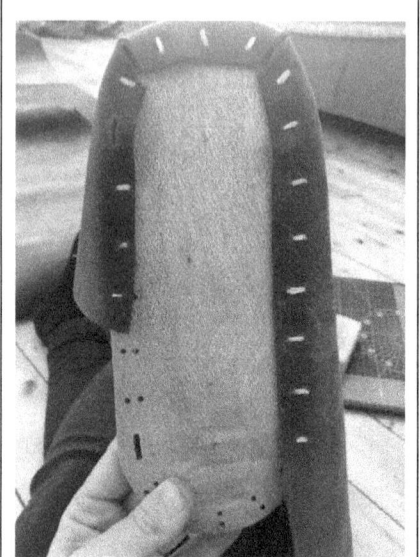 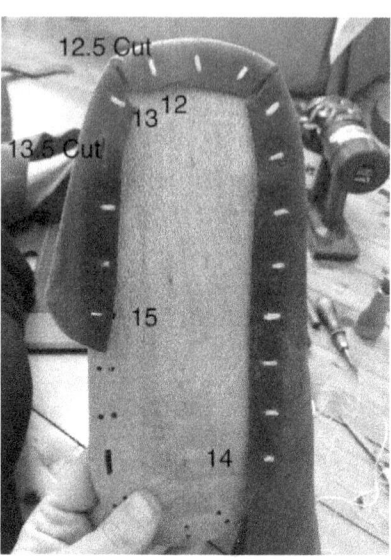

Photos by 130 & 131. Sequence of stitching leather to bottom board, showing the cut outs/darts in the corners.

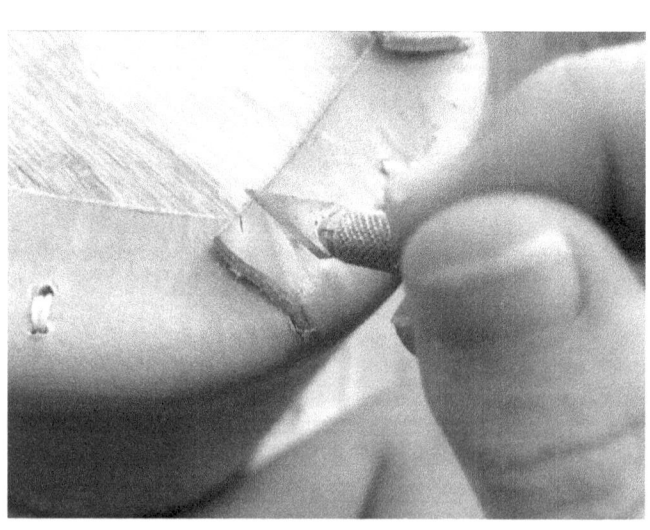

Photo 132. Cut darts in the leather base with a knife.

End join.

1) Overlap ends of the body (at least 2 cm (¾ ")) and sew from the base up to the top edge using a saddle stitch, with stitches 2 cm (¾ ") apart. See Photo 133.

Note: do not stitch up the end join before attaching to the board, you will have trouble seeing, let alone sew the body to the bottom.

2) Pull each end of the thread to the inside of the back pack, tie a '*reef knot*' and pass thread ends back outside the backpack.

Photos 133. Showing the edging covering the upright join of the ends.

Top edge of body – strengthening strip.

The bare edge of 3mm ($1/8$") veggie tanned leather is not that self-supporting hence a strip of leather is sewn to the top of the top edge of the body of the back pack.

1) Measure and cut strips using a straightedge and or strip cutter.
2) Consider the top of the backpack and if it might need trimming to make a good shape for the rim and the board to sit flat on top. You may wish to angle the board away from the body to allow snow to fall off rather than accumulate on the board. See Appendix 10.

3) Line up the edge so that the strengthening strip over laps joins the back of the backpack.
4) Soak strips in cold water for a few minutes before shaping over the edge of the backpack.

Hinges.

1) Mark out and awl four holes in a square on each end of the hinge using a cork block (which prevents damage to the workbench and the awl).
2) Use hole pattern to mark out and awl four holes in the back of the body of the back pack using cork block (which prevents damage to the leather of the back pack). See Photos 134 - 136.
3) Pass one end of the hinge strap through the hole in the lid.
4) Use saddle stitch to attach strap ends to the body of the back pack, starting at the base of the square, and working around the square.

5) Pull each end of the thread to the outside of the back pack, tie a 'reef knot' and pass thread ends back inside the backpack.
6) Repeat for the other hinge strap.

Photos 134. Using the cork block to hold the top of the backpack in place when using an awl to make holes in the back pack.

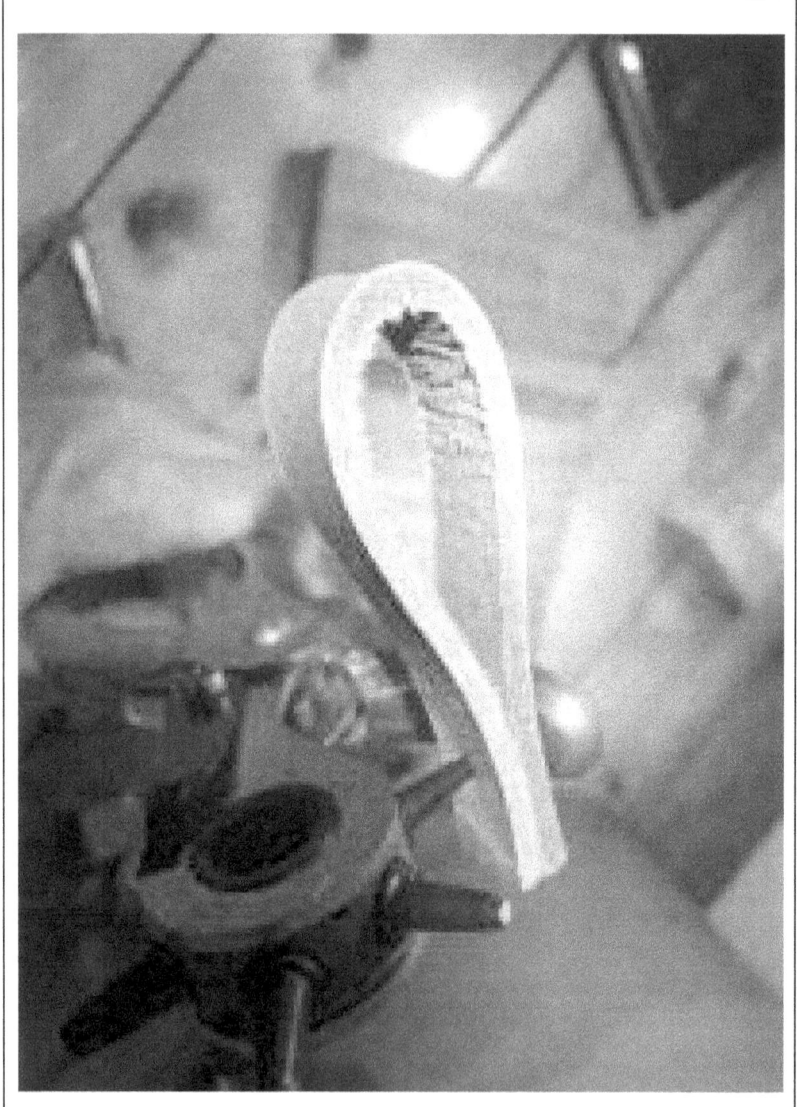

Photos 135. Using a hole punch to make holes in the leather for the hinges.

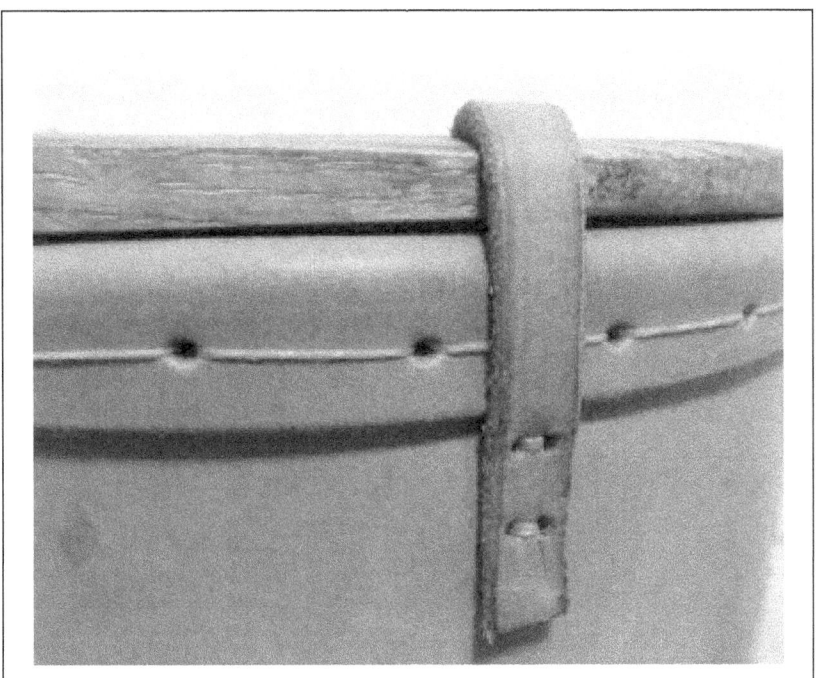
Photos 136. The outside of the leather hinge for the lid.

Photos 137. The back of the back pack before the addition of the shoulder straps. Notice the abutted join on the back, this should have been overlapped.

Shoulder straps (similar to hinges).

Attach Top to backpack.

1) Cut two horizontal slits in the back of the backpack, enlarge the slits to take the shoulder strap near the top of the back pack. See Photo 138.
2) Pass one end of the shoulder strap through the slit in the back of the backpack and then out through the bottom slit.
3) Punch holes in the end of the strap and a section of strap that comes out of the bottom slit. These holes are used to adjust the length of the back strap by tying a leather thong between corresponding sets of holes.
4) Repeat for the top of the other shoulder strap.

Note: the width of the shoulder straps is based on the width of the holes in the base and top boards. See Photo 120 and 121, Appendix 11 for an alternative solutions. (i.e. wider straps or guitar strap).

<u>Attach to bottom of backpack.</u>

1) Cut two sets of horizontal slits in back pack, enlarge to take shoulder straps near bottom of back pack and through bottom overlap, corresponding with holes in bottom board of backpack. See Photo 138.
2) Mark out and awl 4 holes in a square on each end of the shoulder strap using a cork block (which prevents damage to the workbench and the awl).
4) Use saddle stitch to attach shoulder strap ends to each other, starting at the base of the square, and working around the square.
5) Pull each end of thread to the inside, tie a *'reef knot'* and pass thread ends back through the shoulder strap.
6) Repeat for the top of the other shoulder strap.

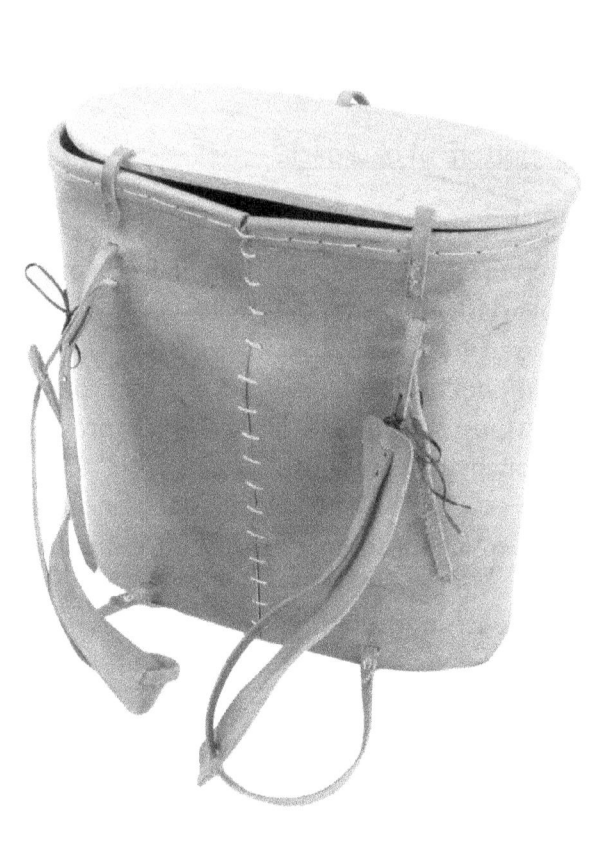

Photo 138. The backpack shows the leather hinges, shoulder straps with the guitar straps added, the black leather ties for the shoulder strap adjustment, and the butted seam up the length of the back pack.

Note 1: the ends of the strengthening strip for the top edge meet at the same spot and the top of the back seam which creates a weak spot, which should be corrected by putting the overlapping join of the strengthening strip at the front of the back pack.

Note 2: for better ergonomics, put the top of the shoulder straps closer to the spine.

Lid front strap.

1) Cut a vertical slit in the front strap with a knife, big enough to take leather toggle.
2) Use a saddle stitch to attach the strap end to the body of the back pack, starting at the base of the square, and working around the square.
3) Pull each end of the thread to the outside of the back pack, tie a *'reef knot'* and pass thread ends back inside the backpack.
4) Pass the end of the front strap up through the slit at the front of the lid.

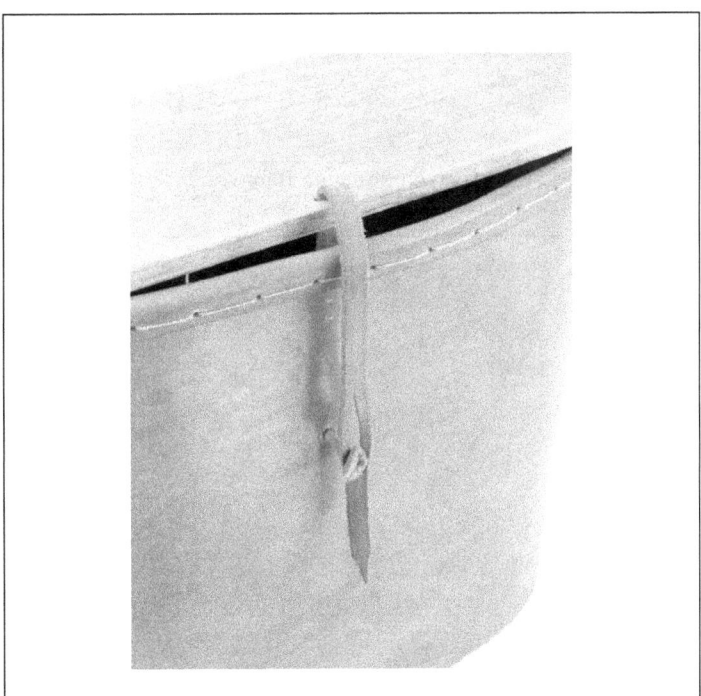

Photo 139. Toggle pokes through the slit in the lid strap, securing the lid.

Toggle.

1) Mark and cut out toggle on 2mm (5oz) thick leather. See Drawing 71 for dimensions for toggle.

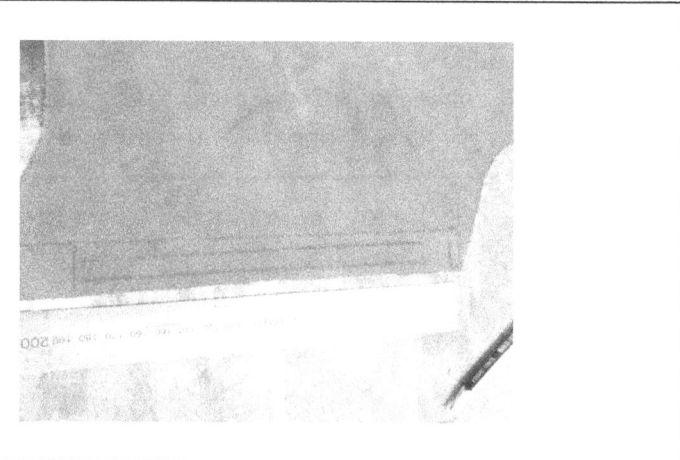

Photo 140. Mark out toggle on 2mm leather.

Photo 141. Cut toggle out with a knife.

2) Feed tail through slit in toggle, pull tail through until the top of the toggle forms a rolled toggle. See Photos 142 and 143.

	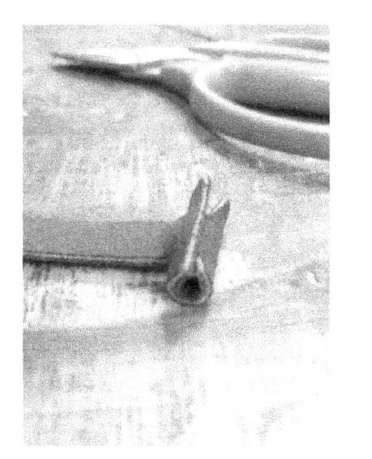
Photo 142. The toggle from the top.	**Photo 143.** The toggle from the side.

3) Cut a slit in the front of the back pack at the full extent of the slit in the lid front strap.
4) Thread tail through slit in front of backpack and tie a half hitch. See Photo 144.

	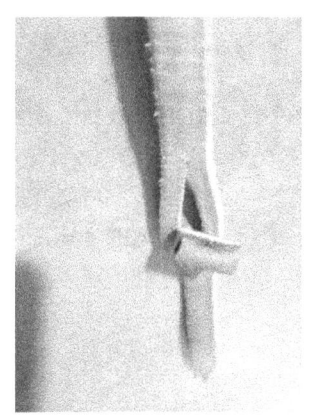
Photo 144. The tail end of the toggle tied in a half hitch.	**Photo 145.** The toggle poked through the slit in the lid strap.

Hedeby Arrows.

By Wayne Robinson.

Hedeby boat grave arrows.	From: Hedeby Boat Chamber grave	**When**: 850 CE
Stored: Viking Museum Haithabu, Schleswig Germany.	**Collection no**: No collection number available at time of publishing.	**Material**: birch shaft, bronze nock, iron heads, copper wire, feather, birch tar.
Size: Various fragments.		

This project is concentrating on making your own interpretation of the arrows from the Hedeby boat chamber grave. The skills you will develop are the same as you would need to make arrows from any of the northern Germanic cultures from the late Neolithic up until the 11th or 12th century CE. The variations will generally be in the shape of the nocks and heads, and I'll provide some options as we go.

Hedeby (German *Haithabu*) was a Danish trading settlement that is now in Schleswig in modern Germany. The second largest trading port of the Viking period, it was occupied from the 8th to the 11th centuries. A boat-chamber grave[28] dating from 850 CE contained a bow and a bundle of some 20 arrows. The arrows had parallel-sided birch shafts, tanged arrowheads, bronze nocks and imprints of the feathers and binding thread in the birch tar glue.

---

[28] Bill (2023).

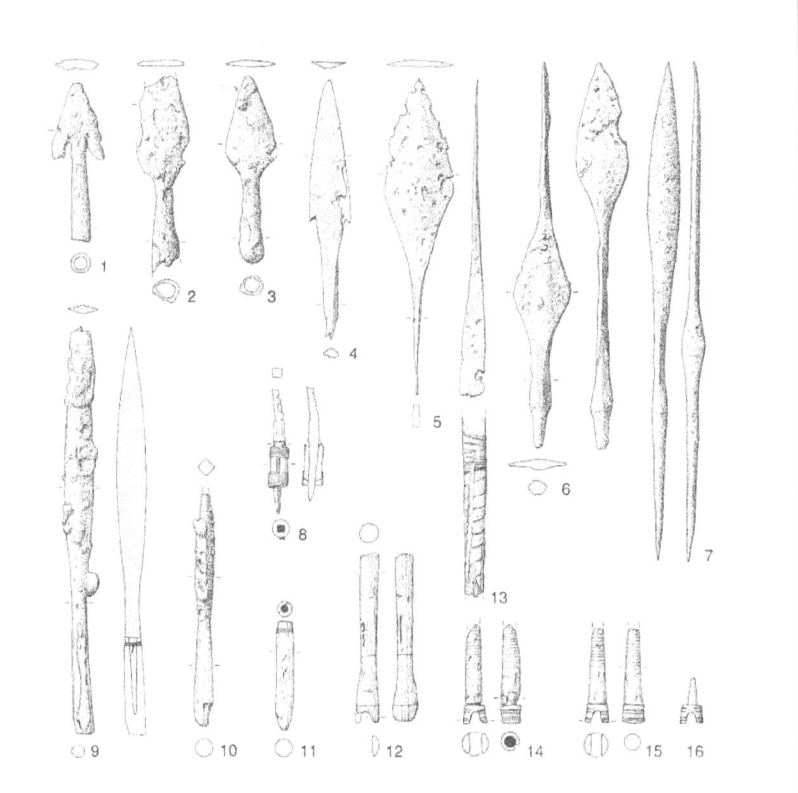

Drawing 72. A sample of arrows from various find locations around Hedeby.
1-3 - short socketed head.
4 - barbed tanged head.
5 - head with a flat tang.
6-7 - twisted leaf-shaped tanged heads.
8 - corroded arrowhead with remains of the shaft and double wire wrapping.
9-11, 14-16 - arrowheads, shaft remains and brass nocks from the boat chamber grave.
12 - nock-end of an arrow with glue residue.
13 - arrow fragments with remains of fletching.

Photo 146. A replica, full length, the arrowhead, fletching and nock.

I've summarised extant arrow finds by archery tradition and period below. These are generalisations and may be way off target for individual finds and locations. Have a look for specific finds that would interest you. The underpinning data for this summary is presented in Appendix 12.

Table 25. Summary of Extant Arrows by Culture.		
Period	Description	Location
Late Iron Age 3rd to 6th C Northern Germanic tradition.	Shafts mainly softwoods, occasional hardwood use. Fletched areas are often reduced in girth. Early in the period most were fletched with four feathers, changing to three by the middle of the Iron Age. Nocks always have a bulbous shape. In some cases, the entire nock is a separate piece of bronze. Mostly leaf-shaped tanged iron or carved bone heads, pitch and linen or sinew binding. Socketed heads are more likely than tanged to the south.	Nydam Illerup Ådal Innlandet ice finds Femund, Norway Oldenburg, Germany
Early	Hardwood or pine shafts;	Oppdal, Trøndelag,

Table 25. Summary of Extant Arrows by Culture.

Period	Description	Location
Medieval Northern Germanic tradition.	resin glue; sinew or plant fibre binding; mostly iron leaf-shaped tanged heads, bone and wooden blunts known. Pine shafts in the north. Nocks bulbous shape. Occasionally bronze nocks.	Norway Hedeby harbour and township Hedeby ship chamber burial
Early Medieval Alemannic / Southern German tradition	Hardwood shafts. Complete shafts measure 55–65 cm (21 ½ –25 ½"). Shaft bobtailed or barrelled, 9–11mm ($^3/_8$ – $^7/_{16}$") diameter at head with even taper to the nock. Barbed flat triangular socketed iron heads, attached with glue and rivets. Binding behind head. Three fletch, parallel cut feathers, birch pitch glue, bound with vegetable bast (linen?) thread with very high number of turns. Bronze nocks.	Oberflacht, Germany Altdorf, Switzerland
Medieval Celtic sites Northern Germanic tradition.	Tanged leaf-shaped heads, early introduction of bodkin points in the late 10th C; hardwood or pine shafts 60-70cm (24-28") long, fletching 12cm (5") long.	Scar, Orkney Wood Quay, Dublin
Eastern/ Eurasian archery tradition	Arrowheads include fire-arrows, barbed and trilobate forms in addition to the more usual leaf-shaped points. Nocks can be made from multiple pieces of wood, shafts very light.	Birka, Sweden

We try to give textual examples as well as extant remains in this series of books. In the context of arrows, it doesn't work very well due to the lack of detail. Most manuscript illuminations represent arrows schematically with a single straight line, and if you're lucky, there'll be another line at the point and a couple of squiggles showing the shape of the fletching.

Table 26. Comparison of Arrows in Art.

Item	Date CE	Collection	Description
Franks Casket (Auzon Casket)	7th C	British Museum Object number 1867,0120.1	Casket lid depicts Egil raining feathery death on his house guests. Seven arrows; five have swept broadheads, one is a wide (almost swallowtail) broadhead and the shape of the other head can't be seen. Fletching is flat/parallel to the shaft and nocks are bulbous. Possible taper from the head to the fletching on the wide headed arrow, but may be an artefact of carving.
Gallican Psalter ('Athelstan' or 'Galba Psalter') BL Cotton MS Galba A XVIII	First half 9th C	British Library Cotton MS Galba A XVIII fol. 14r	Illuminated capital O enclosing the figure of an archer with nocked arrow. Arrowhead diamond shaped with clear medial ridge. Socket or binding shown on the shaft just behind the head. Shaft outlined with two lines, showing narrower end against string, but taper isn't obvious. Fletching is white and parallel sided. Shaftment painted in red-brown, contrasting with the green of the rest of the arrow shaft.
Harley Psalter BL Harley MS 603	1000 CE	British Library Harley MS 603 fol. 2r (See also 6r, 7r, 14r, 25r and	Illumination at top of Psalm 2 depicting the heathens being dashed with a rod of iron, as it were. Group of seven figures being hit with six arrows, two spears and an axe, thrown by a group of the apparently righteous, who have the high

Table 26. Comparison of Arrows in Art.

Item	Date CE	Collection	Description
		64r)	ground (Ps. 2:9). Arrow shaft depicted with a single line, bulbous nocks, no heads shown. Five arrows have flat fletching, one has long triangular fletching with one feather is painted blue while the others are just black lines.
Böksta Runestone, Uppsala, Sweden	c. 1050 CE	In situ	Lithic engraving on granite. Hunting scene of a spearman on horseback and a figure with skis and bow in the bottom left. The arrow is parallel sided with a narrow leaf-shaped head. The shaftment area is missing.
Psalterium Buriense Reg.lat.12	Mid 11th C	Vatican Library	Figure in bottom right corner of fol. 24r. Arrows shown as solid line, head triangular with small barbs, fletching banana or parabolic shape. Nocks bulbous.
Bayeux Tapestry	Prior to 1092 CE	Bayeux Museum, Bayeux, Calvados, Normandy, France	Norman archers with recurved bows depicted in scene 51 to the right of the caption "ET SAPIENTER AD PRELIVM" and in the lower margin of scenes 55 and 56. Additional arrows in shields and Harry's eye in scene 57. Mounted archer in the middle of the cavalry on scene 58. Arrows are straight lines of stitching, fletching where shown is flat/parallel, nocks bulbous. Arrowheads are large and barbed.
Life and Miracles of St Edmund, Bury St Edmunds, England.	1130 CE	Pierpont Morgan Library MS M.736, fol.14r	Large illumination showing, curiously enough, the death of St Edmund. Six archers with longbows; top and bottom loops on the bowstrings clearly

Table 26. Comparison of Arrows in Art.			
Item	Date CE	Collection	Description
			visible. Five arrows are shown drawn to the chest, a further 15 actively enmartyrating St Edmund. All arrows shown with a single straight line, nocks are all bulbous, fletching of 19 of the arrows is flat, the archer at the far end of the front line has banana shaped fletching on his drawn arrow. Heads are diamond shaped and socketed, some appear to also have vestigial barbs.

Construction Instructions.

Materials.

Shaft: It depends on what's available to you, and whether your arrows are just for display or for use with targets. If they are purely for display, dowel may be appropriate. Splitting shafts from a board can be a rewarding, but time consuming, historically accurate method. If you are planning to buy them, get arrow shafts matched for your bow's draw weight, and make sure they are at least 9mm ($\frac{3}{8}$") diameter to match the cast nock.

Binding thread: I often use commercial dressmaking linen thread, but any medium linen thread will do.

Commercial linen sewing thread is perfectly useable for arrow binding. Look for a thread weight of about 40 to 50. I'm using a fine linen weaving thread with a weight of 60 in the photos below because of the additional support from the glue. You can use finer threads if they are glued down for the entire length of the wrap. Using fine thread that is just glued in place at the start and end of the binding (for example, when using fletching tape) will result in the thread breaking in use. It happens the first time they are used with my 50# longbow, every time.

If sinew is available to you, give it a try. I can only get silverside tendon, and while it makes a good bow backing, it isn't much use as a twisted thread.[29]

Binding wire: The original arrows had the points reinforced with a copper-alloy wire. I'm using a clear enamel coated copper wire from the local electronics shop. Most hardware store copper wires are too heavy for the job.

Arrowhead: Tanged arrowheads are more usual throughout the Iron Age in northern Scandinavian finds, with socketed heads becoming more usual as you travel south or west in Europe. Socketed heads are known from Viking sites in England and Ireland. Typically leaf-shaped, forked and small barbed heads are found. See what's available on the Internet near you.[30]

For information about forging your own arrowheads, see Cole (2023).

Nocks: There are a few stores selling bronze copies of Hedeby nocks.[31] A number of this batch have voids inside that I'll fill with a rosin/wax/charcoal mix so it doesn't damage the

---

[29] It's entirely possible my saliva is missing the enzyme needed to activate the sinew and it may work properly for you.

[30] The heads I'm using are from Medieval Fightclub in Australia, https://www.medieval-fightclub.com.au/archery/arrowheads/ .

[31] Mine are from *The Red Knight* (https://www.redknight.co.nz/shop) in New Zealand.

bowstring. If you are unhappy with the quality, it isn't difficult to make your own, just time consuming.[32]

Fletching: If local laws permit, try making your own flights from feathers. Feathers from geese, swans or eagles are the most accurate.

For commercial sources, Trueflight's Bronze Brown turkey feather is a good match for white tailed eagle wing feathers, and their Autumn Brown is almost identical to the peacock primary pinions I bought from the local feather farm.

When selecting feathers for each individual arrow, it makes things easier for binding if you can match the slope on the barbels.

Glue: The originals have birch tar, use it if you can get it. This statement holds true for arrows in the Northern Germanic tradition right back to the Palaeolithic period.[33] Pine tar would be an acceptable substitute if you can get it as a solid rather than dissolved into liquid. I have used brewer's pitch in the past, but can't get that any more either. Bitumen-based roof sealer also works, the technique is slightly different as it solidifies by evaporation rather than cooling. I'll be using the rosin, beeswax and carbon blend in Appendix 13 for this project to get the right look, feel and odour. To be honest, only a few people on the planet will be able to tell if you've just used gloss black paint on the shaftment and applied your usual glue or fletching tape.

---

[32] See Söderberg & Hoffman (1999) and Söderberg (2018),
[33] Kozowyk et al. (2023).

Tools.

Much of the work on the arrows is done with a sharp knife. The knife needs to be shaving sharp for hardwood arrows and even sharper for softwoods, then sharper again for cutting feathers. Hone the knife frequently during use. Jump on YouTube and watch some sharpening videos, then practise until you can repeatedly achieve a sharp edge.

Other tools are: a saw; an awl; drills; pliers and wire cutters; abrasives (optional); files (for self-nocks and cleaning arrowheads); some way of measuring; candle; a can; a stick and some wooden blocks.

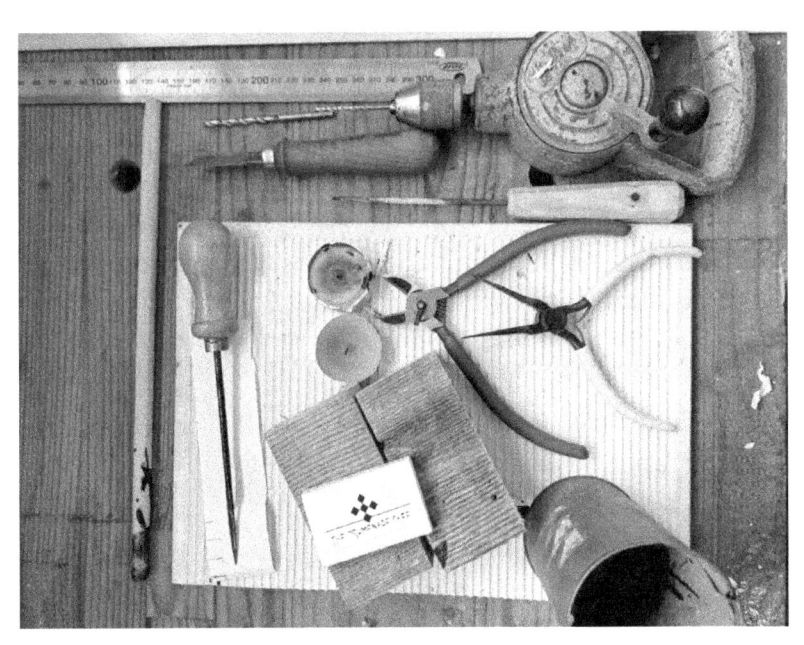

Photo 147. The required tools.

Prepare the shafts

The boat chamber grave's arrow shafts do not have entirely parallel sides. There's a small step where the thread binding starts, so when you use the arrow there's no bump as the binding passes the bow's riser. They taper slightly along the shaftment until they get to a narrow waist, about a half the distance from the end of the binding to the nock. From that point, they are full width again to the nock.

Material required: arrow shafts, nocks

Tools required: saw; sharp knife; rule; pencil; awl; drills; PPE. (Optional: rasp; files; abrasive paper; arrow length jig).

I'm using 1.8m (6') lengths of 9.5mm (⅜") clear pine dowel from the local hardware chain. If you go down this path, try to select the straightest ones with the grain running the full length, avoid any individual dowels heavier or lighter than the others. These will give you two arrow shafts each, plus some off-cuts that can become pegs on your next furniture project. If you are using commercially available wooden arrow shafts, or have dowels in the correct length, go straight to Step 2.

1. Cut shaft to length.
2. Taper the shaftment.
3. Ream nock and point.
4. Attach nocks.

Step 1: cut to length.

Photo 148. I'm using 1.8m (6') lengths of 9.5mm (⅜") clear pine dowel. Get spares, you may find one shaft is too bent to be useable.

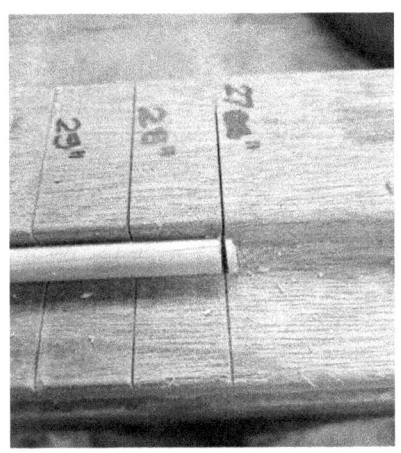

Photo 149. First cut is to trim the end square. A couple of mine had odd grain at the ends, so I took up to 50mm (2") off to get to the straight grain.

Photo 150. Cut to 30" in length. Be careful to avoid any twisted grain. I'm using a jig I made from a bit of spare door architrave and a nail.

Photo 151. One dozen shafts from eight 1.8m (6') dowels. The rejects are at the back, two have too much bow, one shaft has a gum pocket and some interesting grain.

Step 2: mark the centres and drill for the head and nock. The easiest way is to lay a stick about half the thickness of the shaft and press the end of the shaft against it. Draw a line, then rotate the shaft slightly and draw another line. When you've gone the whole way around the shaft, you'll have a small central area within the marks.

Photo 152. Mark the centres of both the nock and point end of the shaft.

Photo 153. Bore the hole for the nock. I start the hole with an awl.

Photo 154. Finish with a drill bit held in a hand chuck or drill. Make sure to clamp the shaft securely. I'm also testing the nock fit in this picture.

Photo 155. The shaftment marked for tapering

Step 3: mark the shaftment. Work out dimensions by looking at Drawing 72 on the first page of this chapter. Numbers 12 and 13 are the boat burial arrows. I'm using 127mm (5") for the feathers and 38mm (1½") space back from the nock to the waist. There's a 10mm ($^3/_8$") section before the feathers, which gives a total tapered length of 200mm (7 $^7/_8$"). I mark one, then use it to transfer the dimensions to the others with the knife. I've used pencil in these photos so it shows up better.

Step 4: cut the waist.

	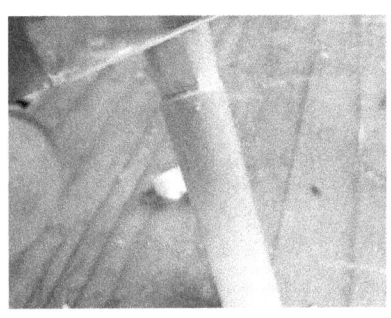
Photo 156. First cut is vertical along the line at the end of the binding. Press the knife firmly and roll the arrow shaft backwards and forwards to cut to a depth of about 1mm ($^1/_{32}$"). The number isn't important, as long as it's about the same as the total height of the thread, the base of the feather and a little extra for glue.	**Photo 157.** Second cut is a relief cut at an angle back towards the first vertical cut. This stops the rest of the arrow from chipping when you start to taper the shaftment.

	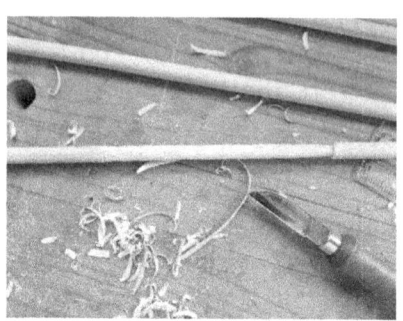
Photo 158. Third cut is a stop cut at the waist. This is to stop the taper cuts from progressing further down into the parts of the nock that we want to keep.	**Photo 159.** Taper the shaftment. Whittle, scrape, sand or file from the first cut back along the arrow to the waste area. You should be aiming to remove 1/3 to 1/2 the shaft at the waist.
	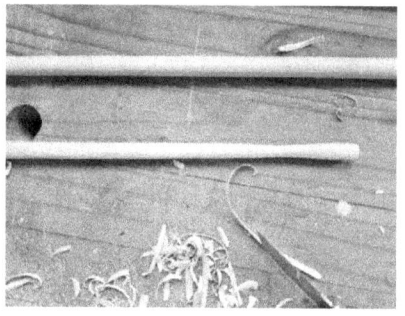
Photo 160. Shape the nock. Reduce the diameter of the end to match the base of the nock (in my case, 7.5mm), then cut an even taper back to the waist.	**Photo 161.** Shape the waist. The waist should be a neat transition from the shaftment taper to that of the nock. Sanding can work well here.

Prepare the feathers.

Material required: feathers.

Tools required: knife; rule; pencil.

Split, trim sides, cut to length. Scrape and/or sand the soft portion of the quill away. Commercially prepared fletching will already have most of this done, you may need to just tidy a small amount.

Attach the nock and head.

	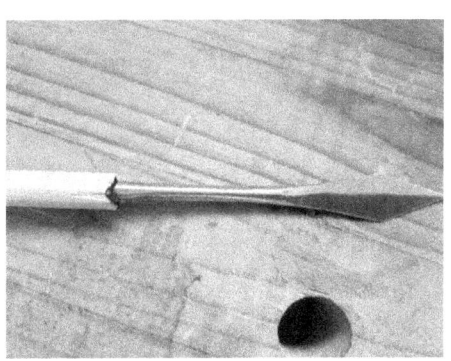
Photo 162. Gluing the nock insert. A bit of squeeze out is probably desirable. It will chip off easily enough when it is set.	**Photo 163.** Gluing the head in place. We'll taper the shaft to match the head later.

Material required: prepared nock; arrowhead; pre-drilled arrow shafts; glue.

Tools required: heat source (a tealight candle is perfect).

Melt the glue and dip the tang of the nock in it. Press the tang of the nock into the hole at the correct end of the arrow and hold it for a few seconds until it sets.

Caution.
It's important to pay attention to the direction of the grain when setting the nock. The groove in the nock should be at right angles to the growth rings in the arrow shaft. If the grain along the shaft isn't straight, any places where the grain comes out the side should be facing up so that if the arrow breaks in the bow, the broken section will be pushed away from the archer's bow arm.

If you are doing self-nocks (see **Variations**, below), cut them now before fitting the heads. The process for setting the head is the same as the nock, just with a little more glue. The blade of the arrowhead should be in the same plane as the string groove in the nock. You have a few seconds to twist the head into the correct alignment. Look along the arrow from the nock while you are doing it.

Fletching.

Material required: prepared feathers and arrow shafts.

Tools required: knife; heat source (a tealight candle is perfect); disposable paint brush or spreading stick; strip of paper; pencil.

If you are making a three-fletch arrow, remember that the cock feather is attached at right angles to the string groove in the nock and the side will depend on whether the archer is left- or right-handed. If you are doing four-fletch arrows, the feathers are all at 90 degree spacing, and are at 45 degrees from the string groove in the nock.

Spread on a layer or two of your chosen glue. Have a look at the original ones to get an idea of how much glue to use, it should be an even, thin cover, not thick and lumpy and looking like the road surface in front of your house.

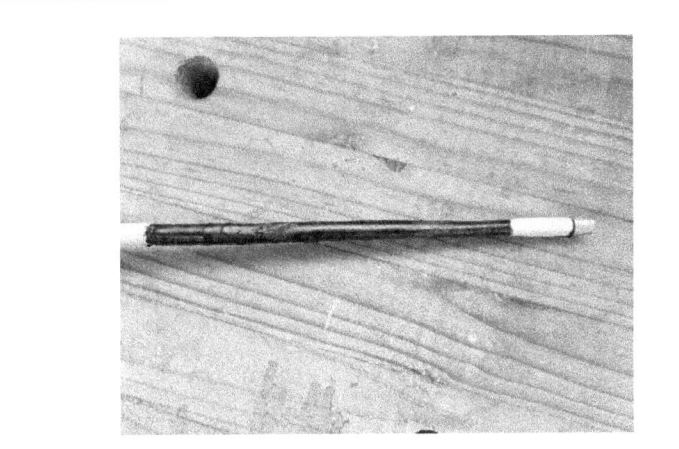

Photo 164. The glue covers the entire shaftment and up over the waist to the point where the binding ends.

The easiest way to work out where the feathers go is to wrap a narrow strip of paper around the arrow shaft. Mark a line on both layers of the paper where they overlap, then unroll it flat again. Mark two points at equal distances between the start and finish marks.

	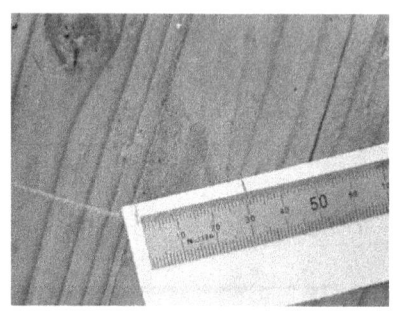
Photo 165. Wrap a strip of paper around the arrow and mark the same point on both layers.	**Photo 166.** Mark two additional points between the first marks.
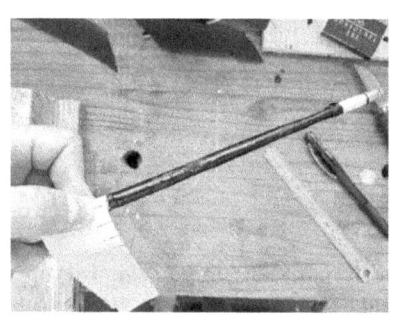	
Photo 167. Align the first mark for the cock feather perpendicular to the axis of the string groove in the nock.	**Photo 168.** Remelting the glue to attach the feathers.

Soften the glue with gentle heating and press the feathers in place. Remember that there is a 10mm ($^3/_8$″) wrap of thread before the feathers start. Slide the slip of paper to cover the first 10mm ($^3/_8$″) of glue and align the front of the feather with the paper tape. You only need to get the first third or so of each feather glued in place at this stage. If you need to re-soften the glue, hold the arrow over a candle while taking care to not burn any already attached feathers.

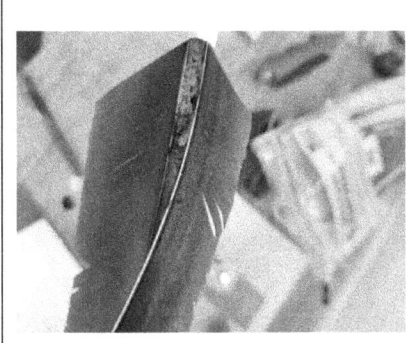 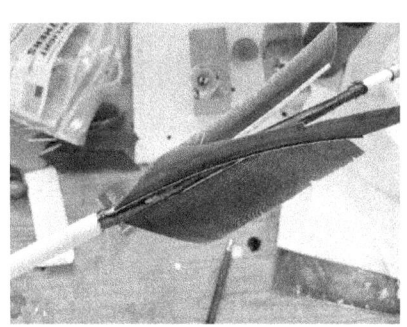

Photo 169. Paper overlaps glue by 10mm, feathers aligned with the edge of the paper.	**Photo 170.** Attached feathers ready for binding.

If you're using a glue that hardens over a longer period of time, use pins at the front and back of each feather to hold the feather in place, or use a fletching jig to hold it in place.

Fletch binding.

Material required: prepared arrow; thread.

Tools required: knife and/or scissors; heat source.

Let's quickly discuss the thread and then we can get on with the fun stuff. The originals from Hedeby were bound with a plant-fibre thread. It seems no chemical analysis has been done, but linen is the most likely answer, nettle/ramie is also possible. The arrow in Drawing 72. labelled [13] has an S-wrap.

It's now time to work out which way your thread binding is going to wrap. Life's a little easier if you know which side the feathers came from so that you aren't binding against the grain of the feather.[34] If they are from the right wing, use a Z-warp; if from the left, use an S-wrap. If you don't know, look at the ends of the barbels to see which way they slope. Wrap the binding the same way; you'll soon know if you are wrapping against the grain as the feathers will fight against you.

To do a Z-wrap, hold the arrow side on with the head pointing to the left. Wrap the thread away from you, over the top of the shaft, down the far side and bring it towards you on the underside. S-wrap is the opposite, start wrapping the thread underneath the arrow, bringing it towards you over the top.

Wrap the thread over the start of the shaftment, then up over the leading edge of the fletches. You'll never have another fletching cut from an arrow if the front edge of the feather is completely covered.

---

[34] Right now, there are a dozen fletchers composing emails in their heads about how if the grain makes a difference, the binding thread is too thick.*
*There are also at least four archaeologists who have never bound an arrow in their lives composing similar emails about how S-wrap always indicates a left-handed fletcher. (see Gardiner et al., 2005).

 **Photo 171.** Starting the wrap. This one is a Z-wrap.	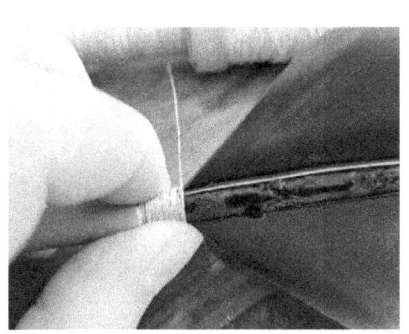 **Photo 172.** Wrap the front of the shaftment, then over the leading edge of the feathers.
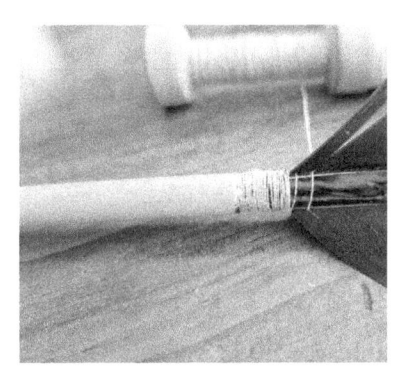 **Photo 173.** Continue to wrap up through the feathers.	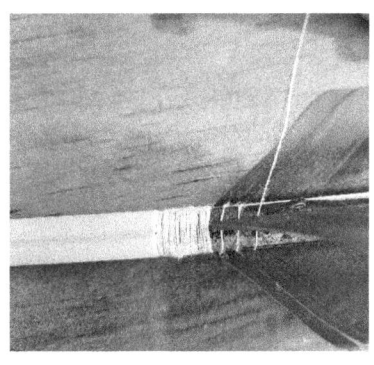 **Photo 174.** It's easier to keep the angle constant if you look down on the current feather.

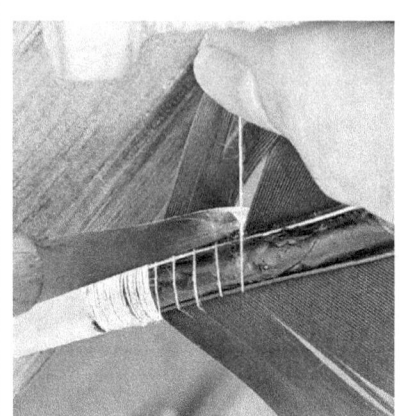 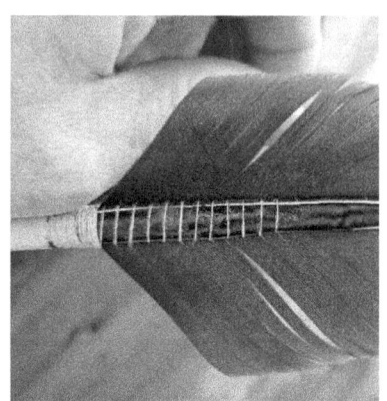

Photo 175. If you are having trouble getting the right spacing, use a fine pointed knife to separate the feather.

Photo 176. Straighten the un-glued section of the feather as you go.

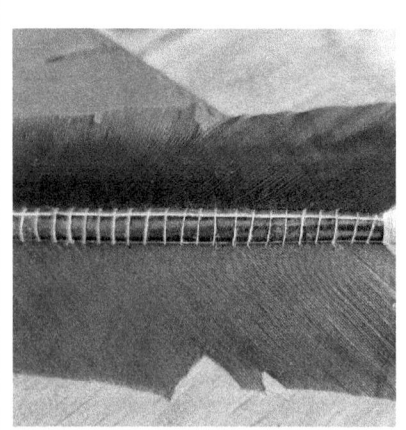 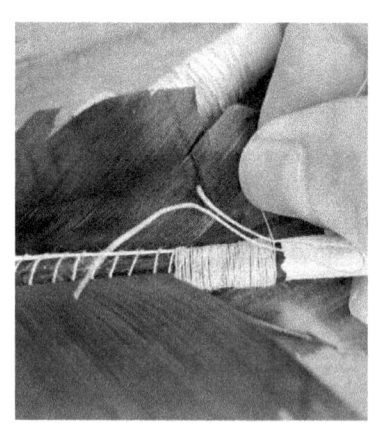

Photo 177. Binding the back of the shaftment.

Photo 178. Winding over a separate loop of thread.

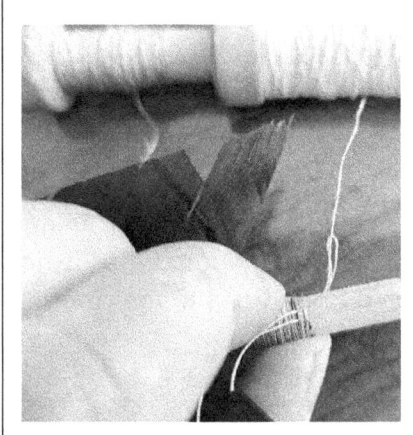	
Photo 179. Tail cut and tucked through the thread loop.	**Photo 180.** The tail tucked under the wrap.

1. Start by pressing the end of the thread into the pitch at right angles to the wrap direction. The heat from your thumb should be enough to soften the pitch and stick the thread in place.
2. Wrap the front of the shaftment with threads wound closely together, then continue over the leading edge of the feathers. Try to not cross over previous threads.
3. Wrap the full length of the feather. You're chasing 4-5mm between wraps (5-6 turns per inch). Try to keep even tension on the thread and don't be afraid to unwrap it and do it again. Keep straightening the feathers as you go.
4. Continue off the back of the feather and bind the back of the shaftment to whatever point beyond the waist that you've decided to go. Put a separate thread loop under the last three to five wraps (see Photo 179). Cut the thread when you finish, leaving a tail at least 25mm (1") long.

5. Tuck the tail through the loop, and pull both of the free ends of the loop while maintaining tension on the tail. The loop will pull out and the tail should tuck under the last windings. Carefully trim the tail flush with the binding.

You can leave the arrow at this stage until you have bound all of them. The final step is re-melting the glue so that it flows into the thread and fully under the feathers. If you're using a non-heat method, skip the next part.

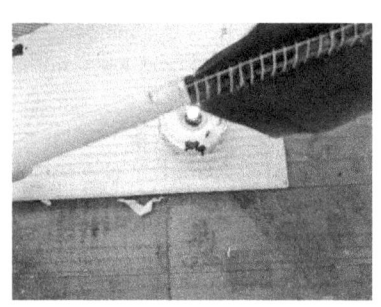	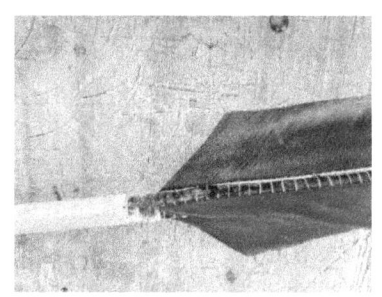
Photo 181. Start gently heating the glue. Try not to burn the feathers.	**Photo 182.** You can see the glue starting to wick into the thread.
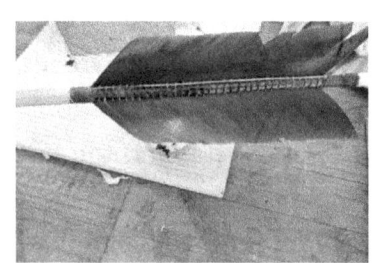	
Photo 183. Once you've done one side, repeat for the other two.	**Photo 184.** Finished. I did burn a feather, but it isn't the end of the world because they get trimmed later.

6. Gently heat the binding to melt the glue. A single candle is sufficient. You'll be able to hear and smell the glue melting before you see it. You could use a heat gun if you prefer, but beware of runs in the glue.
7. Keep the arrow moving so nothing gets burnt. I do the space between two feathers completely, then move on to the next space. I singed one feather because I was paying attention to the camera instead of the flame.
8. Repeat…

Trim feathers.
Once the binding is glued, it's time to trim the feathers.

Material required: prepared arrow.

Tools required: knife and straight edge or scissors; wooden block optional.

I use a wooden block that is about the same height as the arrow and lay the fletch I want to cut on it. I line up the straight edge (aluminium 25 x 13 mm angle (aluminium 1" x ½" angle)) and press down, then cut the feather with a sharp knife.

You can use scissors instead, although I have difficulty keeping the cut straight. Good sewing scissors with a serrated blade work well because they support the feather and stop it spreading or moving while it's being cut. I recommend that you do some test cuts in the unwanted part of the feather to gain some confidence before doing the final trimming.

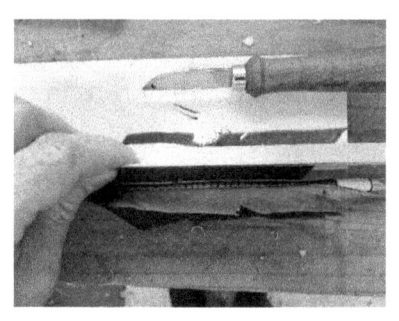

| Photo 185. Scissors with one serrated blade like this work well. | Photo 186. But I prefer a straight edge and sharp knife. |

Head binding.

Material required: prepared arrow; copper wire.

Tools required: knife, smooth jaw pliers; wire cutters; sand paper (optional).

Before binding, the arrow shaft needs to be shaped to match the arrowhead. If you are using wide tanged heads rather than small square cross-section heads, like I'm using here, you won't need to do this step.

There's no need to measure here. Move back about two finger widths and start shaving down to the head. Start with doing four tapers, each at 90 degrees to the others, then work on the high points giving you eight tapered surfaces. I did one more set to get 16 surfaces and then scraped it round, but if you're going to sand it round, you can probably get away with eight surfaces.

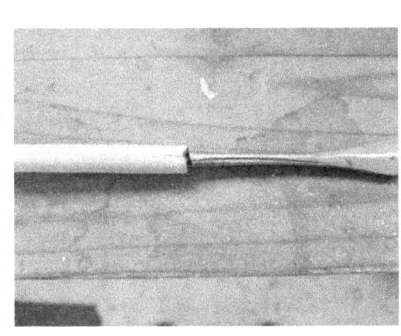	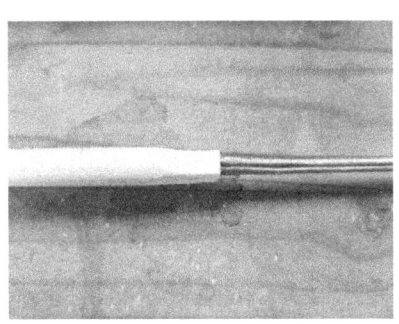
Photo 187. This time I remembered to do a 'before' photo..	**Photo 188.** Tapered with four planes.
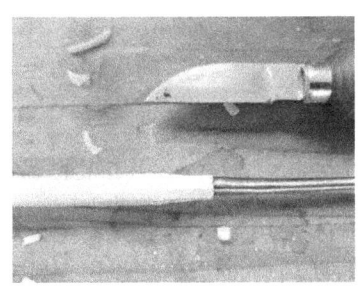	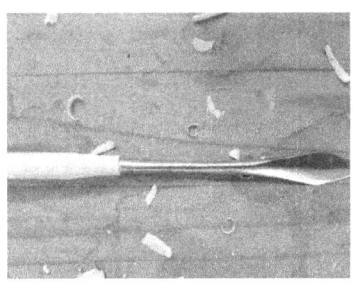
Photo 189. Tapered with 8 surfaces.	**Photo 190.** Finished taper. There is still a small shoulder of wood where it meets the arrowhead

As the arrows from the boat chamber grave were found as fragments, we don't really know whether the twists in the wire were on the bow side, on the hand side or some other direction. I'm doing it in line with the cock feather because the arrow sits flat on the table that way. The wire I used was 0.5mm (20 SWG) enamelled copper wire from the local electronics store. You may find you need to go heavier for a heavier bow. This size was tested to work up to a 45# draw. The enamel will keep the copper bright and stop it corroding. It's used for winding transformers, motors and inductors. I couldn't get an accurate measurement for the wire originally used, but this looks about right compared to the drawing.

1. Put a right-angle bend in the wire. It needs to be long enough to do both sets of twists, so allow at least 50mm (2"). If you are using heavier wire, you may need more length.
2. Lay the bent wire along the arrow, with the running end coming off at right angles.
3. Do five or six wraps starting from the narrow end and heading towards the wide part of the arrow. The originals are inconsistent in the number of wraps, but all are five or six. Keep the wraps close together and make sure they all cross over the bent part of the wire.
4. Cross the running wire over the bent wire, then twist them together five times. Use the pliers to keep tension on the wires, and try to keep them tight and in line with the original bent wire. You can see in the photos that I've drifted around the arrow a little. At least one of the originals has this feature as well.
5. Do another five or six wraps around the arrow, and when it crosses over the bent wire, twist them together another five times.
6. Cut the wire ends neatly, and press them into the wood of the arrow so that they sit flat. You can neaten the wraps and twists slightly if you need to, and as with the fletch binding, don't be afraid to undo it and start again if you aren't happy with it.

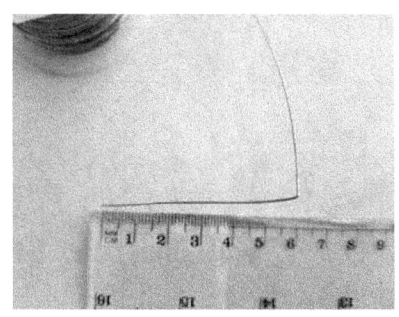

Photo 191. First bend in the wire. The running wire is heading up the page.

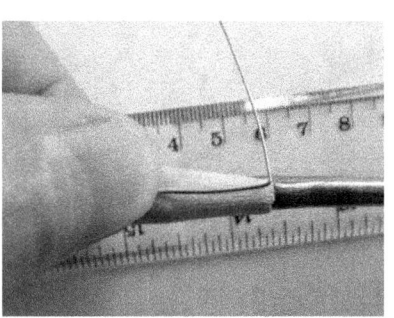

Photo 192. Laying it along the arrow. The cut end is under my thumb, the reel off the top of the photo.

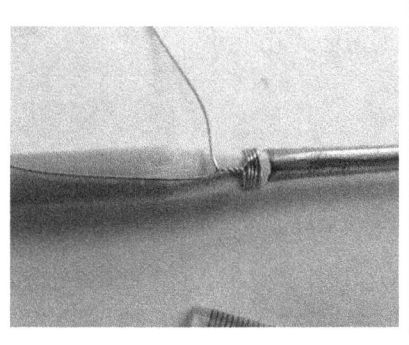

Photo 193. Five wraps and five twists. You can see how I've let the bent wire twist towards me under the wraps.

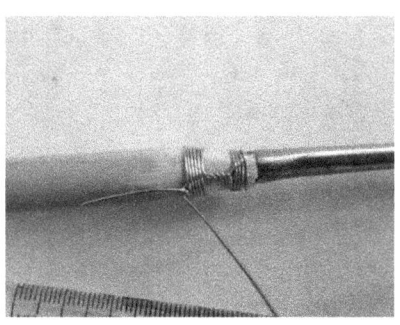

Photo 194. Second set of wraps with the ends just crossed over.

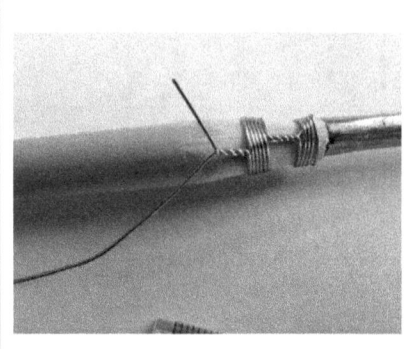	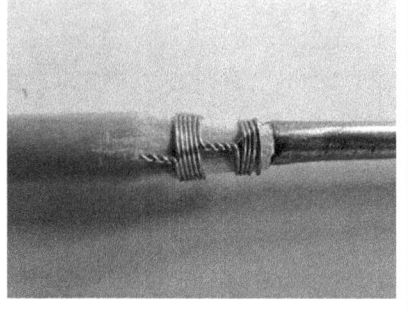
Photo 195. Final set of twists. Again, I've pulled the bent wire towards me.	**Photo 196.** Finished head binding.

I'll redo the head binding on this arrow, but thought it useful to show my mistakes so I could talk about them.

Variations.

Sinew Binding.

If sinew is available to you, give it a try. I can only get silverside tendon and while it makes a good bow backing, it isn't much use as a twisted thread. There are some good YouTube videos on making thread from sinew.

Alternative heads.

Forked.

Small forked heads have been found in wild deer hunting contexts (two at the Langfonne Ice Patch dated 850 CE and another nine in Målselv, Storfjord, Kåfjord and Nordreisa municipalities, all between 850 and 1300 CE).[35] Experiments with reproductions have shown the narrow-forked arrow shot from a reproduction bow penetrates the target with sufficient force to break the animal's spine.

Paulsen (1999) defines these as type E2.

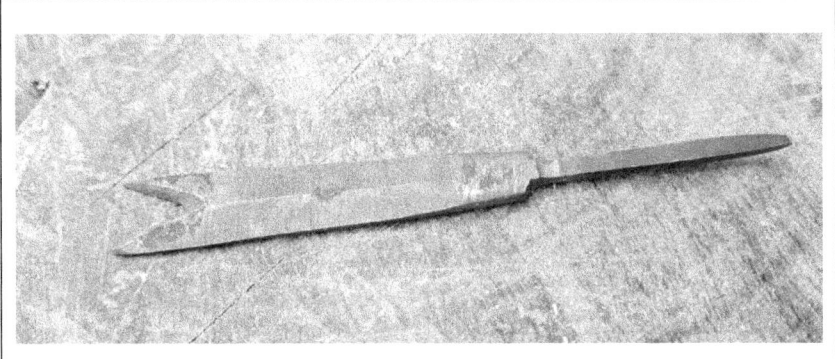

Photo 197. Paulsen type E2 small forked tanged arrowhead from Medieval Fightclub.

Bone/antler/shell.

Skeletal materials have been used to make arrowheads at least since the neolithic period. In Scandinavian and Northern German contexts, this continued until the 6th century, with a blade usually being leaf-shaped. In southern and Eastern Europe, barbed bone heads are also found.

Three Bronze Age arrowheads made from freshwater pearl mussel (*Margaritifera margaritifera*) shells have been found on the Lendbreen glacier in Norway (Mathisen, 2023).

---

[35] Secrets of the Ice (2023)

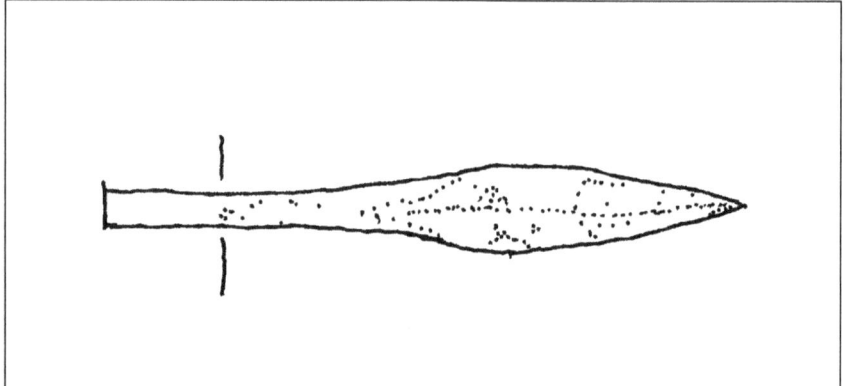

Drawing No. 73: Bone arrowhead from Norway, 1st to 3rd century CE. The other side is concave and follows the inner surface of the bone. Depth of insertion into the arrow shaft indicated, a slot was sawn into the shaft and the arrowhead was secured with pitch and bound with thread.

Socketed.

Despite there being some socketed arrowheads found at Hedeby, socketed arrowheads are unusual in Scandinavian Viking contexts due to the amount of metal required to make the sockets. Generally, tanged arrowheads are found in places where bog iron is the main source of metal. When iron is available from ore, socketed heads predominate.

The working parts of the arrowhead are the same shape for a given place and period, regardless of whether the head is tanged or socketed.

Blunts.

Normally assumed to be used for hunting birds and small game, the presence of at least 13 blunt headed arrows under the water of Hedeby harbour raises the possibility that they were also used for fishing. Those from Hedeby harbour and township mostly resemble the conical Bryggen 29614 with blunt heads integral to the arrow shaft, two taper towards the point as well as back to the shaft.

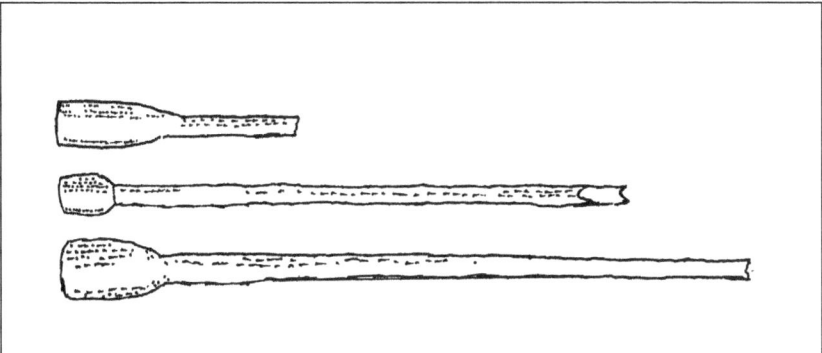

Drawing No. 74: Finds from Bryggen, Bergen, Norway, during excavations 1955-68. Finds number (top to bottom) 29614, 27382, 17308.

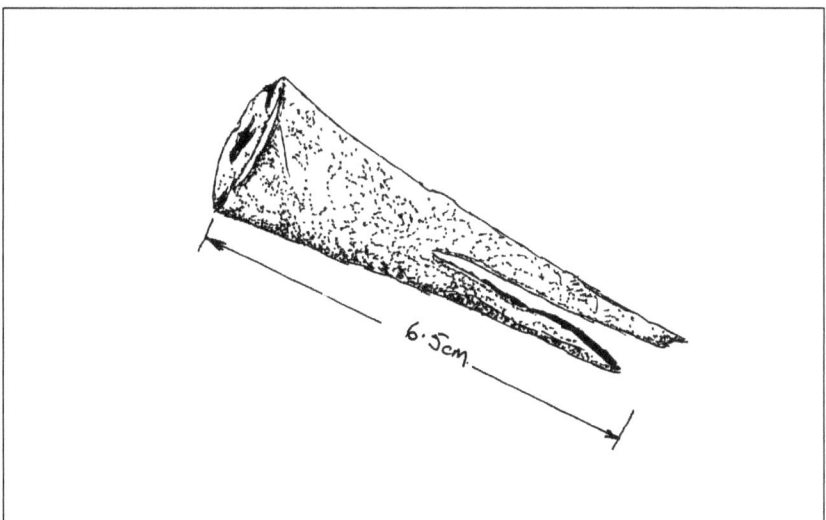

Drawing No. 75. Bone blunt arrowhead from Valsgard 7. Drawn by the author after a photograph supplied by Matt Bunker. (6.5cm = $2\ ^9/_{16}$")

Foreshafts: (short heavier section of hardwood spliced into the shaft as a repair or for other reasons) are known from 9th century hunting contexts.

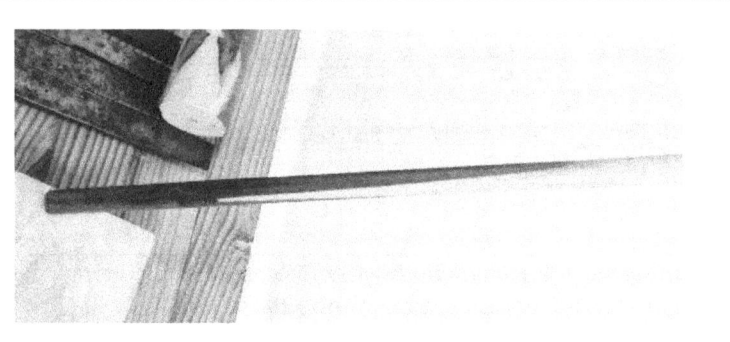

Photo 198. Walnut foreshaft on a medieval ash arrow as a repair. Sometimes they are done with a long wedge shape like this, other times there's a smaller scarf joint. Nocks can be similarly repaired with scarf joints and thread or sinew binding.

Self-nocks.

Separate nocks like those from the boat burial are an anomaly in the archaeological record. Almost all arrows from western European contexts throughout history were self-nocked, including the contemporary arrows found nearby in Hedeby harbour. In this section, I'll take you through the process to make the tapered and bound nock suitable for the northern Germanic/Scandinavian traditions spanning from the neolithic to medieval periods.

Step 1: measure and mark.
> There is so much variation in extant finds that it is almost meaningless to give a firm measurement. The parallel sided area needs to be long enough to support the string groove, but not so long that it gets in the way of your fingers when drawing the arrow back. I just eyeball it, but it is going to be somewhere in the range of 10-12mm ($^3/_8$"-½"). The waist is going to be a similar distance forward of that.

Step 2: cut the string groove.
> I find it easier to cut the groove before doing any tapering. If the other way works for you, do it that way instead. It is vitally important that the groove cuts across the growth rings of the wood. This stops the bow string splitting the arrow when it is released. There're a few ways of cutting the groove. I use a file, then open the sides out with a knife. You could use a rod-saw, three hacksaw blades taped together or even drill a 3mm ($^1/_8$") hole through the back of the arrow and then cut down to the hole with a knife.

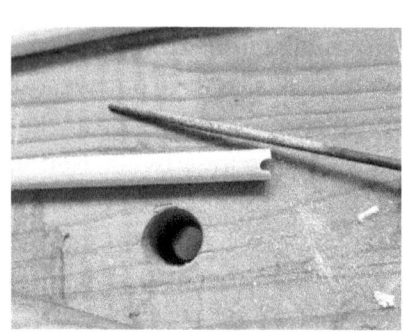	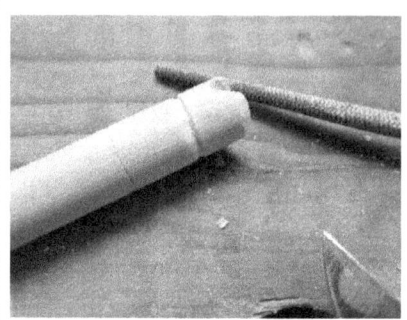
Photo 199. I've used a 3mm ($^1/_8$") rat-tail file to cut the grove to about a 6mm (¼") depth and then eased the edges with a knife.	**Photo 200.** Relief cuts at the nock shoulder. Keep these shallow.

Step 3: cut the shoulder of the nock.

> As in the main section above, the first cut is vertical at a shallow depth, followed by a series of shallow relief cuts. The relief cut depth is the same as the thickness of the binding thread, in my case, 0.8mm ($^1/_{32}$"). The relief cuts prevent a split or tear-out running to the parallel part of the nock.

Step 4: cut the waist of the nock.

> The process is the same as for all the other cuts – a main vertical cut, followed by a series of shallow relief cuts. In this case, it's considerably deeper and the relief cuts are made from both sides of the line. Keep cutting from the shoulder to the waist to shape the nock. You can see from in the facets shown in Photo No 203 below how I've used four sets of increasingly steep cuts.

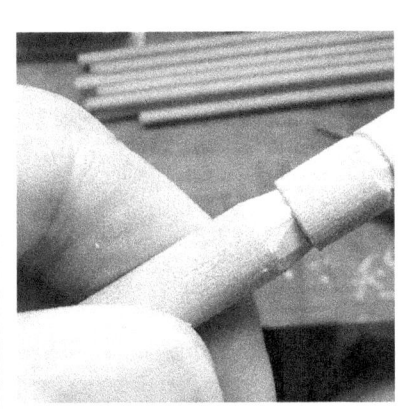	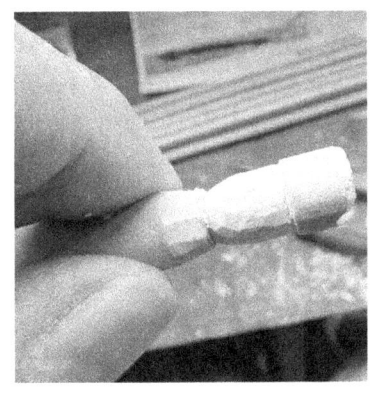
Photo 201. Depth cut and first set of relief cuts done on the waist.	**Photo 202.** Relief cuts being made progressively deeper towards the waist.

Step 5: Taper the shaftment.

Having already established the correct depth at the waist, it's easier to now work back towards the start of the shaftment in a series of decreasingly deep cuts. The front of the shaftment is worked out the same way as with the solid nock but is slightly shorter because the waist is already done: I'm using 125mm (5") for the feathers and 32mm (1 ¼") back from the end of the feather to the end of the binding. There's a 10mm (³/₈") section before the feathers, which gives a total worked length of 167mm (6 ⁵/₈").

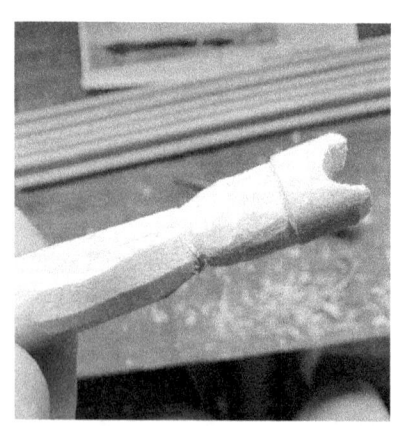 

Photo 203. Increasing the taper from the waist back along the shaftment. My knife always points towards the waist for this set of cuts.	**Photo 204.** Continue working back along the shaftment. Do one cut, then do a similar one on the opposite side. Rotate 90 degrees and do opposite cuts to square the shaft, then take the corners off to make it octagonal.

Photo 205. You should establish the start of the shaftment and depth as in Photos number 160 and 161 above. Continue tapering the shaftment until you go full length and at the desired depth. You may need to do the last set of cuts back towards the start of the shaftment.	**Photo 206** Turn the knife on the side and scrape along the high points to smooth the taper and nock. You may have to pay attention to the direction of the grain and scrape towards the head on one side of the shaft and towards the nock on the other side.

Put the feathers on the same way as we did with the bronze nocks. The binding is also the same, but continues all the way up to the step on the nock.

Photo 207. Finished self-nock binding after heating. The feathers are out of frame to the left.

Acknowledgement.

Thanks to Andrea Redden for the use of her copy of Owen et al (1999) and Matt Bunker for information and his assistance on the original arrows.

Appendices.

Appendix 1 - Typology of locks.

Table 27. Typology for locks (as you are looking at the outside of the lock).

Number of hasps	Hasp position(s)	Typology code	Example
1	Left A	1A	Kaagenden - Denmark
	Centre B	1B	Lejre – Grave 321
	Right C	1C	None found
	Left with snib	1D	Fyrkat - Denmark
2	Left and right A	2A	Mastermyr - Sweden
3	Left, centre and right A	3A	Oseberg 149
Other			
Spring displacement at right angles to lock plate		4A	Oseberg 178
Spring displacement at Parallel to lock plate		4B	Mastermyr lock no. 4

Note: Type 1C is *'None found'* as far as part of this short survey.

Appendix 2 - Trapezoid chest comparison, updated from Viking – Volume 1 (2021).

Table 28. Trapezoid chest comparison.

Place	Dated CE	Collection	Material	Dimensions
Oseberg farm, Tonsberg, Vestfold, Norway	800 – 850	Viking Ship Museum, Oslo, Norway. No. 149	Oak and iron	L (base 156cm (61 $^{27}/_{64}$")), top 104cm (40 $^{15}/_{16}$")), W (base 36cm (14 $^{11}/_{64}$")), top 28cm (11 $^{1}/_{32}$")), H 41cm (16 $^{9}/_{64}$").
Oseberg farm, Tonsberg, Vestfold, Norway	800 – 850	Viking Ship Museum, Oslo, Norway. No. 156.	Oak and iron	L (base 113cm (44 $^{31}/_{64}$"), top 108cm (42 $^{33}/_{64}$")), W (base 29cm (11 $^{27}/_{64}$")), top 32cm (12 $^{19}/_{32}$")), H 35cm (13 $^{25}/_{32}$").
Oseberg farm, Tonsberg, Vestfold, Norway	800 – 850	Viking Ship Museum, Oslo, Norway. No. 178.	Oak and iron.	L (base 66.5cm (26 $^{3}/_{16}$"), top 52cm (20 $^{15}/_{32}$")), W (base 24cm (9 $^{29}/_{64}$"), top 21cm (8 $^{17}/_{64}$")), H 31cm (12 $^{13}/_{64}$").
Hedeby Harbour, Germany	Pre-982	Viking Museum Haithabu	Oak and iron	L (base 52cm (20 $^{15}/_{32}$"), top 42cm (16 $^{17}/_{32}$")), W (base 23cm (9 $^{1}/_{16}$"), top 22cm (8 $^{21}/_{32}$")), H 27cm (10 $^{5}/_{8}$").
Mästermyr, Sproge parish, Gotland, Sweden	1000	Staten Historiska Museum, Stockholm,	Oak and iron	L (base 92cm (36 $^{7}/_{32}$"), top 88cm (34 $^{41}/_{64}$")), W (base 25.6cm (10 $^{5}/_{64}$"), top 24cm (9 $^{29}/_{64}$")), H 24.6cm (9 $^{11}/_{16}$").

Townfoot Farm, Cumwhitton, Cumbria, England	10th Century	Sweden, Ref. 21592 Grave 85, Tulee House Museum, England.	Acer sp. (Maple) and iron	L (base 46cm (18 $^7/_{64}$"), top 38cm (14 $^{61}/_{64}$")), W (base 16cm (6 $^{19}/_{64}$"), top 11cm (4 $^{21}/_{64}$")), H 20cm (7 $^7/_8$").

Appendix 3 – Updated Coppergate Mallet measurements from Viking – Volume 1 (2021).

In the first issue of Viking - Volume 1 (2021) the measurements provided for the mallet were incorrect, the second issue corrected that error. This is just in case you missed the first correction.

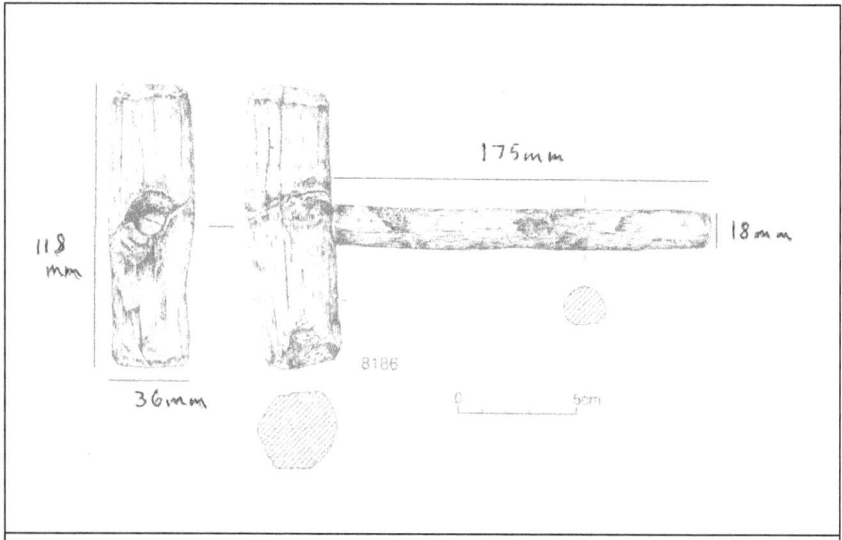

Drawing 76. The Coppergate mallet (in mm) with the correct measurements.

Appendix 4 – Alternative hasp plate for Hedeby chest

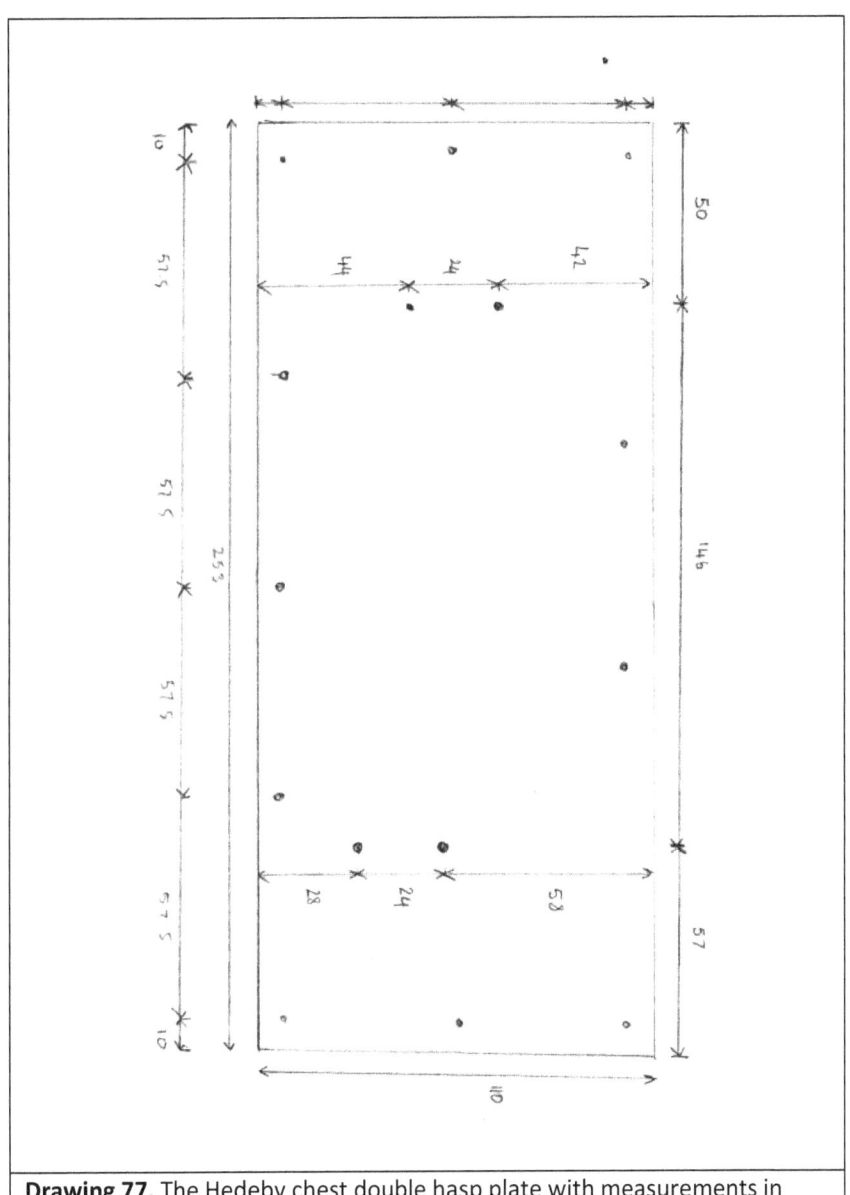

Drawing 77. The Hedeby chest double hasp plate with measurements in mm.

Appendix 5 – Hedeby chest – Small version.

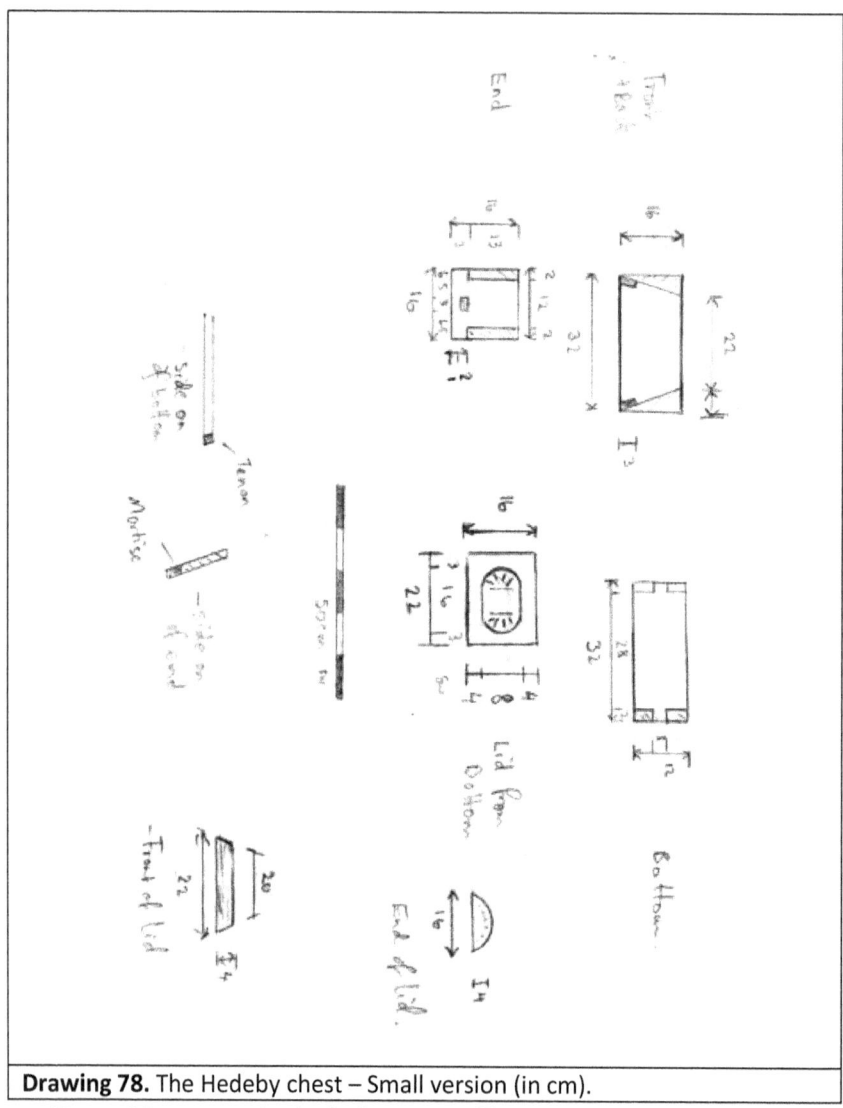

Drawing 78. The Hedeby chest – Small version (in cm).

Note: I have not included tenon off set in these drawings.

Appendix 6 – Hedeby chest – Large version.

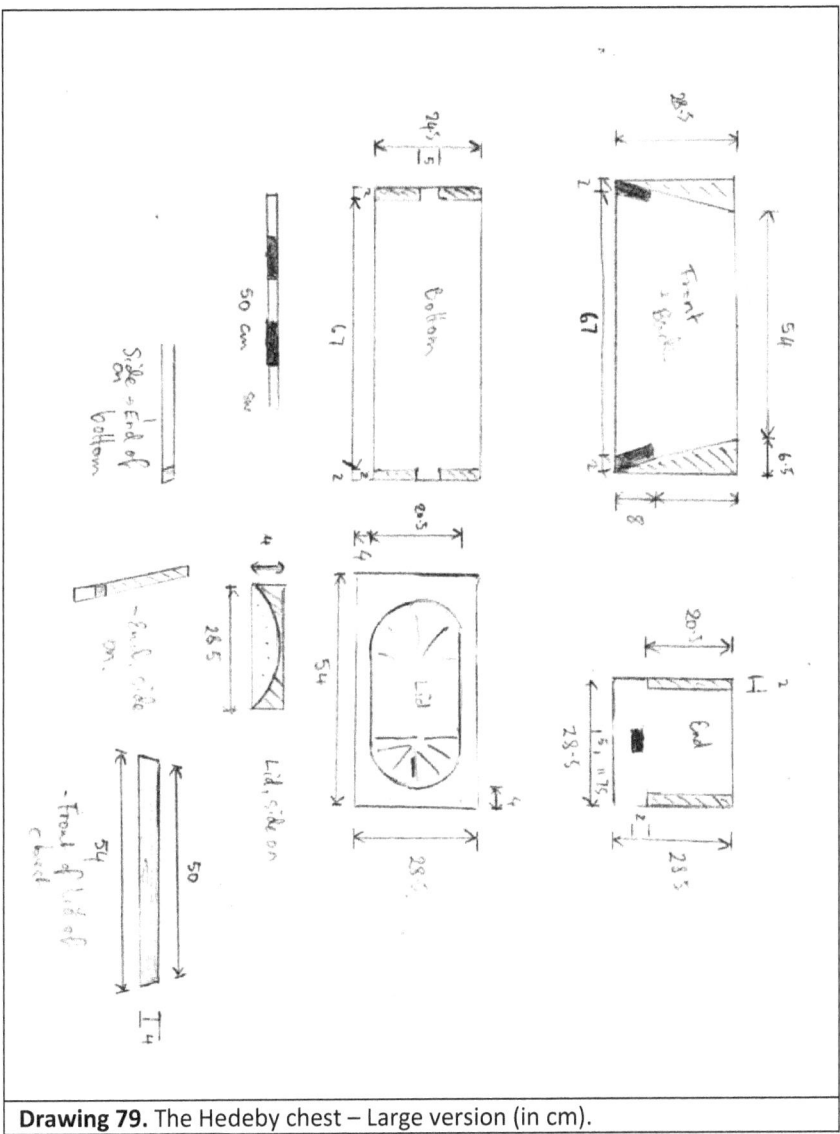

Drawing 79. The Hedeby chest – Large version (in cm).

Note: I have not included tenon off set in these drawings.

Appendix 7. – Gokstad bed. Wider slat plans – when you need more support.

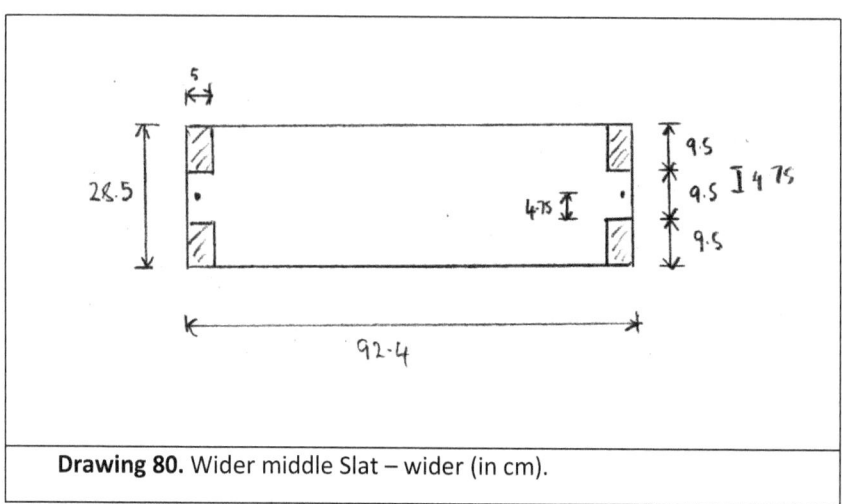

Drawing 80. Wider middle Slat – wider (in cm).

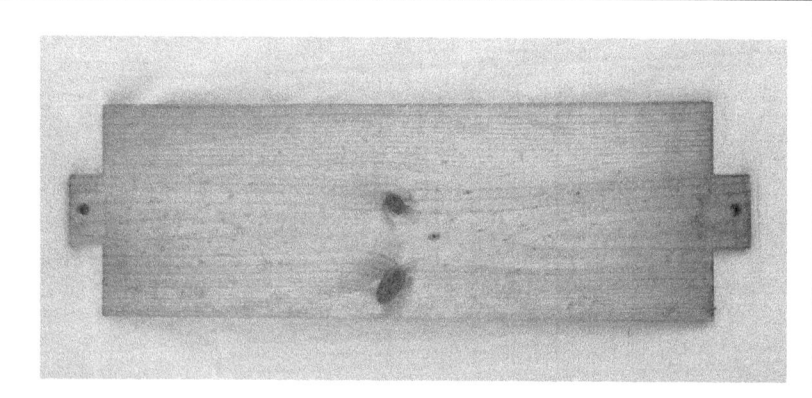

Photo 208. Wider middle slat but the same size slat can be used for the rest of the slats if more support is required.

Appendix 8 – Gokstad backpack – Kids version.

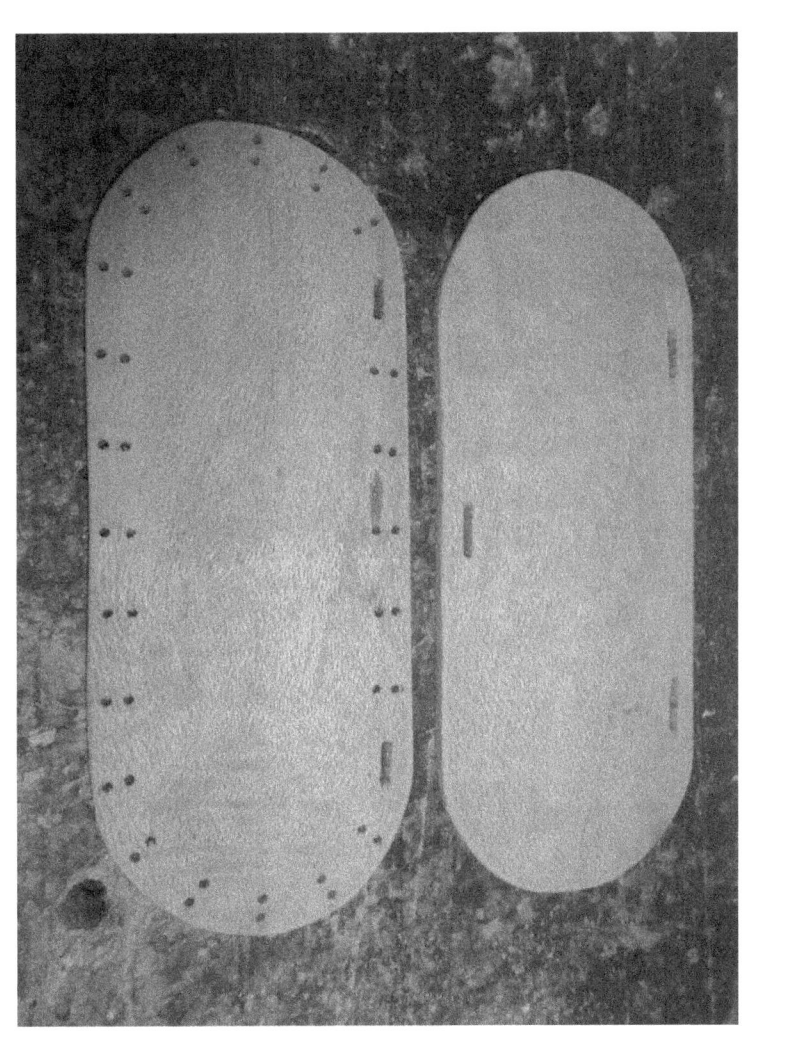

Photo 209. Gokstad backpack Boards – Kids version.

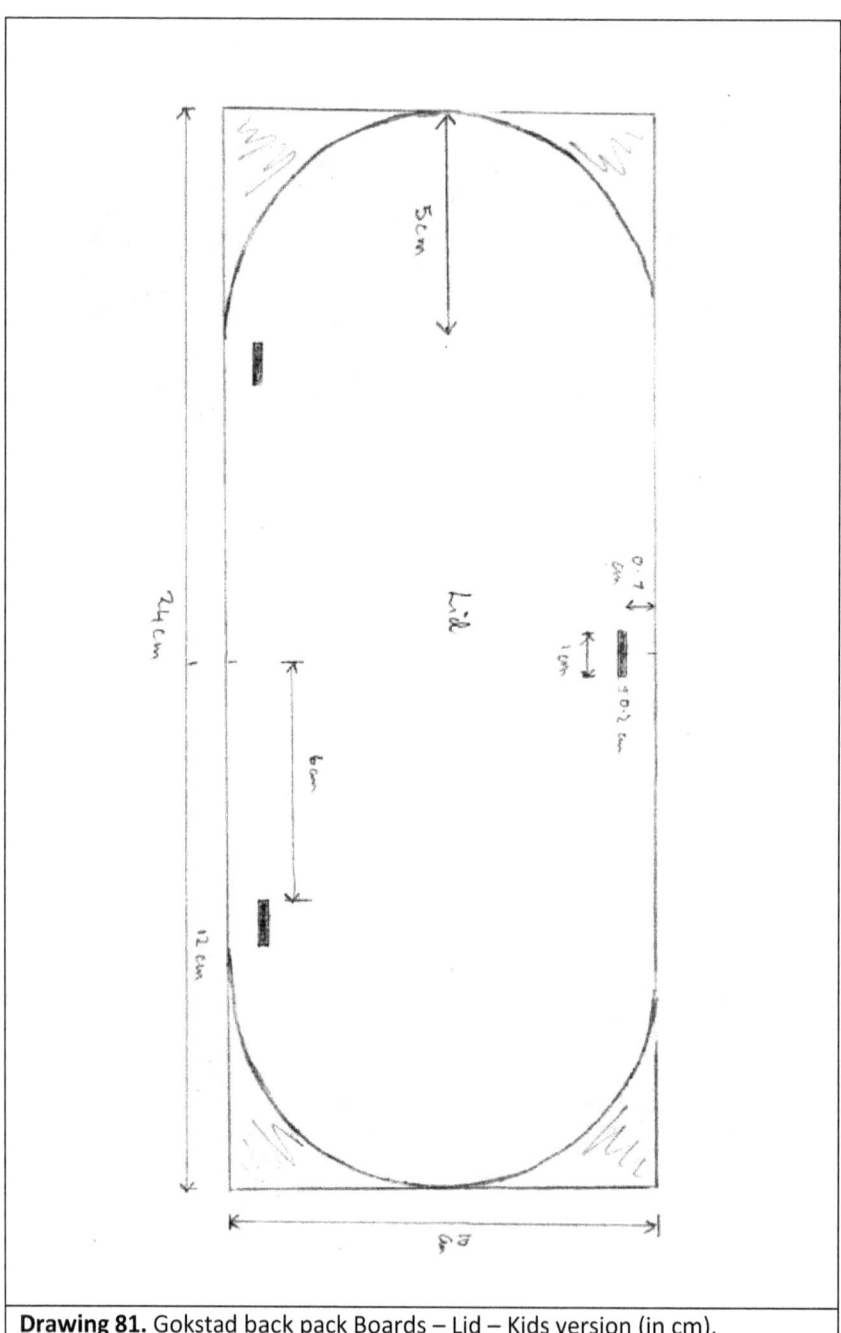

Drawing 81. Gokstad back pack Boards – Lid – Kids version (in cm).

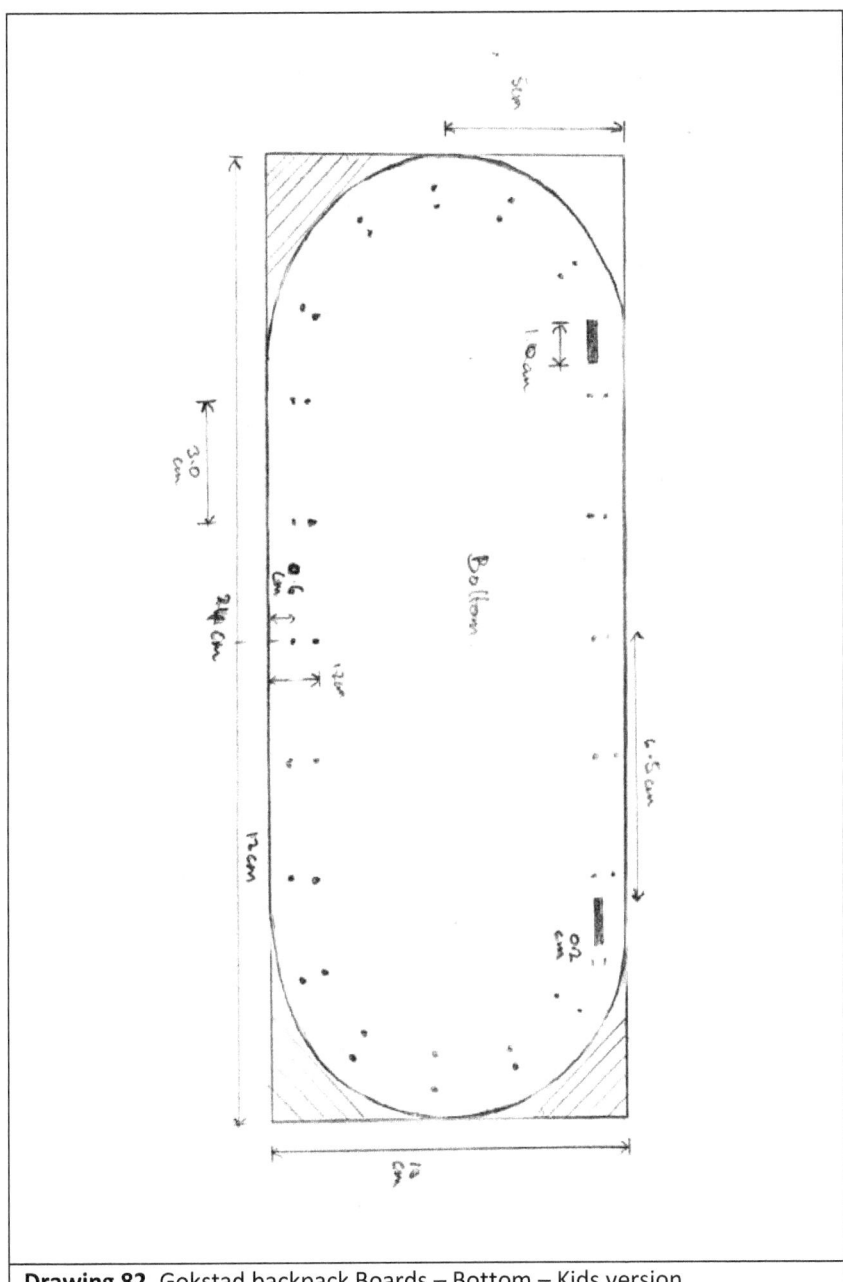

Drawing 82. Gokstad backpack Boards – Bottom – Kids version

Table 29. Dimensions of leather work in 2mm (6oz) veggie tan leather	
Body (includes overlap)	62 x 26cm (24 ½" x 10 ¼")
Rim strengthening strap (includes overlap)	62 x 5cm (24 ½" x 2")
Shoulder straps *2	52 x 1cm (20 ½" x ⅜")
Lid hinges	16 x 1cm (6 5/16" x ⅜")
Lid closure strap	22 x 1cm (8 ¾" x ⅜")
Leather thonging for securing the lid closure strap	12cm x 3mm (5" x ⅛")

Please refer to the article on the larger version of the backpack for construction instructions.

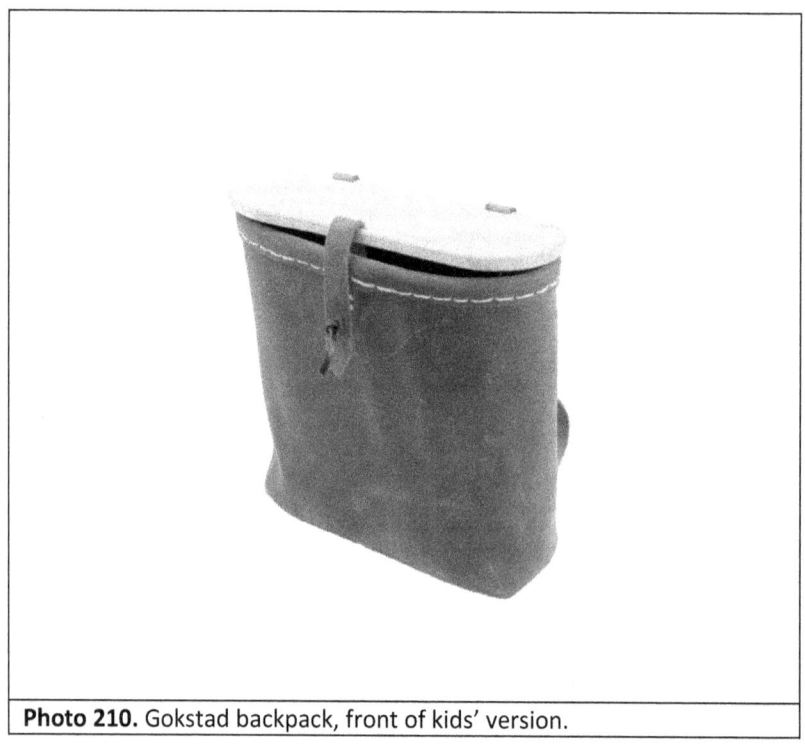

Photo 210. Gokstad backpack, front of kids' version.

Photo 211. Gokstad backpack, back of kids' version.

Photo 212. Gokstad backpacks, full versus kids' version.

Appendix 9 – Larger Oseberg chair.

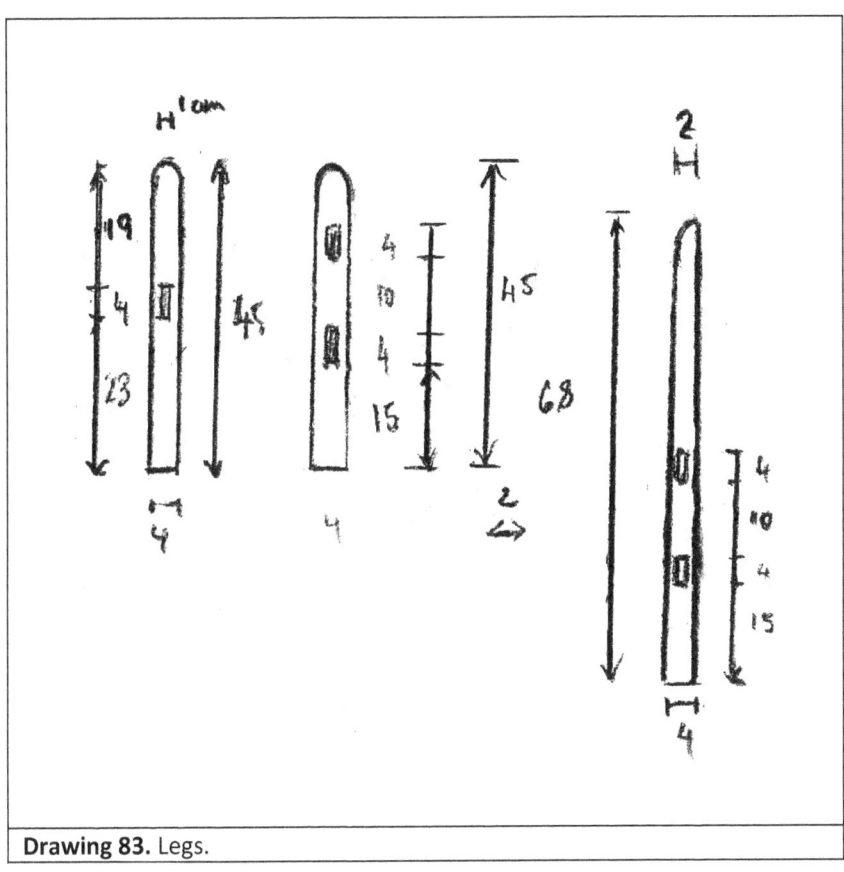

Drawing 83. Legs.

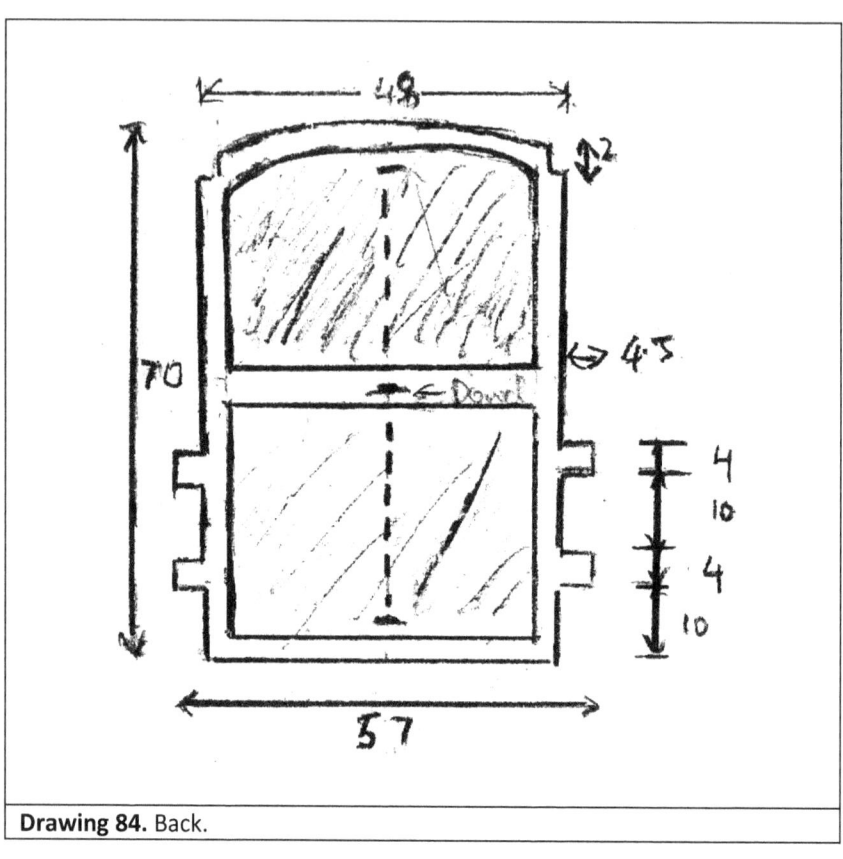

Drawing 84. Back.

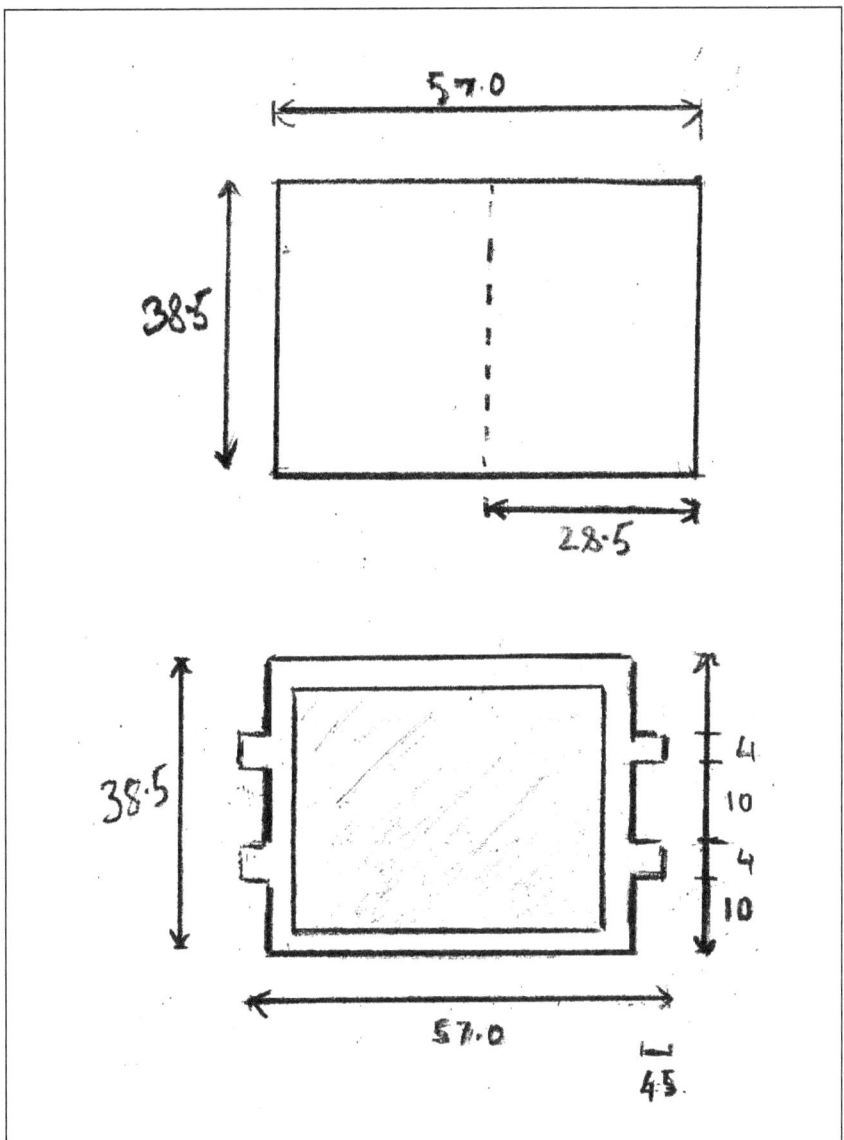

Drawing 85. Front with joint as dotted line. **Drawing 86.** Front with tabs cut and insert chiselled out.

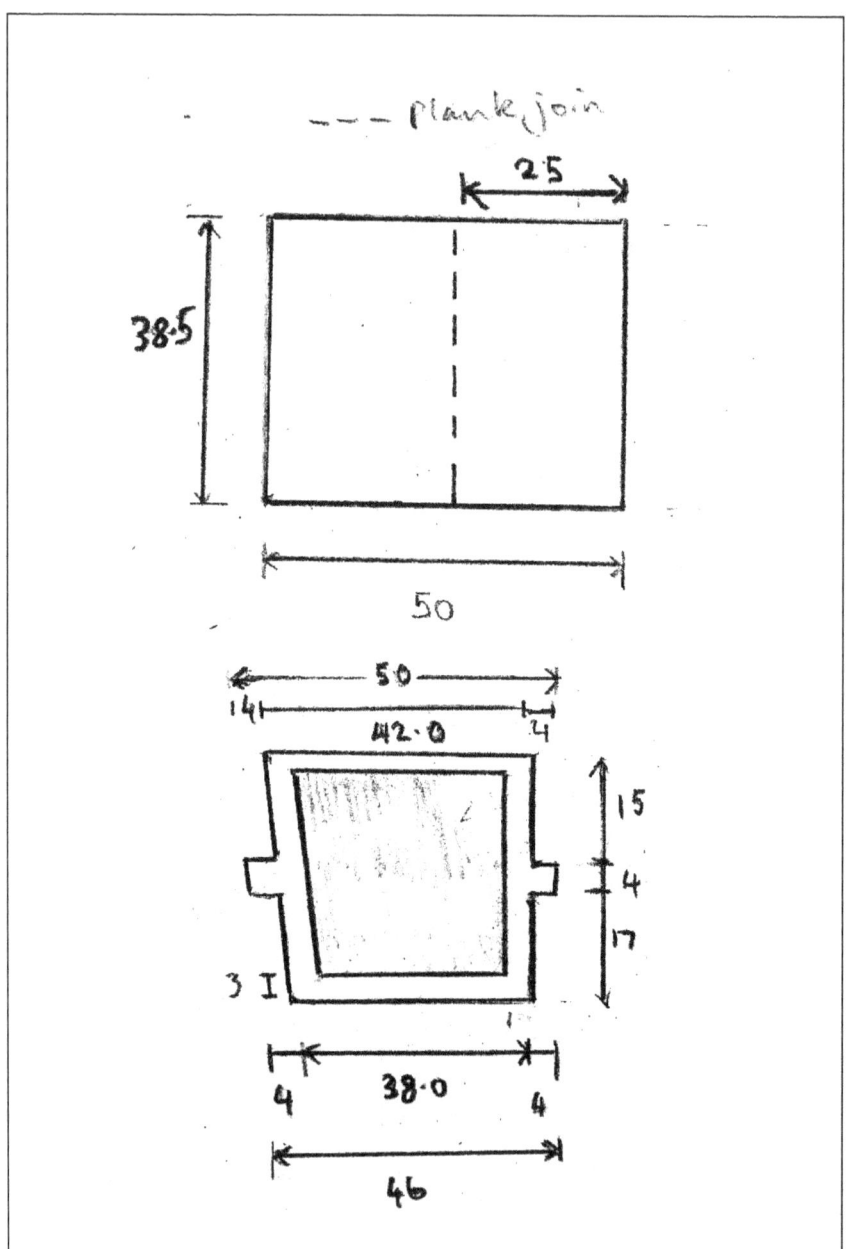

Drawing 87. Side with joint as dotted line. Drawing 88. Side with tabs cut and insert chiselled out.

Appendix 10 - Gokstad Backpack evaluation.

By Steve Mijatovic (member of The Wandering folk – living history group – Australia).

Date: Monday the 30th May 2022. Place: Mt Twynam, Great Dividing Range, in the Snowy Mountains, New South Wales, Australia.

Hi Sven, As promised here is a write up of the trip, your backpack and how it performed. Firstly I have to apologise. Due to a sudden and unpredictable change in the weather I was forced to abandon my chance to take multiple walks and instead work on extracting the event attendees. This meant that I was only able to take the pack on a single walk and for reasons below only on half of it.
Overall scores Function - 10/10 Comfort - 10/10 Practicality - 7/10 Design - 6/10 Function - The pack is great, it's big and it's roomy and it does exactly what it should do.
Comfort - Even made for a larger man the wide straps and low weight make carrying it a joy. It doesn't wobble around while walking and you can genuinely forget it is on your back. I was able to run and jump in it with no issues.
Practicality - We start to lose a few points here as despite its cavernous carrying capacity it lacks a real way to attach anything further to it. You can't really strap down a rolled up shelter or blanket on top of or underneath it or tie anything to the outside. In addition to the above if you are planning to wear a cloak with the pack you are either forced to wear it sash fashion or over the top of the pack. Neither of these options then gives you the full warmth and protection of the cloak. This would likely be less of an issue with the smaller original sized pack. (It was for this reason that I removed the pack half way through the hike. We were starting to climb Mt Twynam and the snow was coming in and I believed I needed the full cloak

coverage). Design - Nothing really surprising here, the biggest downside was the size of the lid which literally allowed snow to fall directly in the pack. I had to stop several times as the pack got heavier to scoop out snow and everything inside got wet. An easy fix. The unscaled nature of this replica made wearing a cloak with it near impossible (see above) It needs some sort of chest strap to distribute weight to full effect, again an easy fix. The pack itself has distorted a bit from the wet and the snow. A dent has appeared in the leather on the back up the top from the weight of the lid and it is no longer nice and oval. Lastly the leather strap that goes through the slot in the lid swelled in the wet and the lid became very hard to open, an easy fix by widening the slot.

Photo 213. Backpack in use. By James Moss.

Appendix 11 – Gokstad Backpack – An alternative shoulder strap arrangements for comfort.

The width of the shoulder straps is based on the width of the holes in the base and top boards, this width of 1 cm may cause discomfort to the user. Solutions may include the attachment of wider straps (which would require longer slits in the back of the back pack and the wooden bottom) or the addition of a guitar strap to the existing thin shoulder straps.

A guitar strap is a piece of material rectangular in shape with two slits in either end and the ends of the shoulder strap are threaded through these slits, which provides better protection to the shoulders of the back pack user by distributing the load over a larger surface area.

See photos 104 & 105.

Optional Shoulder Pieces – 38 * 6cm (15 x 2 ½"") in 3mm (8oz) veggie tanned leather.

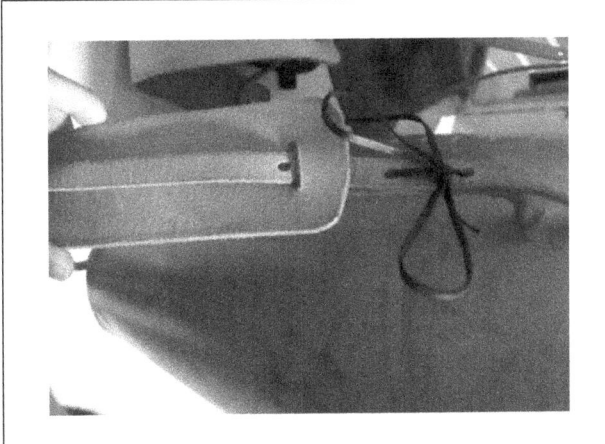

Photos 214. Shoulder strap adjustment and guitar strap.

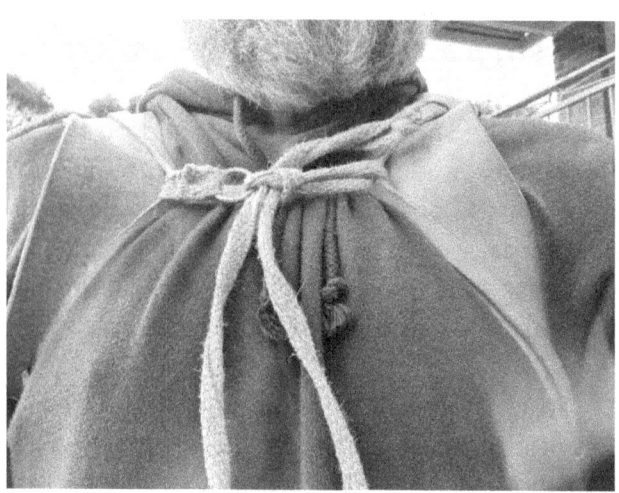
Photo 215. Cinch strap between shoulder straps at front may make the shoulder strap more secure.

Appendix 12 – Extant arrow finds.

Table 30. Comparison of Extant Arrows. Unless otherwise noted, arrows are made in the Northern Germanic/Scandinavian tradition.

Place	Date	Collection	Description
Nydam	3rd to 4th C	Museumsinsel Schloss Gottorf	Almost 200 arrows or fragments. Dated to the 3rd to 4th centuries, strictly speaking the late Iron Age, but their shape and manufacture represent a Northern Germanic tradition. Shafts were mainly made from pine, a few from ash. Their length averages 75–80 cm (29.5–31.5 in.). The widest part of 9–12 mm is in the middle, from which the shafts taper towards both ends. The fletched area is often particularly reduced in girth, so the layer of birch pitch used as glue did not add additional thickness. By far the majority of arrows were fletched with four feathers of 8–12 cm ($3\,^{1}/_{16}$–$4\,^{3}/_{4}$ in.) length each, which were pulled off the quill rather than split. A very narrow whipping of natural fibres – most likely flax or hemp The nock ends are always of bulbous shape, to offer enough material for the string groove to be cut in. In some cases, the entire nock is a separate piece of bronze. (a) flat, triangular, barbed arrowheads, and (b) leaf-shaped bladed heads were both used for hunting and warfare, while (c) long, square or rhomboid bodkins are mostly for war. Heads could be socketed or tanged.

Table 30. Comparison of Extant Arrows. Unless otherwise noted, arrows are made in the Northern Germanic/Scandinavian tradition.

Place	Date	Collection	Description
			Bone arrowheads found at Nydam imitate contemporary iron points.
Langfonne, Norway	4160BCE–1340CE No finds date from the period from 110BCE to 300CE	Museum of Cultural History, University of Oslo	68 arrows and five isolated arrowheads. 29 of the 31 arrows from the late iron age/early medieval period are complete. Average length is 59cm (23 ¼"). Bronze age shafts tend to be linden with bone or antler heads, iron age/medieval are mostly birch. Occasional hardwood foreshafts. Some nocks show field repairs using scarf joints, glue and binding. All heads tanged; sinew or thread binding behind the head and on the shaftment; traces of pitch.[36] Some older arrows (c.1500BP) from the Innlandet ice are 4-fletch. 22 arrows with the fletching preserved to various degrees, including about 40 fletches total. Binding is 4-6 turns at the start of the fletching and continues past the end of the fletching to the nock. Fletching is cut flat, or a sort-of parabolic shape with the back edge clipped at right angles to the shaft.
Illerup Ådal	3rd C CE	Moesgård Museum	Complete arrows – leaf-shaped tanged iron heads or carved bone heads, pitch and linen or sinew binding, evidence of the feathers

[36] Pilø et al. (2020)

Table 30. Comparison of Extant Arrows. Unless otherwise noted, arrows are made in the Northern Germanic/Scandinavian tradition.

Place	Date	Collection	Description
Oppdal, Trøndelag, Norway.	400-600 CE	NTNU Vitenskapsmuseet Trondheim	remain on the shafts. Birch, pine shafts; resin glue; sinew binding; mostly leaf-shaped tanged heads, one socketed head appears to be a late example from the site.[37]
Högum, Medelpad, Sweden	late C5th	Lost?	36 arrows with red paint on their shafts[38]
Vimose, Denmark	1st to 7th C, most items 2nd-3rd C	Given as gifts to foreign heads of state in the 19th C.[39]	Many tanged leaf-shaped arrowheads, some long trilobate bodkins
Thorsberg, Northern Germany	5th C?	Museumsinsel Schloss Gottorf	Arrow shafts 13 mm (½") diameter, 66-89 cm (26-35 inches) long
Oberflacht, Germany	6th-7th C	Arrows lost since discovery in the 19th C	Alemannic tradition. Fragments, plus 18 complete arrows: mostly birch. Complete shafts measure 55–65 cm (21 ½ –25 ½ "), associated bows showed draw length about 24 inches. Shaft bobtailed, 9–11mm (3/8 - 7/16") diameter at head with an even taper to the nock end. No heads found, but shafts were stepped

---

[37] Callanan
[38] Rau, p.143
[39] Jensen (2020), p. 69

Table 30. Comparison of Extant Arrows. Unless otherwise noted, arrows are made in the Northern Germanic/Scandinavian tradition.

Place	Date	Collection	Description
Altdorf, Switzerland	7th C	Uri Historical Museum, Altdorf, Switzerland	and tapered for socketed heads, reddish glue and tiny nails evident to attach heads. Three fletch, parallel cut feathers glued with birch pitch and bound with vegetable bast (linen?) thread with very high number of turns. No nocks found implies they were likely metal and recovered for reuse along with the heads. Alemannic tradition. Eight arrow shafts, diameter 9-11mm ($3/8$ – $7/16$") ash, honeysuckle, hazel. Shafts tapered at head, some evidence of binding thread behind head. Barbed flat triangular socketed iron heads. Shaftment and nock areas missing.[40]
Femund, Norway	800–1000 CE	?	Birch shaft; tanged head; sinew binding covered with birch bark at the head end.
Valsgärde ship burial 6, 7 and 8	7th C	The Swedish History Museum	Sharp iron, and blunt arrowheads, made of bone.
Valsgärde ship burial 13	710–750 CE	The Swedish History Museum	Sharp iron arrowheads
Hedeby ship chamber burial	c. 850 CE	Wikinger Museum Haithabu	Birch, yew shafts; tanged arrowheads with brass wire binding. At least nine have brass nocks[41] Birch tar adhesive, imprint shows binding starts approx 10mm ($3/8$") from the beginning of the keel

---

[40] Rau
[41] Petersen p104

Table 30. Comparison of Extant Arrows. Unless otherwise noted, arrows are made in the Northern Germanic/Scandinavian tradition.

Place	Date	Collection	Description
			and winds around the shaft at intervals of 4 to 6 mm ($3/16 - 1/4$") to the end.
Hedeby settlement and harbour	825-1100 CE	Wikinger Museum Haithabu	Birch, yew; some fletching simply glued on with birch tar, others have thread binding. Thirteen wooden blunt heads were found in the harbour, 11 were conical, two tapered in either direction from the widest part. Another 45 blunts were found in the settlement, L of head: 31-82mm; D of head: 9-35mm (21mm average); D of shaft: 6-14mm (9mm average). That's the old quarter to half inch shaft with the average bang on $3/8$".
Scar, Orkney	875-950 CE	The Orkney Museum, Kirkwall, Orkney	Eight arrows with tanged leaf heads; Scots pine shafts split from a larger billet and worked round, estimated 60-70cm (23 1/2 - 27 1/2") long from imprint in the sand. Surviving length of shaft 12cm (4 3/4").
Oldenburg, Germany	9th C	State Museum for Nature and Man in Oldenburg	Two brass nocks like those from Hedeby[42]
Gjermundbu	c. 970 CE	Historical Museum - Oslo	Eight arrowheads total, four leaf-shaped, shouldered tanged arrowheads from the male burial.
Birka	10th C	Birka Viking Museum	450 arrows recorded to date. The Birka garrison finds show an

---

[42] Petersen p96

Table 30. Comparison of Extant Arrows. Unless otherwise noted, arrows are made in the Northern Germanic/Scandinavian tradition.

Place	Date	Collection	Description
			intersection of the Germanic/Scandinavian with the Eastern/Eurasian archery tradition. Arrowheads include fire-arrows and trilobate forms in addition to the more usual leaf-shaped points.[43]
Wood Quay/Dublin	10th-12th C CE	National Museum of Dublin	Birch, Scots pine, willow shafts 60-70cm (23 ½ - 27 ½") long; fletching 12cm (4 ¾") long. Haplin (2008) argues that other finds in Dublin show the introduction of bodkin points in the late 10th C was in response to the rise in mail armour.

---

[43] Lundström et al. pp108-9

Appendix 13 - Making your own pitch glue.

By Wayne Robinson.

Many of the reports of archaeological digs from this period refer to birch tar used as a glue on objects like arrows. This is often an assertion based on the known trade of birch tar, rather than any chemical analysis of the finds. Pfeifer and Claußen (2015) make a compelling case for the use of local conifer resin, with carbon from the extraction method adding to the strength of the product. Cetwińska and Sadło (2021) found from further experimentation that adding beeswax to the resin/carbon glue added significantly to the strength, shock resistance and working time of the adhesive. They defend the use of beeswax when it hasn't been documented in the archaeological record. Nobody has looked for the chemical markers of beeswax in analyses to date.

Cetwińska and Sadło (2021) found that a ratio 5:4:1 rosin (colophony) / beeswax / ground charcoal by weight was optimal to match the properties of birch tar. Pfeifer and Claußen, (2015) used a 3:1:1 ratio, citing other sources using that ratio and noting that it's stronger than the tar but is also more brittle.

In this appendix I'll take you through the process of making pitch glue if you don't live in an area where you can get birch tar.

Materials required: rosin/colophony; beeswax; ground charcoal (or carbon black pigment from the same shop as the rosin).

Photo 216. The materials required.

My rosin came from a calligraphy warehouse. You don't need to pay a premium extra for sporting or music instrument grade rosin. The charcoal came from the front yard[44] and I swapped some used travertine marble for some bees wax with the local apiarist. This glue worked out cheaper than brand name wood glue from the hardware store.

Tools required: a heat source (a pair of tealight candles is enough); heat protection for the workbench (I'm using a spare ceramic tile); support for the container (I used a couple of spare pieces of Oregon); calibrated stick; kitchen scales (don't spill the charcoal on it); something to grind the charcoal with; disposable container (a tin can works well).

---

[44] We have a charcoal layer left by an ancient bushfire

Photo 217. tools required. I had to swap the scales for some that would measure small enough amounts. Add two smooth stones for grinding charcoal.

Most modern canned foods use a lacquer or paint lining, so test it with the candles underneath before you add any of the expensive ingredients to see if it burns off with this amount of heat. Burnt lining will add extra carbon to the mix and make it too brittle. I ended up changing cans for another that had a tin plate lining.

 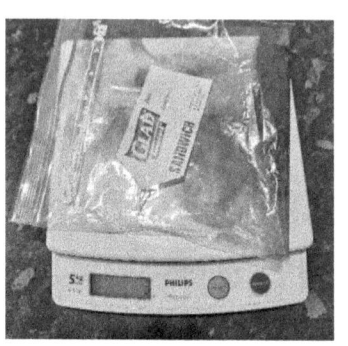

Photo 218. charcoal grinding with a mortar and pestle	**Photo 219.** weighing the charcoal

I'm grinding the charcoal in the photos using a lab mortar and pestle because I already have them. Best not use the good herb or coffee grinder - a round rock works well when grinding the charcoal against a flat rock or piece of tile. The charcoal needs to be finely ground but don't be obsessive about it unless you have a really deep need to.

I didn't know how much I would need, so I took the easiest path. I had 3g (0.1 oz) of charcoal already ground, so I used 15g (0.5 oz) of rosin and 12g (0.4 oz) of wax. Don't worry about matching my quantities, use whatever amount you have, and keep to the same ratio.

Photo 220. melting the rosin
Photo 221. liquid rosin and beeswax
Photo 222. adding charcoal
Photo 223. the finished glue

Melt the rosin, add the beeswax and when it becomes liquid, add the charcoal, stirring with the stick throughout.

> **Safety tip:** Molten rosin burns deeply, and sticks to the burn. If you do manage to burn yourself, irrigate with plenty of cold water for at least 5 minutes to cool both the burn and the pitch. The cooled pitch may peel away from the burn, but if it doesn't, don't pull it. Cover the burn and seek medical assistance.

Leave the glue to sit until it hardens into a sticky semi-liquid state before use. This may take anything up to 30 minutes depending on how much heat you used and the ambient temperature. It only took a couple of minutes for me because the two candles had barely enough heat to melt the rosin.

Appendix 14 - Useful conversions.

Table 31. Metric to customary and imperial conversions.	
1 metre = 100 cm	39.3701 inches / 3.28 feet / 1.09 yard
1 centimetre = 10 mm	0.3937 inch
1 millimetre	0.03937 inch
1 yard = 3 feet	91.44 cm
1 foot = 12 inches	30.48 cm
1 inch	2.54 cm
Volume	
1 litre	4 metric cups / 1000 ml
1 litre	1.06 US quarts / 33.8 US fl oz.
1 litre	0.88 Imperial quart / 35.2 Imp fl. oz.
1 US quart	4 US cups / 32 US fl oz. / 946 ml
1 Imperial quart	4 Imp cups / 40 Imp fl.oz. / 1136 ml
1 US cup	240 ml
1 metric cup	250 ml
1 Imperial cup	284 ml
1 US teaspoon	4.9 ml
1 metric teaspoon	5 ml
1 Imperial teaspoon	5.9 ml
Weight	
1kg = 1000 g	2.2 lb
1 lb	0.454 kg
1 oz	28.35 g
Leather thickness	
0.8 – 1.2 mm	2 – 3 oz
1.2 – 1.6 mm	3 – 4 oz
2.8 – 3.2 mm	7 – 8 oz
5.5 – 6.4 mm	14 – 15 oz

Closest customary fraction to metric size:

Metric	Closest gauge number	Closest inch
0.8mm	20ga	1/32"
1.2 mm	18ga	
1.6 mm	16ga	$\frac{1}{16}$"
3 mm	10-11ga	$\frac{1}{8}$"
6 mm	4ga	¼"
1 cm/10 mm		$\frac{3}{8}$"
19mm		¾"
25 mm		1"

Solvents.

Australia and New Zealand mineral turpentine is the same as the USA's mineral spirit and the UK's white spirit. Do not use Australian white spirit (drycleaning solvent) or Australian white oil (pesticide).

Gum Turpentine/ Spirit of Turpentine is a useful if more expensive vegetable-based alternative.

Residents of the state of California will need to formulate their own oil-based timber treatment with an approved solvent or obtain something acceptable from commercial sources.

Linseed oil may be sold as flaxseed oil in some jurisdictions.

About the authors.

Stephen Francis 'Sven' Wyley.

Born in the town of Colac (Victoria, Australia) and now lives in Melbourne (Victoria), son of a nurse and a fibrous plaster, worked in analytical and research science (from EPA to CSIRO) for 25 years, then moved in occupational health and safety because safety paid more and he had desire to make the world a safer place one workplace at a time, and now is a self-employed author, craftsperson and lexicographer.

Sports and martial arts figured predominantly in his life which included Freestyle wrestling (represented Australia), Archery (Longbow, Victorian State champion and competed at the nationals), Fencing (foil, epee and sabre at intervarsity competitions), and attaining a blue belt in Shudokan Aikido.

A living historian and re-enactor since joining the New Varangian Guard Inc. in 1984, then started Sven the Merchant (a business making and selling medieval goods mainly consisting of furniture, arrows and leatherwork) in 2004.

In his spare time he runs workshops helping people make their own gear, carries out research on design, makes replicas, and writes books on how to make your own furniture, tools etc. Lexicography sees Stephen working on a book on Military Architecture.

And to support and enhance people's understanding the author has made and uploaded many videos to YouTube about using and maintaining tools, and making furniture.

45

https://sites.google.com/site/svenskildbiter/
https://www.youtube.com/channel/UCYaAcfT70zRoQv2RzNC829A

---

[45] Stephen Francis Wyley, not to be confused with his cousin or an actor in Ireland of the same name.

Sean 'Bjorn the Blacksmith' Boyle.

Place born: Melbourne, Australia

Principle job: IT Consulting

Starting re-enacting in: 2014

Current club: New Varangian Guard, Vlachernai Garrison

Interests: Viking Age blacksmithing tools, practices, and materials. Reproductions of early medieval tools, weapons, and domestic artefacts. A particular interest in early medieval axes, axe typologies, and archaeological finds.

Darren Delany

Darren was born and bred in Newcastle (NSW), is a long time member of Fire and Steel of Australia (since 1989) after starting with 1066 in 1983. Darren is a committed re-enactor of Dark Ages history, a presenter of living history displays, craftsperson of very high quality replication of historical artefacts, and not a bad bloke by halves. Darren's passion is researching the lost arts and immersing himself in living history activities which gets him in touch with his ancestors.

Brodie Henry

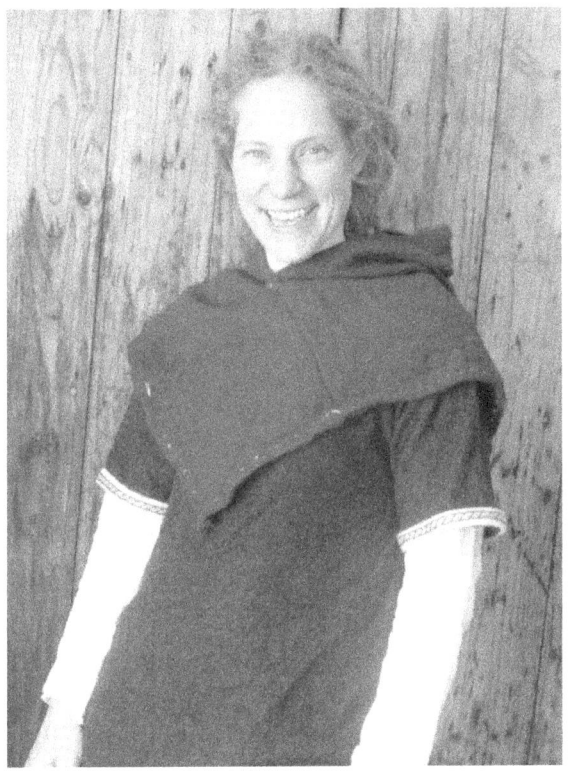

Brodie joined New Varangian Guard, Vlachernai branch, in 2019 with a strong interest in leather craft after many years of making costume armour and accessories. She has dabbled in tanning with various techniques and is still learning. Brodie She enjoys the reconstruction process and the puzzle of trying to work out why historical peoples did things the way they did. Brodie is teaching her son the skills of craft and combat and they can be seen together in the encampment village at public displays. Outside re-enactment Brodie is a Registered Music Therapist and works at a special school.

Shannon Joyce

Shannon has been re-enacting for a number of years now. Her lifelong interest in history and handicrafts has combined with her desire for a deeper understanding of her cultural roots and has resulted in her diving head first into the Viking Age. Shannon has a passion for the material culture of this period with a focus on objects that would have been used daily in domestic life; especially those involved in the production and use of textiles and food preparation. She hopes to show that historical crafting is possible even when access to authentic materials may be restricted.

Shannon is an active member of Europa Re-enactment Association in the Blue Mountains west of Sydney.
https://www.facebook.com/KatlaKnarrabringa

Wayne Robinson

Wayne Robinson and one of Robert Mindum's shoe horns.

Wayne Robinson is the product of an upbringing by three generations of his family. He occasionally claims to be descended from his father. He worked in technical development roles in a variety of industries. Accidentally retired, Wayne is working on the Renaissance Person thing, although the sonnets are proving to be an embuggerance.

A re-enactor of some vintage, having joined 1066 in 1982 and going on to be a member at different times (and occasionally, founder) of more re-enactment groups than can possibly be healthy. He is currently a member of: The Pike and Musket Society concentrating on the middle class London militia of 13 November, 1642 and; The Company of the Staple based on a merchant company in Calais in 1376.

He is sufficiently skilled in ancient, medieval and early modern period leather work, fletching, paint, woodwork and metalwork to bluff convincingly. Much to his own surprise, he finds himself to be a world authority on the carved horn work of Robert Mindum (active 1593-1613).

Publications include: The Reverend's Big Book of Leather (2005) and The Reverend's Big Blogge of Leather (2009); A Catalogue of Shoe Horns by Robert Mindum (2014 -); The Opus of Robert Mindum- 1593 to 1613 (2018 -); a small part in Wyley, Robinson and Joyce's Historic Viking Replicas Vol 1 (2021); with The Double Armed Man - a New Invention in preparation, based on a series of articles about William Neade's 1623 method of arming pikemen with longbows.

Stephen Sinclair

Born and raised on the river in country South Australia, I spent my youth *'apparently'* having way too much fun and making bad decisions. So when, at the age of 16, I packed my bag, left home and moved to the city to pursue the Coopering Apprenticeship I had applied for, my poor old Dad could neither hide his pure joy that I was leaving or his concerned disappointment at yet another bad decision about to be made by me. A supposedly dying trade with a rapidly declining future would, under normal circumstances, have totally justified his concerns, but sometimes 'you just gotta do what you gotta do!!'

After 49 years as a Cooper I have not one regret. This trade has taken me all around the world, it has led me to the best restaurants and allowed me to dine with some of the most significant players in the game. I have made lifelong friends in many amazing places, experienced so many differing aspects of Coopering being performed on this planet. I have been Production Manager of the largest commercial cooperage in the southern hemisphere and, today, am happily self-employed (kept occupied) with my own small 'Cottage' business – The Village Cooper – focusing on authentic historic period coopering.

Although not strictly a re-enactor myself, I have an insatiable interest in the history of Coopering and how it has been woven into the structural fabric of general life throughout virtually every recorded time period of Human progress.

That one 'bad' decision made all those years ago turned out to be the best decision I could have ever made!! It provided the platform that allowed me to spend my life being myself!

So, is it a dying trade? Probably so, but not while I'm still 'having way too much fun!!'

Bibliography.

Archaeology.

Almgren, O. (1907). "Vikingatidsgrafvar i Sagån vid Sala", in *Fornvännen, Journal of Swedish Antiquarian Research,* 1907, 1-19. Sweden : Kungl. Vitterhets historie och antikvitetsakademien.
https://pub.raa.se/dokumentation/750776a5-0672-4a77-8569-acd028579b36

Blomqvist, R., & Mårtensson, A. W. (1963). *Thulegrävningen 1961 : en berättelse om vad grävningarna för Thulehuset i Lund avslöjade*. Sweden, Lund : Kulturhistoriska museet.

Brisbane, M. A., & Judelson, Katherine. (1992). *The archaeology of Novgorod, Russia : recent results from the town and its hinterland / edited by Mark A. Brisbane* ; translated by Katharine Judelson. Great Britain, Lincoln : Society for Medieval Archaeology.

Kalmring, Sven. (2010). "Of Thieves, Counterfeiters and Homicides Crime in Hedeby and Birka". *Fornvännen, Journal of Swedish Antiquarian Research*. 105. 281-290. Sweden : Kungl. Vitterhets historie och antikvitetsakademien.
https://app.raa.se/open/arkivsok/resolve/80cf55da-e18c-46c4-83c4-c38d5e0d0c47

Morris, Carole A. et al. (2000). *Archaeology of York: Craft, Industry and Everyday Life: Wood and Woodworking in Anglo-Scandinavian and Medieval York.* The Archaeology of York Vol. 17 fasc. 13. Great Britain, York : Council for British Archaeology for York Archaeological Trust
https://www.collections.yorkarchaeologicaltrust.co.uk/s/collections/item/74502#lg=1&slide=0

Nicolaysen, Nicolay and Krag, Thomas. (1882) *Langskibet fra Gokstad ved Sandefjord = The viking-ship discovered at Gokstad in Norway / beskrevet af N. Nicolaysen ; [with English translation by Thomas Krag].* Norway, Oslo, Christiana : A. Cammermeyer.

Schietzel, Kurt, (2021). *Spurensuche Haithabu : archäologische Spurensuche in der frühmittelalterlichen Ansiedlung Haithabu ; Dokumentation und Chronik 1963 - 2013*. Germany, Neumünster : Wachholtz Verlag.

Vlasatý, T. (2016). *4.2.4.20 Bag-handles.* http://sagy.vikingove.cz/wp-content/uploads/2016/02/bag-handles.pdf. Projekt Forlog - Reenactment and science.

Watson, J., Graham, K., Gao, J., Schaeder, U., Skinner, L., Jones, J. and Fell, V. (2011). T*ownfoot Farm, Cumwhitton, Cumbria : Investigative Conservation of Material from the Viking Cemetery: archaeological conservation report*. Great Britain, Fort Cumberland : Historic England.
https://doi.org/10.5284/1033948

Westphal, F. (2006). *Die Holzfunde von Haithabu*. Germany, Neumünster : Wachholtz Verlag.

Arrows.

Gardiner, J., Allen, M.J., Alburger, M.A. and others. (2005). *Before the Mast – Life and Death Aboard the Mary Rose* (Archaeology of the Mary Rose Volume 4). Great Britain, Portsmouth : The Mary Rose Trust.

Hansard, G. A. (1841). *The Book of Archery*. United Kingdom. London, : Bohn.

Ottaway, Patrick (1992). *Anglo-Scandinavian Ironwork from Coppergate*. The Archaeology of York Vol. 17 fasc. 06. Great

Britain, York : Council for British Archaeology for York Archaeological Trust.
https://www.collections.yorkarchaeologicaltrust.co.uk/s/collections/item/74495

Owen, Olwyn; Dalland, Magnar; Historic Scotland. (1999). *Scar, A Viking Boat Burial on Sanday, Orkney*. Great Britain, East Linton : Tuckwell Press in association with Historic Scotland.

Paulsen, H. (1999). "Pfeil und Bogen in Haithabu" (Bow and arrow in Hedeby) in Geibig, A. and Paulsen, H. (1999). *Neue Ausgrabungen in Haithabu; Band 33: Das archäologische Fundmaterial VI 1999*. Germany, Neumünster : Wachholtz Verlag.

Pedersen, Anne (2014*). Dead Warriors in Living Memory. A study of weapon and equestrian burials in Viking-age Denmark, AD 800-1000*. Publications from the National Museum. Studies in Archaeology & History Vol. 20:1 2 Jelling Series. Sweden, Stockholm : Nationalmuseet.

Schietzel, K. (2022). *Unearthing Hedeby*. Germany, Neumünster : Wachholtz Verlag.

Söderberg, A. & Hoffman, O. (1999). Blowing new life in old technology - Viking Age bronze casting in *Viking heritage newsletter*. 1999 (6), pp13-16.

Blacksmithing.

Blindheim, C. (1962). "Smedgraven fra Bygland i Morgedal". [The Smedgraven from Bygland in Morgedal]. *Viking - Journal of Norse Archeology* 26. 25-80. Norway, Oslo : Norwegian Archaeological Society.
https://www.duo.uio.no/handle/10852/37586

Harries, D., & Heer, B., (2006). *Basic Blacksmithing – An Introduction to toolmaking*. Great Britain, London : Intermediate Technology Publications Ltd.

Sims, L. (2006). *The Backyard Blacksmith, Tradition techniques for the modern smith*. USA, Massachusetts, Beverly : Quarry Books Inc.

Furniture.

Croom, A.T. (2007). *Roman Furniture*, Great Britain, Cheltenham : The History Press.

Diehl, D. (1997). *Constructing Medieval Furniture, Plans and Instructions with Historical Notes*. USA, Pennsylvania, Mechanicsburg : Stackpole Books.

Diehl, D & Donnelly, M. (1999). *Medieval Furniture, Plans and Instructions for Historical Reproductions*. Pennsylvania, Mechanicsburg : Stackpole Books.

Diehl, D & Donnelly, M. (2012). *Medieval and Renaissance Furniture, Plans and Instructions for Historical Reproductions*. Pennsylvania, Mechanicsburg : Stackpole Books.

Gilbert, Vicenc & Lopez, Josep (2002) *Woodworking class Cabinetmaking*. Great Britain, London : Batsford, Batsford Books.

Krogh, Knud j. & Voss, O. (1961). *Fra hedenskab til kristendom i Hørning* [From Paganism to Christianity in Hørning]. 3-34. Denmark, Copenhagen : Nationalmuseets Arbejdsmark.

Metalwork.

Biddle, M. (1990). *Object and economy in medieval Winchester*. Great Britain, Oxford, Clarendon Press | USA, New York : Oxford University Press.

Goodall, Ian H. (2012). *Ironwork in Medieval Britain*. Society for Medieval Archaeology Monograph No. 31. Great Britain : Society for Medieval Archaeology

Other.

Cetwińska, A.; Sadło, M. (2021, November 25). Beeswax an Addition to the Production of European Stone Age Adhesives. In *EXARC Journal* Issue 2021/04.
https://exarc.net/ark:/88735/10605

SPfeifer, Werner; Claußen, Marco. (2015, November 30) Experiments on Possible Stone Age Glue Types. In *EXARC Journal* Issue 2015/4. https://exarc.net/ark:/88735/10222

Rundkvist, Martin & Williams, Howard. (2008, November). "A Viking Boat Grave with Amber Gaming Pieces Excavated at Skamby, Ostergotland, Sweden". *Medieval Archaeology*. 52. 69-102. DOI: http://dx.doi.org/10.1179/174581708x335440

Smoothing board.

Batey, C. (1994). "A Viking whalebone plaque fragment and linen smoother". *Glasgow Archaeological Journal, 19*, 109-113. Scotland, Glasgow : Glasgow Archaeological Society. http://www.jstor.org/stable/44945066

Graham-Campbell, J. (1980). *Viking Artefacts: A select Catalogue.* London : British Museum Press.

Isaksen, E. (2012). *Hvalbeinsplater fra yngre jernalder: En analyse av hvalbeinsplatenes kontekst og funksjon.* [Master's thesis, Universitetet i Tromsø] Norway, UiT Munin. https://munin.uit.no/handle/10037/4308

Owen, O., & Dalland, M. (1999). *Scar : a Viking Boat Burial on Sanday, Orkney / Olwyn Owen and Magnar Dalland, with Contributions from Anne Allen [and Others] ; and with Illustration by Sylvia Stevenson and Christina Umwin, and Artefact Photography by Michael Brooks.* Great Britain East Linton : Tuckwell Press in association with Historic Scotland.

Petersen, J. (1951). *Vikingetidens Redskaper.* Norway, Oslo : Norske Videnskaps-Akademi.

Reinicke, T. (2015). *A whalebone plaque from the collection of the British Museum.* ['Vikings and Material Culture' course paper] Academia. https://www.academia.edu/12070380/A_Whalebone_Plaque_from_the_Collection_of_the_British_Museum

Vikings.

Almgren, et al. (1991). *The Viking.* USA, New York : Crescent Books.

Arwidsson, G. & Berg, G. (1983). *The Mästermyr Find, a Viking Age Tool Chest from Gotland.* Sweden, Stockholm : Almqvist & Wiksell.

Graham-Campbell, James. (1989). *The Viking World*, London : Windward.

Graham-Campbell, J. & Kidd, D. (1980). *The Vikings*, Great Britain, London : British Museum Publications Ltd.

O'Meadhra, U. (2018). "Unfinished and unused. A new look at two iconic antler finds from Sigtuna, the 'Mammen' Sword-guard and the 'Sigtuna Viking'." *Situne Dei 2018*. 6-33. Sweden : Årsskrift för Sigtunaforskning och historisk arkeologi.
https://arkiv.sigtunamuseum.se/wp-content/uploads/2019/10/Situne-Dei_2018_UOmeadhra.pdf

Raymond, C. (2017, May 30). "Reflections on Birka and Hedeby Bags." *Loose Threads: Yet Another Costuming Blog*. [blog post] http://cathyscostumeblog.blogspot.com/2017/05/reflections-on-birka-and-hedeby-bags.html

Roesdahl, E. (1991). *The Vikings.* Great Britain, London: Allen Lane | The Penguin Press.

Roesdahl & Wilson [editors]. (1992). *Viking to Crusader - The Scandinavians and Europe 800 -1200.* Sweden, Uddevalla : Bohusla¨ningens Boktryckeri.

Svärdström, E. (1974). *Lödöserunor om kärlek och vänskap* [Lödöse runes about love and friendship]. Fornvännen, Årg, 69, 35-40.
Wilson, D. & Fell, C. [editors] (1980). *The Northern World*, Great Britain, London : Thames and Hudson.

Weaving.

Ewing, T. (2007). *Viking Clothing.* Great Britain, Cheltenham : The History Press.

Hayeur Smith, M. (2020). *The Valkyries' Loom: the archaeology of cloth production and female power in the North Atlantic.* Gainesville : University of Florida Press.

Rabiega, K. (2019). *Viking Dress Code: textile and leather clothing in Scandinavia.* Poland : Triglav Publishing.

Rogers, P. W. (1997). *Textile Production at 16-22 Coppergate.* The Archaeology of York Vol. 17 fasc. 11. Great Britain, York : Council for British Archaeology for York Archaeological Trust. https://www.collections.yorkarchaeologicaltrust.co.uk/s/collections/item/74500

Further Reading.

Abbott, M., (1991). *Green Woodwork: Working with wood the Natural Way*, Great Britain, Wiltshire : Guild of Master Craftsman Publications.

Biddle, M. (1965). "Excavations at Winchester 1964: 3rd Interim Report." *Antiquarian Journal, Issue 2*, 1965, September. 230 – 264. Great Britain, London : The Society of Antiquaries of London | Cambridge University Press. DOI: https://doi.org/10.1017/S0003581500052537

Biddle, M. and Quick, R, N. (1962). '*Excavations near Winchester Cathedral*, 1961" *Archaeological Journal, 119*. 150 - 194. United Kingdom, London : The Office of the Royal Archaeological Institute of Great Britain and Ireland. DOI: https://doi.org/10.1017/S0003581500052537

Birkebaek, F. (1982). *Danmarkshistorien, Vikingetiden*. Denmark, Kobenhavn : Sesam.

Corkhill, T. (1980). *The Complete Dictionary of Wood*. USA, New York : Marboro Books.

Foley, D. (1962). *Toys through the Age*. USA, Philadelphia : Chilton Books.

Fridstrøm, E., *(1985). The Viking Age Wood Carvers, Their Tools and Techniques*. Norway, Oslo : Universitetets Oldsaksamlings Skrifter.

Goodall, Ian H. (1995). "Lock Furniture, hasps and keys, in Norwich Households, the Medieval and post Medieval finds from Norwich Survey Excavations, 1971-1978". *East Anglian Archaeology, 58*. 148-155. United Kingdom, Norfolk : East Anglian Archaeology.

Gosling, K., (1989). "The Runic Material from Tønsberg" in *Universitets Oldsaksamling Årbok* 1986/88. 175–87. Oslo, Norway : Utgitt ved Samlingens bestyrer.

Hoffman, Marta [editor]. Narte N.B. and Ponting, K.G. "Beds and Bedclothes in Medieval Norway," *in Cloth and Clothing in Medieval Europe*: Essays in Memory of Professor E.M. Carus-Wilson. United Kingdom, London : Henemann Educational Books. (Pasold Studies in Textile History 2. ISBN 0-435-32382-2)

Johnson, H., (1980). *The International Book of Wood*. United Kingdom, London : Mitchell Beazley.

Kolchin, B.A. (1989). *Wooden Artifacts from Medieval Novgorod*. United Kingdom, Oxford : BAR.

Lang, J.T. & Caulfield, D. (1988). *Viking Age Decorated Wood*. Ireland, Dublin : Royal Irish Academy.

Mercer, E., (1969). *Furniture 700 – 1700*. United Kingdom, London : Weidenfeld & Nicolson.

Mould, Q., Carlisle, I. & Cameron, E. (2003) *Leather and Leatherworking in Anglo-Scandinavian and Medieval York*. The Archaeology of York Vol. 17 fasc. 16. Great Britain, York : York Archaeological Trust.
https://www.collections.yorkarchaeologicaltrust.co.uk/s/collections/item/74505

Olsen, O. (1977) *Fyrkat: En jysk vikingeborg*. Denmark, Kobenhavn : HHJ Lynge & Søn | Det kgl. nordiske Oldskriftselskab

Oughton, F. (1985). *Viking Carving: How to do it*. Great Britain : Mansard Press.

Svärdström, E., (1982). *Lödöse: västsvensk medeltidsstad*. [Lödöse: western Swedish medieval town.] Sweden, Stockholm : Almqvist & Wiksell International.

Theophilus (Author), John G. Hawthorne, C. S. Smith (Translators), (1979 August 1,). *On Divers Arts*. USA, Chicago : Dover Art.

Werner, A., (1999). *London Bodies The Changing Shape of Londoners from Prehistoric Times to the Present Day*. United Kingdom, London : HMSO | Museum of London.

Wyley, S., (2014) *A Few Things Re-enactors can do to make their encampments better – Inspector General of the Encampment Inspectorate*.

Wyley, S., Robinson, W., Joyce, S., *Historical replica construction in Wood & Metal. Viking Volume 1*, Australia, Victoria, Burwood : Intertype.

Links.

Antikythera Mechanism.

Bruderer, H. (2020, April 1). "The Antikythera Mechanism". *Communications of the ACM.* (2020, April 1). 63 (4). 108-115. DOI: https://doi.org/10.1145/3368855
https://cacm.acm.org/magazines/2020/4/243649-the-antikythera-mechanism/fulltext

Antikythera - Anticythère - Αντικύθηρα - 安提凯希拉 (2011, June 26). *The Antikythera Mechanism - 2D* [Video]. YouTube. https://youtu.be/UpLcnAlpVRA
    Antikythera Mechanism reconstruction by Swiss clockmaker Hublot.

Computer History Magazine. (2015, May 23). *Secrets of the Antikythera Mechanism: Session 1* [Video]. YouTube. https://www.youtube.com/watch?v=cSh551cdIEY

Arrows.

Bill, Jan R. (2023) [trans: Fellows-Jensen, Gillian]. *Haithabu ship burial*. Retrieved 13 April 2023, from
https://www.vikingeskibsmuseet.dk/en/professions/education/the-longships/findings-of-longships-from-the-viking-age/haithabu-ship-burial

Bishop, M. C.; Coulston, J.C.N. (2006) *Roman Military Equipment. From the Punic Wars to the Fall of Rome, second edition*. Great Britain, Oxford : Oxbow Books. https://doi.org/10.2307/j.ctvh1dtw2.

Callanan, M. (2013). Melting Snow Patches Reveal Neolithic Archery. In: *Antiquity*. 87 (337). 728-745.

https://www.academia.edu/11986064/Melting_snow_patches_reveal_Neolithic_archery accessed 19 April 2023.

Callanan, M. (2012). Central Norwegian Snow Patch Archaeology: Patterns Past and Present. In: *Arctic*, 65, 178–188. JSTOR. http://www.jstor.org/stable/41638617

Callanan, M. (2014). Bronze Age Arrows from Norwegian Alpine Snow Patches. In: *Journal of Glacial Archaeology*. Vol.1. 25-49. https://www.academia.edu/12644052/Bronze_Age_Arrows_from_Norwegian_Alpine_Snow_Patches accessed 19 April 2023

Cetwińska, A.; Sadło, M. (2021, November 25). Beeswax an Addition to the Production of European Stone Age Adhesives. In *EXARC Journal* 2021/04. https://exarc.net/ark:/88735/10605

Cole, H. (2023). Scandinavian Arrowheads of the Viking Age, Their Manufacture and Distribution. In *EXARC Journal* 2023/02 https://exarc.net/issue-2023-2/at/scandinavian-arrowheads-viking-age

Farbregd, O. (1972). Pilefunn fra Oppdalsfjella. In: *Det Kgl. Norske Videnskabers Selskab, Museet, Miscellanea / senere endret navn til Gunneria; 5*. NTNU Vitenskapsmuseet. Retrieved 19 April 2023 from http://hdl.handle.net/11250/271921 [English language summary of finds, pp 105-108]

Gjerde, J.M. (2019). Alta (Norway), Rock Art of. In: *Encyclopedia of Global Archaeology*. Springer, Cham. https://doi.org/10.1007/978-3-319-51726-1_2815-1

Jensen, Xenia Pauli. (2009). *North Germanic archery. The practical approach – results and perspectives*. Retrieved 21 August 2014, from http://www.academia.edu/1479148/North_Germanic_archery._The_practical_approach_-_results_and_perspectives

Jensen, Xenia Pauli. (2020). Weapons in bogs and wetlands: weapon cult and warfare. In *Journal of Roman Military Equipment Studies* **21** 2020. England, United Kingdom: The Association for Roman Military Equipment Studies by the Armatura Press. https://www.academia.edu/79299064/Weapons_in_bogs_and_wetlands

Kozowyk, P.R.B., Fajardo, S. & Langejans, G.H.J. (2023). Scaling Palaeolithic tar production processes exponentially increases behavioural complexity. *Sci Rep* **13**, 14709 2023. https://doi.org/10.1038/s41598-023-41963-z

Lindbom, P. (1994). Pilspetsarna från Valsgärde 13 (The arrowheads from Valsgärde 13). *Tidskrift för arkeologi (Tor) 27*, 1994. Sweden: Almqvist och Wiksell. Retrieved 19 April 2023, from https://www.academia.edu/11729177/Pilspetsarna_fr%C3%A5n_Valsg%C3%A4rde_13_Tor_27_1994

Ljungkvist, J. (2009). Valsgärde ~ Development and change of a burial ground over 1300 years. In: Norr, S. *Valsgärde Studies: the Place and its People, Past and Present*. p. 13-55. Uppsala (2008). Retrieved 19 April 2023, from http://www.diva-portal.org/smash/get/diva2:127069/FULLTEXT01.pdf

Lundström, F., Hedenstierna-Jonson, C., and Holmquist, L. (2010) Eastern archery in Birka's Garrison. In: *The martial society. Aspects of warriors, fortifications and social change*. pp. 105-116. Retrieved 13 April 2023, from https://www.academia.edu/1429936/Eastern_archery_in_Birka_s_Garrison

Mathisen, Georg. (2023, February 20). *Archaeologists surprised when 3,500 year old arrowheads made of shells melted out of the ice in the Norwegian mountains*. Norway, Oslo: ScienceNorway.no. https://www.sciencenorway.no/archaeology-bronze-age-glaciers/archaeologists-surprised-when-3500-year-old-arrowheads-made-of-shells-melted-out-of-the-ice-in-the-norwegian-mountains/2157675

Pilø, L. H., Barrett, J. H., Eiken, T., Finstad, E., Grønning, S., Post-Melbye, J. R., Nesje, A., Rosvold, J., Solli, B., & Ødegård, R. S. (2021). Interpreting archaeological site-formation processes at a mountain ice patch: A case study from Langfonne, Norway. *The Holocene*, 31(3), 469–482. https://doi.org/10.1177/0959683620972775

Pfeifer, Werner; Claußen, Marco. (2015, November 30) Experiments on Possible Stone Age Glue Types. *EXARC Journal* Issue 2015/4. https://exarc.net/ark:/88735/10222

Rau, Andreas (2007). *Remarks on finds of Wooden Quivers from Nydam Mose, Southern Jutland, Denmark*. Arch. Baltica 8, 2007, 141–154.
https://www.academia.edu/1812945/Remarks_on_finds_of_w

ooden_quivers_from_Nydam_mose_Southern_Jutland._Archaeologica_Baltica_8_2007 accessed 5 April 2017.

Secrets of the ice, [secretsoftheice] (2023,19 April). *A unique find: A forked iron arrowhead mounted on a short foreshaft.* [Instagram, also comment by Sommerseth, I., [arkeologing] (2023,19 April)].
https://www.instagram.com/p/CrLbjozNWWW/

Secrets of the ice, (2019, 28 August). *We love bone arrowheads, especially when they are still attached to their shaft.* [Facebook].
https://www.facebook.com/secretsoftheice/posts/pfbid0Eerq MT8YqtqKpAnM1HoFeMta2ZJvWvYm827QbSfzY8FkuMsFyh48v Yw9pndAEwPwl

Söderberg, A. (2018, November 15). Viking jewellery mould making. Experimental and reconstructive aspects, in *EXARC Journal* Issue 2018/4. Retrieved from
https://exarc.net/ark:/88735/1037 .

The Trustees of the British Museum. (2021). *Casket | British Museum*. Retrieved 10 June 2023, from
https://www.britishmuseum.org/collection/object/H_1867-0120-1

Medieval Manuscripts.

Bayeux Tapestry (2017; Eleventh century) Credentials: City of Bayeux, DRAC Normandie, University of Caen Normandie, CNRS, ENSICAEN ; La Fabrique de patrimoines en Normandie. [Digital representation]
https://www.bayeuxmuseum.com/en/the-bayeux-tapestry/discover-the-bayeux-tapestry/explore-online/

Biblioteca Apostolica Vaticana. Reg.lat.12, Psalterium Buriense, cum kalendario, canticis, litaniis, precibus. [Digitised manuscript]. Vatican City: Vatican Library.
https://digi.vatlib.it/mss/detail/Reg.lat.12

British Library. Harley MS 603, Psalter ('The Harley Psalter'). [Digitised manuscript]. *Catalogue of Illuminated Manuscripts*. London, United Kingdom: British Library.
http://www.bl.uk/manuscripts/FullDisplay.aspx?ref=Harley_MS_603

British Library. Cotton MS Galba A XVIII, Gallican Psalter ('Athelstan' or 'Galba Psalter'). [Digitised manuscript]. *Catalogue of Illuminated Manuscripts*. London, United Kingdom: British Library.
https://www.bl.uk/manuscripts/FullDisplay.aspx?ref=Cotton_MS_galba_a_xviii

Pierpont Morgan Library (c. 1130) *Miscellany on the life of St. Edmund* MS M.736. [Digitised manuscript]. Bury St Edmunds, United Kingdom ; New York, USA.
https://www.themorgan.org/collection/Life-and-Miracles-of-St-Edmund

Beds.

Speake, G. (2014). "A Saxon Bed Burial on Swallowcliffe Down: Excavations by F de M Vatcher". English Heritage (2014) *English Heritage Archaeological Monographs* [data-set]. York: Archaeology Data Service [distributor]
https://doi.org/10.5284/1028203

disaibirkilundi. (2020, August 8). Online Class: Woodworking 101 with HL Alasdair Part 3 – Gokstad Bed. Early Sweden.
https://earlySweden.wordpress.com/2020/08/08/online-class-woodworking-101-with-hl-alasdair-part-3-gokstad-bed/

Vikingskip Museet. (n.d.). *The Gokstad boat.*
https://www.vikingeskibsmuseet.dk/en/professions/boatyard/building-projects/the-gokstad-boat accessed 6 May 2023.

Bedell, J. (2019, June 8). The Singer's Grave at Trossingen, 580 AD. bensozia.
https://benedante.blogspot.com/2019/06/the-singers-grave-at-trossingen-580-ad.html

Blacksmithing.

Barndon, R. & Olsen, A. B. (2018). "En grav med smedverktøy fra tidlig vikingtid på Nordheim i Sogndal. En analyse av gravgods, handlingsrekker og symbolikk". *VIKING*. 81 63. Norway : Norsk Arkeologisk Årbok. DOI:
https://doi.org/10.5617/viking.6480
A tomb with forging tools from the early Viking age at Nordheim in Sogndal. An analysis of grave goods, series of actions and symbolism.

Rullestad, Silje Sandø. (2007). *Den norrøne jernaldersmeden i tekst og kontekst* [The Norse Iron Age blacksmith in text and

context]. [Master's Thesis, Universitetet i Oslo]
https://www.duo.uio.no/bitstream/handle/10852/23174/Masteroppgave-07.pdf

Nordahl, M. (2015, January 15). A viking blacksmith buried with his tools, Norway Oslo : sciencenorway.no.
https://sciencenorway.no/archeology-forskningno-norway/a-viking-blacksmith-buried-with-his-tools/1412894
A news report on the find of a grave of a blacksmith in Sogndalsdalen, Norway.
Livius. (2015, April 26) Viking blacksmith grave even greater than expected. *The History Blog.*
http://www.thehistoryblog.com/archives/36178

Ježek, Martin . (2015). "The Disappearance of European Smiths' Burials". *Cambridge Archaeological Journal* 25(01):121-143. DOI:10.1017/S095977431400064X
https://www.researchgate.net/publication/276508678_The_Disappearance_of_European_Smiths%27_Burials

Vodyasov, Evgeny & Zaitceva, Olga. (2019). Early medieval (5th – 10th centuries) burials with blacksmith tools in Western Siberia. *Eesti Arheoloogia Ajakiri* [Estonian Archaeology Journal] 23(1). 20-38.
https://www.ceeol.com/search/article-detail?id=748151

Game boards.

Arzani, Alessandro. (2021) "Atypical" markings on hnefatafl boards. *Abbas Agraphicus.*
https://abbasagraphicus.files.wordpress.com/2021/05/atypical-markings-on-hnefatafl-boards.pdf

Arzani, Alessandro. (2021). "Atypical" markings on hnefatafl boards PT. 2. *Abbas*

Agraphicus.https://abbasagraphicus.files.wordpress.com/2021/05/atypical-markings-on-hnefatafl-boards-pt2-2.pdf

Vikings in the East Midlands. (2024). United Kingdom, Nottingham : University of Nottingham. https://emidsvikings.ac.uk/

World Tree Project. (2024). Ireland, Cork : University College of Cork. https://www.worldtreeproject.org/

Other.

MrFord4210. (2020, April 30). 1066 *The Battle of Hastings Re-enactment - Normans versus Anglo Saxons at Battle, Sussex, England* [Video]. YouTube. https://youtu.be/GdgmVNZ97RY?si=PJYTLB6Iq1owHW1y.

Bayeux Museum. (n.d.) *Explore the Bayeux tapestry online*. https://www.bayeuxmuseum.com/en/the-bayeux-tapestry/discover-the-bayeux-tapestry/explore-online/

Cetwińska, A.; Sadło, M. (2021, November 25). Beeswax an addition to the production of European stone age adhesives. *EXARC Journal* Issue 2021/04. https://exarc.net/ark:/88735/10605

EXARC. (n.d.) Topic: Experimental Archaeology. https://exarc.net/experimental-archaeology

Larsdatter, Karen. (n.d.) *Chests and Trunks*. Medieval and Renaissance Culture - The Linkspages at Larsdatter.com. http://www.larsdatter.com/chests.htm accessed 25/04/2010.

UnitConverters.net, (2008 – 2020). *Length Conversion,* https://www.unitconverters.net/length-converter.html

Bill, Jan. (2011, November 8). *Revisiting Gokstad Interdisciplinary investigations of a find complex excavated in the 19th century.* [conference paper] https://www.researchgate.net/publication/281118137_Revisiting_Gokstad_Interdisciplinary_investigations_of_a_find_complex_excavated_in_the_19th_century

Recochem | Diggers. (2020, September 16). Safety Datasheet - Paint Stripper. Issue 6. https://diggersaustralia.com.au/wp-content/uploads/sds/Paint%20Stripper%20v6.pdf

Pfeifer, Werner; Claußen, Marco. (2015, November 30) Experiments on possible stone age glue types. In *EXARC Journal* Issue 2015/4. https://exarc.net/ark:/88735/10222

Vlasatý, T, (2017). *The man from Voll An example of a well-preserved Norwegian male grave, Marobud.* https://www.academia.edu/32458579/The_man_from_Voll_An_example_of_a_well-preserved_Norwegian_male_grave accessed 26 March 2022.

Runes.

Looijenga, Tineke. (2003). Oldest Runic Inscriptions [doctoral dissertation, University of Groningen].
https://www.academia.edu/5030830/Texts_and_Contexts_of_the_Oldest_Runic_Inscriptions accessed 16 October 2021.

Nichols, C. (2021, August 31). The Jelling Stones and the birth of Denmark. *Scandinavian Archaeology*.
https://www.scandinavianarchaeology.com/the-jelling-stones-and-the-birth-of-denmark/

Imer, L. M., Kitzler Åhfeldt, L., & Zedig, H. (2023). A lady of leadership: 3D-scanning of runestones in search of Queen Thyra and the Jelling Dynasty. *Antiquity*, *97*(395), 1262–1278. doi:https://doi.org/10.15184/aqy.2023.108

Sutton Hoo Helm.

British Museum. (n.d.). helmet—Object: The Sutton Hoo Helmet.
https://www.britishmuseum.org/collection/object/H_1939-1010-93 accessed 23 August 2021.

Khan Academy. (n.d.). The Sutton Hoo Helmet. Course: Medieval Europe + Byzantine. Unit 6: Early Medieval. Lesson 1 England. [course notes]
https://www.khanacademy.org/humanities/medieval-world/early-medieval-art/early-medieval-objects/a/the-sutton-hoo-helmet accessed 23 August 2021

Viking.

Reenactment a věda. (n.d.). *Project Forlog*. DOI: https://doi.org/10.59500/forlog

Nationalmuseet i København. (n.d.). The chamber-graves of the Viking Age. https://en.natmus.dk/historical-knowledge/denmark/prehistoric-period-until-1050-ad/the-viking-age/the-grave-from-mammen/the-chamber-graves-of-the-viking-age/ accessed 22 May 2022

Vikingeskibsmuseet. (n.d.) Ship reconstruction at the museum's boatyard. https://www.vikingeskibsmuseet.dk/en/professions/boatyard/experimental-archaeological-research/ship-reconstruction accessed 23 August 2021.

Sørensen, T. & Dael, M. R. (2020). Roar Ege: The Lifecycle of a Reconstructed Viking Ship. *EXARC Journal* Issue 2020/2. https://exarc.net/issue-2020-2/ea/roar-ege-lifecycle-reconstructed-viking-ship

Wyley. S. F. (2020). *A collation of Viking names*. Sven Skildbiter. https://sites.google.com/site/svenskildbiter/home/viking-names accessed 25 August 2021.

House Greydragon. (2003). Visit to Sweden's Museum of National Antiquities (Historiska Museet). https://www.greydragon.org/trips/stockholm/index3.html accessed 5/09/2021.

RAMUNI - Viking Crafts and Reenactment. (2022, March 22). Viking Crafts Guide (Ep. 3) Backpack from Gokstad| Viking Tutorial | Viking Bushcraft [video]. Youtube.

https://www.youtube.com/watch?v=9Nov0dB6QVk
Weaving.

State Historical Museum, Sweden. (n.d.) Weaving knife – acquisition number 27600. https://samlingar.shm.se/object/62735E26-9F58-487E-BC91-2CD9B49F133B accessed 4 March 2024.

SHM 29750:542 is the inventory no. of the copy of Gamla Lödöse knife - https://mis.historiska.se/mis/sok/bild.asp?uid=349811 Downloaded 15 May 2023

British Museum. (n.d.). *weaving-batten*. [Weaving Batten, AngloSaxon, 6th Century, Museum number 1963,1108.98.] https://www.britishmuseum.org/collection/object/H_1963-1108-98 accessed 4 July 2021

British Museum. (n.d.). *weaving-batten*. [Weaving Batten, AngloSaxon, 5-7th Century, Museum number 1995,0102.184.] https://www.britishmuseum.org/collection/object/H_1995-0102-184_1 accessed 4 July 2021

British Museum. (n.d.). *weaving-batten*. [Weaving Batten, Viking, 9th Century, Museum number 1894,1105.45.] https://www.britishmuseum.org/collection/object/H_1894-1105-45 accessed 4 July 2021

Archaeological Institute of America. (2017, September 17). Viking-Era Weaver's Sword Discovered in Ireland. *Archaeology*. https://www.archaeology.org/news/5946-170926-ireland-weaver-sword accessed 17 October 2021.

Roche, B. (2018, May 24). *Viking houses from 1070 found in Cork dig at former Beamish & Crawford brewery*. Ireland, Dublin

: The Irish Times DAC. https://www.irishtimes.com/news/ireland/irish-news/viking-houses-from-1070-found-in-cork-dig-at-former-beamish-crawford-brewery-1.3506033 accessed 27 December 2021.

Lewins, S. (2003). *The Ancient Craft of Tablet Weaving – Getting Started.* https://www.shelaghlewins.com/tablet_weaving/TW01/TW01.htm accessed 19 November 2021.

Woodwork.

Baker, Garry & Jennifer. (2013). *Oseberg chair.* Thatshim & Indunna. https://sites.google.com/site/thasthimindunna/home/recreations/chair

Larsdatter, Karen. (n.d.) *Chairs.* Medieval and Renaissance Culture - The Linkspages at Larsdatter.com. http://www.larsdatter.com/chairs.htm accessed 3 July 2021

Schuster, Robb. (Halvgrimr) (n.d.). *The Gokstad 'Back Pack'.* Accessed from https://web.archive.org/web/20150811145706/http:/web.missouri.edu/~rls555/SCA/research/gokbkpk/gokbkpk.htm

Photographs.

Table 31. Photographs			
Number	Description	Credit	Page no.
1	Weaving knife in use for tablet weaving. Photo by Shannon Joyce.	Katrina 'Kat' Lambert	Cover photo
2	Hammer head making by Bjørn the Blacksmith.	Sean Boyle	13
3	Dwarven brothers Eitri and Brokk, Hylestad Stave Church Norway,	Wikimedia commons.	16
4	Byzantine ivory casket panel depicting Adam and Eve 10-11C.	https://www.metmuseum.org/art/collection/search/464020 Met Museum public domain images.	16
5	Blacksmith tools from Smoge Norway (900-950 CE). Photo DF.2092 Norway Digital Museum.	Photo DF.2092 Norway Digital Museum.	17
6	Bag bellows, Byzantine ivory casket.	https://www.metmuseum.org/art/collection/search/464020 Met Museum public domain images.	20
7	Accordion bellows, Hylestad Stave Church Norway..	Wikimedia commons.	20

8	A forge stone depicting the face of Loki. Snaptun Norway (1000 CE),	Wikimedia commons.	21
9	Reproduction Viking Age anvils by Bjørn the Blacksmith. Left to right: Rectilinear, 2 x rectilinear with bick and bick only.	Sean Boyle	22
10	Period hammers by Bjørn the Blacksmith. Left to right: Dog's head, small cross pein, large cross pein.	Sean Boyle	23
11	Period mandrel jaw tongs by Bjørn the Blacksmith. The type of tongs most found in archaeological excavations.	Sean Boyle	23
12	Nail headers by Bjørn the Blacksmith. Top: For round profiled nails. Bottom: For square profiled nails.	Sean Boyle	24
13	Drift, Chisel, punches, rove with punched hole and file by Bjørn the Blacksmith.	Sean Boyle	25
14	A finger gauge in use to mark out a line in pencil, never use ink.	B.Wyley	36
15	Tabby Weave	Shannon Joyce	48
16	2/2 Twill Weave	Shannon Joyce	48
17	Broken Twill Weave (Herringbone).	Shannon Joyce	49
18	Diamond Twill Weave	Shannon Joyce	49
19	Bone weaving tablet – threaded up	Shannon Joyce	51
20	Tablet woven bands based on patterns from Birka (Sweden)	Shannon Joyce	52
21	The Gamla Lödöse weaving knife	Swedish History Museum. https://www.flickr.com/photos/historiska/ CC BY 2.0 DEED Attribution 2.0 Generic	57

22	The Gamla Lödöse weaving knife – Replica in front of the original at the display at the Melbourne Museum (2019).	Katrina 'Kat' Lambert	58
23	The Gamla Lödöse weaving knife replica being used for tablet weaving.	Shannon Joyce	58
24	The Gamla Lödöse weaving knife – Using tracing paper to transfer the outline of the weaving knife onto the timber.	Stephen Wyley	64
25	The Gamla Lödöse weaving knife – Knife cut out and shape refined to match original.	Stephen Wyley	65
26	The Gamla Lödöse weaving knife – Runes traced onto the blade before cutting.	Stephen Wyley	65
27	The Gamla Lödöse weaving knife – Cut runes highlighted with charcoal.	Stephen Wyley	68
28	The Gamla Lödöse weaving knife – Using a nail with a triangular shaped nail to punch the two rows of triangular shaped nail holes.	Stephen Wyley	69
29	Oseberg Chair - A replica of the chair in pine.	Shannon Joyce	71
30	Oseberg Chair Replica – side, showing recess cut 2-3mm ($5/_{64}$" - $1/_8$") into outer face of front.	Stephen Wyley	78
31	Oseberg Chair Replica – side, showing recess cut 2-3mm ($5/_{64}$" - $1/_8$") into outer face of side.	Stephen Wyley	80
32	Oseberg Chair Replica – The back, in two sections connected and the recesses in both sections.	Stephen Wyley	83
33	Oseberg Chair Replica – The front legs with mortises.	Stephen Wyley	85
34	Oseberg Chair Replica – The front legs getting the rebate chiselled out.	Stephen Wyley	85
35	Oseberg Chair Replica – The back tenons are marked out only to 1cm (3/8") to fit thinner legs.	Stephen Wyley	88
36	Oseberg Chair Replica – The back connected to the back legs, showing the recesses.	Stephen Wyley	90

37	Oseberg Chair Replica – All the parts connected, awaiting the rope woven seat.	Stephen Wyley	91
38	Oseberg Chair Replica – The back connected to the back legs with dowels and glue, showing the recesses.	Stephen Wyley	92
39	Hedeby Chest - Original	http://www.vikingage.org/wiki/images/5/5e/Hedeby_Chest-2.JPG CC BY-NC-SA 3.0 DEED Attribution-NonCommercial-ShareAlike 3.0 Unported	96
40	Hedeby Chest Replica – Front ¾.	Morgan Wyley	96
41	Hedeby Chest Replica – Front right corner of chest.	Sarah Brown	105
42	Hedeby Chest Replica with lid open	Morgan Wyley	107
43	Lock based Winchester lock (front).	Stephen Wyley	117
44	Lock based Winchester lock (Back).	Stephen Wyley	117
45	Key based on Winchester, Hampshire, 1065-1085 CE.	Stephen Wyley	127
46	The Horning table with a brass bowl and wash cloth.	Morgan Wyley	131
47	The Horning table - Gluing two boards together with sash clamps and an anvil (the anvil is an optional extra, its stops the boards bending upwards.	Stephen Wyley	135
48	The Horning table - Braces glued and nailed in place.	Stephen Wyley	136
49	The Horning table - Using a spade bite on	Stephen	137

	a drill to drill leg holes.	Wyley	
50	The Horning table - Using a drawknife to carve down the leg from square to round.	Stephen Wyley	139
51	The Horning table - Trimming down the leg with a knife to fit the leg hole.	B.Wyley	139
52	The Horning table - Nocking in the legs with a mallet.	Stephen Wyley	140
53	The Horning table - Legs in place on the table top.	Stephen Wyley	140
54	The Horning table - Cutting lines with 'V' gauge and a ruler as a straight edge.	Stephen Wyley	142
55	The Horning table - Dowels through the sides into the table top.	Stephen Wyley	144
56	The Gokstad Bed – The original.	Viking Ship Museum, Oslo, Norway.	145
57	The Gokstad Bed – The replica of the bed, Legs in cedar, the rest is in pine. In this version all the slats are pegged.	Stephen Wyley	146
58	The Gokstad Bed – Tenon with mortice of head / foot board.	Stephen Wyley	150
59	The Gokstad Bed – Sawing the top of the leg. Cutting the lozenge.	Stephen Wyley	152
60	The Gokstad Bed – Leg, showing single mortices for head/foot board.	Stephen Wyley	153
61	The Gokstad Bed – Leg, showing double mortices for the sideboard.	Stephen Wyley	154
62	The Gokstad Bed – Chiselling out the mortices.	Stephen Wyley	156
63	The Gokstad Bed – Leg taper marked out.	Stephen Wyley	157
64	The Gokstad Bed – Tapered leg, sacrifice board held in place by a hold fast onto the workbench and bearded hand axe.	Stephen Wyley	158
65 & 66	The Gokstad Bed – Using an axe and then a plane.	Stephen Wyley	158
67	The Gokstad Bed – Legs cut down to size.	Stephen Wyley	159
68	The Gokstad Bed – Legs fitted to end	Stephen	159

	boards.	Wyley	
69	The Gokstad Bed – One of the sides.	Stephen Wyley	163
70	The Gokstad Bed – Wedges.	Stephen Wyley	164
71	The Gokstad Bed – The slat pegs.	Stephen Wyley	165
72	The Gokstad Bed – The sides and slats are ready for assembly.	Stephen Wyley	166
73	The Gokstad Bed – The sides and slats assembled.	Stephen Wyley	167
74	The Gokstad Bed – The sides and slats inserted into head / leg board.	Stephen Wyley	168
75	The Gokstad Bed – The bed assembled.	Stephen Wyley	169
76	The Gokstad Bed – The corner is wedged.	Stephen Wyley	170
77	The Gokstad Bed – The middle slat is pegged.	Stephen Wyley	171
78	The Gokstad Bed – Sven asleep on his Gokstad bed.	Jonathon Lyon	172
79	Trondheim Hnefatafl board - The remains of the original board, playing pieces and a die.	NTNU Vitenskapsmuseet- Nefatafl fra Trondheim https://commons.wikimedia.org/wiki/Category:Tafl#/media/File:Nefatafl_fra_Trondheim_(19896084560).jpg Photo credit - Åge Hojem, NTNU Science Museum In	173

		collaboration with Halldis Nergaard, Adresseavisa CC BY 2.0 File: Hnefatafl from Trondheim (19896084560).jpg Created: 10 November 2014	
80	Trondheim Nefatafl board - The replica board.	Morgan Wyley	174
81	Trondheim Hnefatafl board - The Main grid marked out	Morgan Wyley	182
82	Trondheim Hnefatafl board - The inner squares are marked out.	Morgan Wyley	182
83	Trondheim Hnefatafl board - The two of the XX's.	Stephen Wyley	183
84	Trondheim Hnefatafl board - . The Centre X, the 'x' is still to be gouged out.	Stephen Wyley	184
85	Trondheim Hnefatafl board - . Lanes chiselled out and gaps between the squares on the right are underway.	Stephen Wyley	184
86	Trondheim Hnefatafl board - . Gouge out the main lines with 'V' gouge	Stephen Wyley	185
87	Trondheim Hnefatafl board - . Gluing and clamping the sides in place.	Stephen Wyley	186
88	Trondheim Hnefatafl board - . Gluing and clamping the sides in place.	Stephen Wyley	187
89	Trondheim Hnefatafl board - Nine man Morris gouged out.	Stephen Wyley	189
90	Trondheim Hnefatafl board - The underside of the replica shows the Nine man morris game, and the cleated nails.	Morgan Wyley	190
91	Trondheim Hnefatafl board - Showing	Unknown	191

		the underside of the board, including repairs with wooden keys on either side of the central rectangle.		
92		Trondheim Hnefatafl board - Game board with glass blue and clear playing pieces, and agate king. Gaming pieces are based on the Rogaland, Norway extant pieces.	Morgan Wyley	192
93		Whalebone plaque. Grytoy, Trondenes, Norway. Bergen (HM) B.272.	Petersen, J, 1951.	193
94		Grytøy Whalebone Plaque – The replica in maple.	Shannon Joyce	195
95		Smoothing stone made from glass from the Viking age, Namsos, Trøndelag (T10653).	Photo by Ole Bjørn Pedersen, NTNU Vitenskapsmuseet, CC BY-SA 4.0	196
96		Grytøy Whalebone Plaque – Design drawn on a piece of timber. Carving of design at bottom has been started.	Shannon Joyce	197
97		Grytøy Whalebone Plaque – The finished board. Top edge and inserts cut.	Shannon Joyce	199
98		Grytøy Whalebone Plaque – The finished board.	Shannon Joyce	201
99		Grytøy Whalebone Plaque – Crumpled linen as a starting point.	Shannon Joyce	202
100		Grytøy Whalebone Plaque – Heating of the smoother in boiling water in a bowl.	Shannon Joyce	203
101	- 108	Grytøy Whalebone Plaque – Results of Smoothing Experiment.	Shannon Joyce	204-207
109		The Oseberg Bucket – original	HTTPS://COMMONS.WIKIMEDIA.ORG/WIKI/FILE:OSLO,_VIKINGSKIPSHUSET_(17).JPG CC BY-SA 4.0 DEED	213

		Attribution-ShareAlike 4.0 International	
110	The Bucket – based on the Oseberg bucket	Bronwyn Sinclair	214
111	The Oseberg Bucket – Tools used in Section A.	Bronwyn Sinclair	220
112	The Oseberg Bucket – Tools used in Section 3.B, C & D.	Bronwyn Sinclair	221
113	The Oseberg Bucket – Rising a bucket.	Bronwyn Sinclair	235
114	The Oseberg Bucket – Working out the end.	Bronwyn Sinclair	237
115	The Oseberg Bucket – The finished groove.	Bronwyn Sinclair	244
116	The Oseberg Bucket – Driving the hoops.	Bronwyn Sinclair	246
116	The Gokstad Backpack – The original	Kulturhistorisk museum in Oslo	258
117	The Gokstad Backpack – The replica	Morgan Wyley	259
118	The Gokstad Backpack – The replica with lid open.	Morgan Wyley	260
119	The Gokstad Backpack – Boards for the top and bottom of the back pack.	Morgan Wyley	259
120	The Gokstad Backpack – The Horse and hound carving.	Gokstad field report	269
121	The Gokstad Backpack – The other geometrical drawings on plates.	Gokstad field report	269
122	The Gokstad Backpack – The dog chasing the horse and woven design carved into the top plate.	Stephen Wyley	270
123	The Gokstad Backpack – Mail ring design carved on the bottom plank.	Stephen Wyley	263
124	The Gokstad Backpack – Wet moulding the body.	Brodie Henry	277
125	The Gokstad Backpack – Folding the body and the rim.	Brodie Henry	278

126	The Gokstad Backpack – Tape used to hold one of the thread while sewing the other end.	Brodie Henry	279
127	The Gokstad Backpack – Tying a reef knot in the top of the bottom, inside the backpack.	Brodie Henry	280
128 &129	The Gokstad Backpack – Sequence of stitching leather to bottom board	Brodie Henry	281
130 & 131	The Gokstad Backpack – Sequence of stitching leather to bottom board,	Brodie Henry	282
132	The Gokstad Backpack – Cut darts in the leather base with a knife.	Brodie Henry	274
133	The Gokstad Backpack – Showing the edging covering the upright join of the ends.	Brodie Henry	283
134	The Gokstad Backpack – Using the cork block to hold the top of the backpack in place.	Brodie Henry	285
135	The Gokstad Backpack – Using a hole punch to make holes in the leather for the hinges.	Brodie Henry	286
136	The Gokstad Backpack – The outside of the leather hinge for the lid.	Brodie Henry	287
137	The Gokstad Backpack – The back of the back pack before the addition of the shoulder straps.	Brodie Henry	280
138	The Gokstad Backpack – The backpack shows the leather hinges, shoulder straps with the Guitar straps added, the black leather ties for the shoulder strap adjustment, and the butted seam up the length of the back pack.	Brodie Henry	290
139	The Gokstad Backpack – Toggle and lid strap.	Brodie Henry	291
140	The Gokstad Backpack – Marking out toggle on 2mm leather	Stephen Wyley	284
141	The Gokstad Backpack – Cut toggle out with a knife.	Stephen Wyley	292
142	The Gokstad Backpack – The toggle from the top.	Stephen Wyley	293
143	The Gokstad Backpack – The toggle from	Stephen	293

	the side.	Wyley	
144	The Gokstad Backpack – The tail end of the toggle tied in a half hitch	Stephen Wyley	293
145	The Gokstad Backpack – The toggle poked through the slit in the lid strap.	Stephen Wyley	293
146	A replica, full length, the arrowhead, fletching and nock.	Wayne & Glenda Robinson	288
147	The Hedeby Arrows – The required tools.	Wayne & Glenda Robinson	296
148 - 151	The Hedeby Arrows – cut to shaft length.	Wayne & Glenda Robinson	306
152 - 155	The Hedeby Arrows – drilling the hole for attaching the nock.	Wayne & Glenda Robinson	306
156 - 161	The Hedeby Arrows – cut the waist	Wayne & Glenda Robinson	308 - 309
162	The Hedeby Arrows – Glue the nock insert.	Wayne & Glenda Robinson	310
163	The Hedeby Arrows – Glue the head in place.	Wayne & Glenda Robinson	310
164 - 170	The Hedeby Arrows – Fletching	Wayne & Glenda Robinson	312 - 314
171 - 184	The Hedeby Arrows – Fletch binding	Wayne & Glenda Robinson	316 - 319
185 - 186	The Hedeby Arrows – Trim feathers.	Wayne & Glenda Robinson	321
187 - 196	The Hedeby Arrows – Head binding	Wayne & Glenda Robinson	322 - 325
197	Paulsen type E2 small forked tanged arrowhead	Wayne & Glenda Robinson	326

198	Walnut foreshaft on a medieval ash arrow as a repair.	Wayne & Glenda Robinson	329
199 - 207	The Hedeby Arrows – Self-nocks.	Wayne & Glenda Robinson	331 - 334
208	Gokstad bed - wider middle slat.	Morgan Wyley	343
209	Gokstad backpack Boards – Kids version.	Brodie Henry	344
210	Gokstad backpack, front of kids version.	Brodie Henry	347
211	Gokstad backpack, back of kids version.	Brodie Henry	348
212	Gokstad backpacks, full versus kids version.	Brodie Henry	349
213	Backpack in use.	James Moss.	352
214	Shoulder strap adjustment and guitar strap.	Steve Mijatovic	353
215	Cinch strap between shoulder straps at front may make the shoulder strap more secure.	Steve Mijatovic	354
216 - 223	Making your own pitch glue.	Wayne Robinson	362 - 365
224	Stephen *'Azaz'* Wyley	Mark McManus	369
225	Sean "*Bjorn the Blacksmith*' Boyle	Inta Mezdreis	371
226	Darren Delany	Stephen Wyley	372
227	Brodie Henry	Stephen Wyley	373
228	Shannon Joyce	J.P.Harris	374
229	Wayne Robinson	Glenda Robinson	375
230	Stephen Sinclair	Bronwyn Sinclair	377

Drawings.

Table 32. Drawings.			
Number	Description	Credit	Page no.
1	Warp-weighted loom	https://commons.wikimedia.org/wiki/File:M%C3%A9tier_vertical_%C3%A0_pesons_2.jpg downloaded 8 February 2024	52
2	The Gamla Lödöse weaving knife, back decoration	Elisabeth Svärdström. Lödöserunor om kärlek och vänskap Fornvännen 35-40 http://kulturarvsdata.se/raa/fornvannen/html/1974_035 Ingår i: samla.raa.se	63
3	The Gamla Lödöse weaving knife, front with measurements and runes.	Stephen Wyley	64
4	Drawing of the Oseberg chair.	Gustafson, Gabriel (1904). Osebergfundet. In: *Aarsberetning af Foreningen til norske Fortidsmindesmærkers Bevaring for 1904*, 107-110.	72
5	Original drawing of Oseberg chair with scale	Gustafson, Gabriel (1904). Osebergfundet. In: *Aarsberetning af Foreningen til norske Fortidsmindesmærkers Bevaring for 1904*, 107-110.	78
6	The Oseberg chair front, showing the four tenons (in cm).	Stephen Wyley	79
7	The front, showing the recessed area (in cm).	Stephen Wyley	80
8	The side, showing	Stephen Wyley	81

	the sloped back and two tenons (in cm).		
9	The side, showing the recessed area (in cm).	Stephen Wyley	82
10 and 11	The back, in two sections (in cm).	Stephen Wyley	84
12	The back, in two sections connected and the recesses in both sections (in cm).	Stephen Wyley	85
13	The front leg (in cm), showing the mortices for side and front tenons.	Stephen Wyley	86
14	The back leg, showing the mortices for side and back tenons (in cm).	Stephen Wyley	89
15	The recesses in the back and front legs (cm), to the depth of 6mm ($^{15}/_{64}$").	Stephen Wyley	91
16	Bottom plan (in cm).	Stephen Wyley	100
17	Tenon at one end of bottom, side on (in mm).	Stephen Wyley	100
18	Line decoration on front and back (in cm).	Stephen Wyley	102
19	Line decoration on ends (in cm).	Stephen Wyley	103
20	End plan (in cm).	Stephen Wyley	104
21	End plan side on	Stephen Wyley	104
22	Front and back (in cm).	Stephen Wyley	106
23	Inside of the lid (in	Stephen Wyley	108

	cm), showing the dugout area.		
24	Lid edge on (in mm), from end.	Stephen Wyley	108
25	Hook and eye hinges (in mm).	Stephen Wyley	111
26	Placement of hinges on back of chest (in cm).	Stephen Wyley	113
27	Placement of fittings on lid of chest (in cm).	Stephen Wyley	114
28	Winchester lock drawing, front (in mm).	Stephen Wyley	117
29	Winchester lock drawing – back (in mm).	Stephen Wyley	118
30	Isometric drawing of the Winchester lock	Gary Bannister	120
31 and 32	Hasp and hook, Short, left side of lock (in mm).	Stephen Wyley	123
33	Staple (in mm), dotted lines are bends.	Stephen Wyley	144
34	Slide (in mm).	Stephen Wyley	126
35	Slide side on (mm), showing the hook and the key engagement area.	Stephen Wyley	127
36	Spring (in mm)	Stephen Wyley	127
37	Key (in mm) based on Winchester, Hampshire, 1065-1085 CE.	Stephen Wyley	129
38	Drawing of the original table	Unknown.	132
39	Brace (in cm).	Stephen Wyley	136
40	Table top, one	Stephen Wyley	137

	piece or two (in cm).		
41	Position of braces on bottom of table top (in cm).	Stephen Wyley	139
42	Legs (in cm).	Stephen Wyley	140
43	Sides (in cm).	Stephen Wyley	143
44	Lines on sides (in mm).	Stephen Wyley	143
45	Scratch tool (in mm),	Stephen Wyley	144
46	The corner join of the sides.	Stephen Wyley	145
47	The corner join of the sides (top view) in cm.	Stephen Wyley	145
48 & 49	Side and end rails (in cm).	Stephen Wyley	151
50	Overall leg measurements	Stephen Wyley	152
51	Details of top of leg	Stephen Wyley	153
52	Central slat	Stephen Wyley	162
53	Other slats	Stephen Wyley	162
54	Side (in cm), detail of end.	Stephen Wyley	163
55	Side (in cm),	Stephen Wyley	164
56	Wedge (in cm),	Stephen Wyley	165
57	Peg (in cm).	Stephen Wyley	166
58	The board plan.	Stephen Wyley	183
59	Centre square detail.	Stephen Wyley	185
60	The underside of the replica with showing the Nine man morris	Stephen Wyley	190
61	Measurements of plaque (in cm).	Shannon Joyce	201
62	Stave jointing guide.	Stephen Sinclair	228
63	Hoop features	Stephen Sinclair	231

64	Stave features.	Stephen Sinclair	237
65	Working out the shape.	Stephen Sinclair	242
66	The Chime.	Stephen Sinclair	242
67	Profiling guide.	Stephen Sinclair	250
68	Desired finish outcome.	Stephen Sinclair	250
69	The boards (in cm).	Stephen Wyley	269
70	Suggested cutting plan.	Brodie Henry	275
71	Piece dimensions (in cm).	Brodie Henry	276
72	Hedeby Arrow	Jankhun (1943) figure 14.	298
73	Bone arrowhead from Norway	By Wayne Robinson, after Secrets of the Ice, 2019.	330
74	Finds from Bryggen	By Wayne Robinson, after Farbregd, 1972.	331
75	Bone blunt arrowhead from Valsgard 7.	By Wayne Robinson after a photograph supplied by Matt Bunker.	332
76	The Coppergate mallet (in mm). with the correct measurements.	Stephen Wyley	342
77	The Hedeby chest double hasp plate	Stephen Wyley	343
78	The Hedeby chest – Small version (in cm).	Stephen Wyley	344
79	The Hedeby chest – Large version (in cm).	Stephen Wyley	341
80	Gokstad bed. Wider slat plans	Stephen Wyley	346
81	Gokstad backpack Boards – Lid – Kids version (in cm).	Stephen Wyley	348
82	Gokstad backpack Boards – Bottom – Kids version	Stephen Wyley	349
83 - 88	Larger version of	Stephen Wyley	350 -

| | Oseberg Chair | | 352 |

Index

Ælfric's Colloquy, 17
anvils, 20
Blackening iron and steel, 11
Carving, 28
Coopering, 207
Coppergate mallet, 336
Egil's saga, 17
Experimental archaeology, 36
Extant arrow finds, 355
finger gauge, 34
Forge welding, 25
Forging, 24
Futhark', 38
glass smoother, 191
Gokstad Backpack evaluation, 351
Good housekeeping, 53
Grytøy Whalebone Plaque., 191
Heat treatment, 26
Hedeby boat grave arrows, 292
Hedeby chest – Large version, 339
Hedeby chest – Small version, 338
Hedeby chest double hasp plate, 337
hierarchy of control, 51
Icelandic Sagas, 14
Kjartan, 12
Larger Oseberg chair, 347
Living historians, 36
locks, 34
Oseberg 156 chest, 45
Oseberg 178 chest, 45
Oseberg bucket, 212
Paracelsus, 51
pitch glue, 361
pleating of linen, 191
Poetic Edda, 14
re-enactor, 36
replica, 37
research, 32
runic alphabet, 38
security, 41
Smelting, 24
smoothing boards, 191
storage, 41
Tablet woven bands, 50
The Gamla Lödöse weaving knife, 55
The Gokstad Backpack, 256
The Gokstad bed, 143
The Hedeby Chest, 92
The Hørning table, 128
The Oseberg chair, 68
The Riddle of Steel, 12
The Trondheim Hnefatafl board, 171
The Winchester lock, 112
toxic substances, 51
Trapezoid chest comparison, 334
Typology for locks, 333
Viking chest lock study, 42
warp-weighted loom, 48
weaving, 46

Forthcoming works.

13th century Volume 1;
- WheelBarrow (Bibl. Sainte-Geneviève MS 1185, fol. 127v) c. 1220-1230) - Stephen Wyley,
- 1225-1250 France, BL Royal MS 20 D V – Legendary- Bench – Stephen Wyley,
- Chest (Castigas de Santa Maria – 1221 – 1284 - Stephen Wyley,
- Shrine of the Adoration of the Magi – Late 12th – 13th century – Hamish Manzi,
- Matthew Paris on his death bed - 1250 - 1259 AD - Stephen Wyley,
- Table (Pathenon – 1200 – 1255) - Stephen Wyley,
- Toy (Leather Ball of Novgorod) – Steven Baker,
- Satchel (Maciejowski – 1240) – Brodie Henry,
- Kitchen (the Maciejowski Meat cleaver, plate 148 – 1240- Sean Boyle,
- Novgorod Awl – Steven Baker.

Next on the list:
- Byzantine Volume 1:
- Viking Volume 3;
- Tudor Volume 1;
- Viking Volume 4.

Along with other titles:

Dictionary of Military Architecture, Fortifications and Field works from the Ancient times to the 21st Century.

Previous volumes.

- Historical replica constructions in Wood and Metal, Viking Volume 1 by Wyley, Robinson and Joyce, 2nd issue in 2022.

- Historical replica constructions, 14th Century Volume 1 by Wyley, Fraser and Robinson, 2023.

www.ingramcontent.com/pod-product-compliance
Lightning Source LLC
Chambersburg PA
CBHW051828230426
43671CB00008B/881